B

G

GW00578098

Bradford Trolleybuses

by

Stanley King

"Bradford is the centre of a spider's web. She sucks in every day an army of workers 15,000 strong. To collect this army and to transport the 7,000 workers who go out from the city, Bradford has one of the best trolleybus services I have ever seen."

"Yorkshire, West Riding,"
by Lettice Cooper
The Country Books Series, 1950

Venture *publications*

© J. S. King February 1994.

ISBN 1 898432 03 1

All rights reserved. Except for normal review purposes no part of this book may be reproduced or utilised in any form or by any means, electrical or mechanical, including photocopying, recording or by an information storage and retrieval system, without the prior consent of the Publishers.

DEDICATION

To men of vision everywhere – especially those who pursue "the trackless way".

Cover illustrations

The Best of British ..... British United Traction vehicles were generally regarded as the best trolleybuses ever built in the United Kingdom, and in Bradford they gained instant popularity when first introduced in 1949. Weymann bodied 758, one of the city's most popular trolleybuses, is seen in 1966 leaving the city centre to begin the long climb to Wibsey. Retired in 1971 after a lifetime of first-class public service it is now preserved at the Sandtoft Transport Centre. The scene of the picture, Victoria Square, is now partly covered by Princes Way and the West Yorkshire police headquarters.
On the rear cover 773, seen top left, is an ex-Notts & Derby BUT 9611T new in 1949 which entered service in Bradford during July 1953. It was Weymann bodied to the end of its career in October 1963. Top right is number 720, one of the 1946 Karrier W utilities as rebodied by East Lancs, having re-entered service in January 1958. The lower illustration was taken on Saturday, 24th June, 1961 as the friends of the Bradford trolleybus undertaking were about to tour parts of the network in specially painted vehicles. They are seen in Well Street at the beginning of the journey and AEC/EEC number 603 of 1934 displays a 1911 style livery of Prussian blue and ivory lined out in gold, buff and black with gilt numerals. The 1938 Karrier/EEC behind, number 687, has reverted to its original ultramarine and cream colours.

Photographs: J. Copland, Cover and Golden Jubilee. J. A. Senior, others.

Typeset and produced electronically for the Publishers by Mopok Graphics, 128, Pikes Lane, Glossop, Derbyshire Printed and bound in Great Britain

CONTENTS

Foreword   4

Author's Preface and Acknowledgments   5

Prelude – Before the Dawn   6

Chapter 1 – Foreign Travels   7

Chapter 2 – The Penny Joss   10

Chapter 3 – Innovation, Frustration

                      and Vindication   16

Chapter 4 – Triumph of the Trolleybus   32

Chapter 5 – War and Austerity   47

Chapter 6 – Silk Purses and Full Coffers   58

Chapter 7 – Change and Decoy   78

Chapter 8 – The Golden Evening   91

Chapter 9 – Auld Lang Syne   94

Chapter 10 – Will ye no Come Back Again   97

Fleet List   100

Notes to the Fleet List   111

The Routes   112

Terminology   114

What Could Have Been   116

Management   117

Maps   118

Chairmen, Convenors & Deputies   120

FOREWORD

by

Ronald Edgley Cox,

M.Sc., C. Eng., F.C.I.T., F.I.E.E., F.I.Mech. E

1935-6	Engineering Assistant, Bradford Corporation Passenger Transport
1936-40	Engineering Assistant, London Passenger Transport Board
1940-43	Assistant Rolling Stock Engineer, Bradford C.P.T.
1943-44	Works Superintendent, Bradford C.P.T.
1944-49	Rolling Stock Engineer, Newcastle-upon-Tyne Corporation Transport
1949	Deputy General Manager, Bolton Corporation Transport
1949-52	General Manager and Engineer, St. Helens Corporation Transport
1952-69	General Manager and Engineer, Walsall Corporation Transport
1969-72	Chief Engineer, West Midlands Passenger Transport Executive.

It is most gratifying to be asked to contribute the Foreword to Mr. King's excellent book on the history of Bradford City Transport's trolleybuses.

I recall the satisfaction I felt early in 1936 when I was engaged as a student apprentice after leaving English Electric and before moving to the London Passenger Transport Board, because it gave me unequalled experience of the performance in service of the motors and control equipment I had been working on previously.

Mr. King has put on record in all the necessary detail the developing trolley vehicle from its early days to the post-war fast and efficient mass transit passenger vehicle and emphasises the importance of the C.T. Humpidge period of the rebuilding and extension of the system resulting in a debt-free undertaking.

Ever since I first took Mr. King round Thornbury Works in, 1941, I have known of his genuine concern for the welfare of the system which still is 'the apple of his eye'. This gives me an unexpected opportunity to pay tribute to the Managers and Engineers who have served with distinction the travelling public of Bradford, and to a small number of personal friends within and without the undertaking who have been steadfast colleagues and supporters (so few are still alive) throughout my career and retirement.

I salute Mr. King's work and outstanding enthusiasm for a just cause, and hope his readers will appreciate his dedication.

R. E. Cox. July 1993

Sadly, Mr R Edgley Cox, seen second left with one of his Walsall vehicles, passed away on January 11th, 1994, just as this book was about to go to press. His long and distinguished career in public transport earned him high esteem and many friendships.

AUTHOR'S PREFACE AND ACKNOWLEDGEMENTS

This is a story of enterprise and ingenuity, of clear vision and quiet determination in the face of obstacles and obstruction.

For six decades the City of Bradford and its travelling public owed more than they ever realised to their dedicated team of passenger transport providers – the managers, engineers, traffic staff, depot and works personnel, overhead line crews, drivers, conductors and conductresses, inspectors and instructors – who ensured the lasting success and popularity of that unique feature of our civic life : the Bradford Trolleybus.

Grateful thanks for help, advice, information and encouragement over many years are due to many people – in particular Messrs. F. Hartley, J. A. Pitts, J. Copland, C. Wright, G. B. Lodge, A. Feather, D. Francis, V. Walsh, A. W. Roberts, D. M. Coates, E. Dean, C. Gumbley and former councillors J. W. Pell and L. Dunne, all of Bradford; Mr. B. M. Robinson and Dr. M. Harrison, of Leeds, Messrs. F. P. Groves and G. H. F. Atkins, of Nottingham; Mr. R. Brook of Huddersfield; Mr. K. Dickinson of Halifax; Mr. J. H. Price of Peterborough; Councillor M. D. Simmons (former chairman, West Yorkshire P.T.A.), Mr. W. G. Cottham and Dr. R. Tebb (Yorkshire Rider), Mr. P. Waller (Ian Allan Ltd.), Bradford City Libraries, the West Yorkshire Archive Service, the Bradford 'Telegraph and Argus' (especially Messrs. A. R. Whitaker and P. Holdsworth), the 'Keighley News' and late friends and colleagues C. T. Humbidge, E. Deakin, C. R. Tattam, K. E. Griffiths, T. M. Franks, E. Oughtibridge, E. Robinson and H. Brearley (Bradford City Transport), Alderman W. Hodgson, Alderman A. S. Downey, J. B. Bentley, R. B. Parr and J. S. Cockshott.

Many thanks also to Mr. R. Edgley Cox for writing the Foreword, Mr. J. W. Holroyd for designing the maps, Waterfront Publications of Poole for setting the main text, D. S. Hellewell for giving the completed work a final once-over and making several valuable comments, Venture Publications Ltd for printing and publishing, and finally to 'Hymns Ancient and Modern', the Authorised Version (1611) and the City Hall carillon for textual inspiration.

J. S. King
Bradford
January 1994

Before the Dawn

When the members of the British Association for the Advancement of Science met for their annual conference in September, 1900, in Bradford their discussions were deep and erudite. They spoke of economics, evolutionary geology, analytical chemistry, thermal metamorphosis, palae-phytology, municipal trading and the function of cells.

Reviewing the astonishing progress made in the fields of social and physical science during Queen Victoria's long reign, Sir Alexander R. Binnie cautiously observed, "Whatever the future may have in store for us we cannot tell", whilst Dr. Joseph Larmor mused thoughtfully on "the great mastery obtained over the last twenty years in the practical manipulation of electric power".

On the fifth day of the conference, mentally (and no doubt bodily) refreshed by a Mayoral garden party and a balloon ascent, the delegates listened with growing interest to a lecture on 'The Electric Trolley Omnibus' presented by Mr. J.W.G. Aldridge, A.M.I.C.E. 'The omnibus we know', commented the press, 'and the trolley tram, but this is a proposal to run vehicles by means of the trolley, without rails, the return current being obtained by a second overhead wire. The trolley runs on the wire and is connected to the omnibus by a flexible cable. The theoretical advantages are obvious, and since it is operating in Paris its equally obvious difficulties cannot be insuperable. Mr. Aldridge's prophecy that the trolley omnibus is the vehicle of the future must be received with respect.'

Christopher John Spencer, the 24 year old Manager of the Bradford City Tramways Department, doubtless noted the novel idea for investigation at a future date. But not yet. Not until trams drawn by horses or hauled by steam had been banished from the city's streets, and not before electric tramways then being laid or still to be planned had reached the limits of economic expansion.

So the Victorian trolleybus was not to be. Nor, for that matter, the Edwardian.

Bradford in 1900: A tranquil scene in Forster Square at quarter past midday. Although no public transport is visible, electric trams introduced two years earlier were operating from the Post Office (centre) along Bolton Road (left centre) while Saltaire to Undercliffe steam trams passed through the Square into Well Street (extreme right). Church Bank is at the right of the Post Office and Canal Road (foreground, bottom left). The central island served as a loading station for trolleybuses from 1939 to 1949 – see photograph on page 47.

C. J. Spencer

Chapter One
Foreign Travels

The Edwardian Age is often regarded as having been a golden decade of tranquil, elegant security appropriately enhanced by cloudless and endless summers. Distance doubtless lends a certain measure of enchantment. Nevertheless, looking back upon half a century of almost uninterrupted progress and prosperity, there was good reason for the City and County Borough of Bradford to feel itself fully part of this glittering scene in which its staple trade of worsted 'tops', yarn and 'pieces' played a predominant role. The magnificent 1904 Exhibition opened by T.R.H. the Prince and Princess of Wales at the stately new Cartwright Hall set the seal on the city's status among English municipalities, and is today considered as having been Bradford's apotheosis.

The Corporation tramways had kept pace with the growing demand for links between the city centre and outlying suburbs and villages. By 1905 the pace had slackened, as all the obviously profitable routes – and several which were not – were now served, and the Tramways Committee were reluctant to embark upon further adventures without guarantees of financial stability. Although the network continued to expand with considerable success until 1914, individual councillors' blandishments for the laying of rails in areas which they happened to represent were firmly rejected. Thus a petition for a tramway from Odsal to the outlying settlement of Oakenshaw was dismissed as 'inexpedient' in January, 1906, and a similar fate befell a request for a line along Canal Road from the city centre to Bolton Woods and Frizinghall despite claims that it would stimulate development there.

C.J. Spencer, in whom his Leeds colleague J.B. Hamilton later claimed to have discerned 'an original of mind' as early as 1895, was well aware of new forms of transport development elsewhere, and was always ready to try a new idea if it seemed practical and beneficial. Railless trolley proposals at Stroud, Gloucestershire, in Kent and in neighbouring Halifax in 1902/3 had aroused interest in the transport fraternity even though the plans had been abandoned for lack of a United Kingdom precedent.

During 1908 the pace of progress quickened significantly. In April, York Corporation were urged by the consulting engineer of the London Electrobus Company to adopt either battery-powered buses or trackless trolley vehicles as an alternative to the installation of electric tramcars; tracklesses, he claimed, were 'in all probability the most economical form of traction on ordinary highways that has yet been devised'. Dundee Corporation, in June, took the extreme step of despatching a delegation to the Continent to study the various forms of trackless transport already in use there. Not that anyone who wished to be taken seriously in the United Kingdom would suggest that tracklesses could be anything other than a means of ascertaining whether a route could ultimately be served by a more conventional form of conveyance. 'If a new movement towards the adoption of what are sometimes called trackless trolley cars were now to take shape,' commented the technical press, 'the circumstance would be peculiar and interesting .... we see no reason why such a system should not be used temporarily in districts where there is not sufficient traffic to justify the immediate construction of tramways.'

The City of Manchester now expressed interest, and clearly if 'Cottonopolis' across the Pennines was taking 'railless' seriously, 'Worstedopolis' would lose nothing by investigating the interesting novelty. With the intention of promoting a Bill in the 1909 Parliamentary session the Tramways Committee made a September safari from Odsal (where the Wyke and Shelf tramways diverged) to the isolated village of Oakenshaw which lay astride the city boundary, returning via Bankfoot along a circumferential road to Undercliffe, at a radius of about two miles from the city centre. A proposal to despatch a deputation to investigate 'the trackless trolley system of haulage in use on the Continent' was vetoed by a disapproving Council in February, 1909, and the Bill itself was similarly rejected at a statutory but farcical Town's Meeting: a similar fate befell the Manchester Bill.

The inconvenience of this setback was emphasised within weeks when a Sheffield deputation set off for the Continent: even worse was to follow in April when a Leeds contingent followed in their wake. The Bill was therefore revived. Taking the view that Parliament could scarcely be expected to sanction a form of transport which no one had seen – especially as Continental practices were seldom considered worthy of emulation in England – the Tramways Committee sought and obtained consent for an expedition.

At this juncture it was learned that a Railless Electric Traction Company had been formed in London to facilitate the introduction of tracklesses to the United Kingdom. Initially the company's advocacy relied on theory, but in September they commenced practical trials of a British-built trackless car built to the Schiemann patent, making use of a specially constructed circuit at the Metropolitan Electric Tramway Company's Hendon depot.

Impressed but undeterred from their purpose the Bradford delegation – the Chairman of the Tramways Committee (Alderman Enoch Priestley), his Deputy (Councillor S.C.T. Neumann), Ald. Wesley Knight, Coun. Palin, Coun. Guy (included for his fluency in foreign tongues and experience of Continental innovation), C.J. Spencer and the City Engineer (W.H.S. Dawson) – departed for the Continent on November 27th, 1909, when, over a period of fifteen days (and at a cost of £261-19-9d) they visited Berlin, Vienna, Munich, Milan, Basle, Mulhausen, Strasbourg, Cologne and Brussels. There they saw tramways which did not impress them and tracklesses that did. Three variations on a theme were available. Max Schiemann's products obtained their traction power supply via single or twin trolley booms mounted on the car roof and pressing on the underside of the overhead live wires. The Mercedes-Stoll current-collector comprised a four-wheel bogie mounted on top of the wires and connected to the car by a long, flexible cable, whilst Dr. A.M. Zani's 'Filovia' sported a single trolley boom supporting an under-running bogie.

Reviewing this galaxy of ingenuity the delegates found their choice easy. The German Schiemann cars with their thunderous iron-shod wheels were dismissed as outdated. Austria's 'Cedes' cars found greater favour as an economical form of transport in rural or outlying areas, although the wooden traction poles were clearly something which would not be countenanced in England.

Unstinted praise was reserved for Dr. Zani's four box-like contraptions whose twin 12 h.p. motors propelled them up a formidable 5.5 mile route from Argegno on the shores of Lake Como to the mountain village of St. Fedele, 1,926ft. above sea level, overlooking the Intelvi valley. Unmade road surfaces and hairpin bends on a 1 in 8 incline with a maximum gradient of 1 in 7.7 posed no problems to them and the patent trolley equipment clung doggedly to the wires even when the vehicles reversed direction. The delegates had been seeking something robust, serviceable and uncomplicated, something which was 'no speculative experiment but a good engineering proposition capable of considerable utilisation': here, in the 'Filovia' (literally translated, 'the wire way') they had found it.

Back in England they found the Board of Trade unimpressed. While Filovia cars might be adequate for Continentals, better standards were required for public transport in England, and nothing heavier than a London Electrobus would gain approval. Taking this obvious hint that the already tested Railless Electric Traction Co. vehicle was more likely to find favour, the Bradford Committee began discussions with the company and with Mr. Munro of Brecknell, Munro and Rogers.

On receipt of the Royal Assent for the parliamentary Bill in August 1910 the Corporation resolved to construct the solitary railless route named in the new Act, namely, the short section from Laisterdyke (adjacent to the main tramcar depot and workshops at Thornbury) to Dudley Hill.

Wisely avoiding the pitfall of incompatibility the Tramways Committee ruled that the overhead construction should be as similar as possible to that used on the tramways. A railless car was ordered from the R.E.T. Co. at a cost of £710 subject to satisfactory performance, and still hankering after a Filovia product, the manager was authorised to buy a chassis from Dr. Zani for £650 and a body (presumably British) for £150. Overruled by the City Council, Mr. Spencer ordered a second R.E.T. car; nevertheless he made further overtures to Dr. Zani in January, 1911, when the Council again stepped in to prevent a further bid for an Italian vehicle, this time at a reduced rate of £667.

These developments were viewed with interest by certain residents of Baildon, a semi-moorland township north of Bradford, whose railway station was inconveniently located and which possessed no road transport worthy of the name. But despite a local petition for tracklesses BaildonUrban District Council.* decided to promote a Bill for a tramway extension from the terminus of Shipley U.D.C.'s Bradford-operated system.

Under the terms of the R.E.T. contract the two Bradford tracklesses were to be delivered not later than March 12th, 1911, to enable a public service to begin in April. Technical problems intervened, and the disappointed Committee had to content themselves with visits to the Hurst Nelson and Dick Kerr works to inspect the bodies and electrical equipment under construction. As the neighbouring Leeds trackless system was now likely to be ready at the same time as their own, they agreed that the opening ceremonies should take place simultaneously – not inappropriately, as the two managers had enjoyed mutual support and encouragement in their negotiations with Parliamentary committees and the Board of Trade.

Meanwhile the newly-designed overhead equipment was being erected by the Tramways Department. Between Thornbury Depot and Laisterdyke negative wires were suspended alongside the tram wires, the existing tram standards being retained albeit with lengthened bracket arms. From Laisterdyke to Dudley Hill conventional Bradford standards with ball-and-spike finials, short bracket arms and decorative wrought-iron scrollwork supported span-wire construction with 1ft. 1in. separation of positive and negative wires.

Normal tramway-type curved-line hangers ('double pull-offs') attached to each other by a wrought-iron bar and globe-strainer were used on curved sections of the route, but for straight sections the Thornbury Works foundry produced a new unequal-arm hanger destined to be used on all subsequent trackless routes for the next twenty years. More makeshift provision was made in Leeds Road (Thornbury to Laisterdyke) comprising tramway 'single pull-off' hangers coupled rigidly by an iron bar. At Dudley Hill where the tracklesses were to share a terminus with the Wakefield Road trams, a turning-circle in the width of the carriageway intersected the tram wires, whereas at Laisterdyke physical contact with the tramway was avoided, a reversing triangle being provided in Latimer Street.

The problem of current collection caused concern. The inadequate performance of conventional trolley bases and heads at the Hendon trials had led the R.E.T. Co. to devise a sprung trolley base with a 4-wheel current collector supported by twin-trolley booms, one ahead of the other.

It may have been this device which C.J. Spencer used for testing purposes on June 7th, before the wires

---

Urban District Councils (U.D.Cs) were small local authorities, 1894 -1974.

were energised; the trolley was fitted to a motor tower-wagon which proceeded under its own power along the new route 'to see how a four-wheeled trolley travels beneath the wires'. The trial was satisfactory, but the cumbersome device was not used in service. On the first trackless car, delivered a few days later and tested along the route on the evening of June 15th to the delight of huge crowds, the trolley booms were mounted side by side and fitted with independent trolley heads. In Leeds, J.B. Hamilton was even more confident than Mr. Spencer: he used normal tramcar trolley-heads with 6in. trolley wheels from the outset, an example soon followed by Bradford.

The two Corporations announced that both systems would open simultaneously at midday on June 20th, 1911.

What Bradford nearly bought: a Filovia trackless seen on an Italian mountain road. Ability to climb nearly 2,000ft. over a 5.5-mile route with hairpin bends and gradients of up to 1 in 7.7 impressed the delegation sent out to investigate.

Chapter Two
The Penny Joss

Euphoria and goodwill attained unprecedented heights on Tuesday, June 20th, 1911. At Laisterdyke the Lord Mayor (Ald. Jacob Moser) in a brief ceremony on board No. 240, the first of the new railless cars, praised the 'progressive and enterprising men at the head of affairs' before he 'closed a switch which turned on the current and set the car moving'. In this modest fashion – the operation of a 'canopy switch' above the driver's head – began an adventurous enterprise which, after toil and tribulation, was to bring fame to the city and decades of unsurpassed travel facilities to its citizens.

And yet it does not seem that the civic leaders travelled in triumph to Dudley Hill and back: lunch beckoned, and the lunch was at Leeds Town Hall, more than an hour's journey away. Two years previously Bradford had played host to their Leeds colleagues at the opening of the unique dual-gauge tramcar service between the two cities: now the compliment was being returned, and the Bradford party – the Lord Mayor and certain of his aldermen, councillors and chief officials – were to travel by special tramcar to Leeds. The menu must have been attractive, as they did not linger for official photographs at Laisterdyke.

Mellowed by the meal they exchanged inter-city courtesies – an event so unusual that it was recorded in detail. Ald. Enoch Priestley of Bradford described Bradford and Leeds as "neighbours and friends with common interests"; the Lord Mayor of Leeds "rejoiced to have the company of Bradford in every good work", and the Sheffield tramways chairman (Sir W. Clegg) in proposing "Success to Railless Trolley Traction" ruled that both cities could "claim to have started the system in this country together".

No doubt this last remark was prompted by C.J. Spencer's jocular apology that his watch had been five minutes fast, and J.B. Hamilton's instant reply that his had been almost half a day fast!*

Meanwhile, its historic journey completed, No. 240 returned to Thornbury Depot. Back in London Major Pringle, the Board of Trade Inspecting Officer, wrote a report to his superiors recommending their approval of the Bradford trackless subject to improvements to one of the two foot brakes which had failed to hold the car on a 1 in 15 gradient. The recipient of the report (Mr. Thomas) pondered whether to withhold approval pending alterations to the brake and receipt of a report from the electrical inspector, Mr.

* C.J.S., 29/3/1930: "By reason of my watch being five minutes fast, Bradford was slightly before Leeds in inaugurating trackless vehicles".

Possibly the first day of public service, June 24th 1911: eager passengers await the departure of Railless No. 240, one of the first pair of vehicles. from Laisterdyke. The Driver is James Hogg and the conductor Henry Laurence Nogers, who was later killed in the Battle of the Somme.
B.C.T.

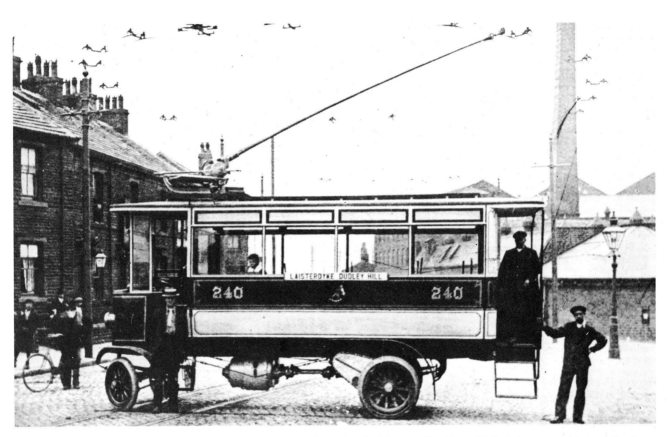

Car No. 240 at Dudley Hill Terminus. As well as the loop of overhead wiring to allow the vehicle to turn, passing over the tram track, this view shows how the pair of motors were slung beneath the chassis frame, with a combination of shaft, worm and enclosed chain drive to the rear wheels. Note the steep steps to the narrow rear platform. **B.C.T.**

A.P. Trotter. These doubts having been overruled, the certificate was issued on June 21st (providentially, as although Mr. Trotter inspected and approved the electrical installations on that day, he did not publish his report until September 23rd!).

Numbered at the end of the tramcar series, No. 240 was a neat 28-seat car mounted on solid rubber tyres, powered by two 20 h.p. motors each with individual drive to the rear wheel. The small cab housed a hand-operated power controller, steering wheel, foot and hand brakes and two canopy switches of opposite polarity; the rear platform was open. Seats were lightly upholstered in hide, with minimal padded back-rests, and the car was painted in the Corporation colours of Prussian blue (lined out in gold leaf and white) and ivory (with brown lining), red patterned corner-posts, red-oxide roof and black wheels, mudguards and trolley booms.

Red-and-white shaded gilt fleet numbers and the City coat-of-arms completed a handsome and serviceable livery. Immediately upon receipt of the Board of Trade certificate, the solitary car began an hourly service between Laisterdyke and Dudley Hill on Saturday, June 24th, the day's takings being a modest £3 for a total mileage of 55, but visiting Keighley Corporation delegates were so impressed that before the end of the month they had decided to 'go trackless'.

The second car, No. 241, arrived either late July or early August thus enabling a half-hourly service to be run at a penny fare. No photograph of this car has ever been traced, but of course it was identical with No. 240, and both were identical with the Leeds cars except in livery details and the fact that the latter had forward entrances for one-man operation as befitted a rural service.

Enthusiasm reigned at the Tramways Committee's July meeting. Tenders for two further tracklesses were authorised, and Mr. Spencer was asked to consider extending the route at both ends – to Bankfoot and Bolton – as well as the long hoped-for services to Oakenshaw, Bolton Woods and Frizinghall and a semi-circular route from All Saints' Road to Peel Park. Councillors pressed for other ventures: Hall Lane (East Bowling) to Rooley Lane via Bowling Hall Road; Thornton to Denholme and Greengates (tram terminus) to Thackley. A provisional order for a few of the above was duly sought.

When the euphoria had evaporated, teething troubles became apparent. Both ends of the existing route were paved with granite setts, but the intervening section consisted of the waterbound limestone macadam to be found outside most towns in the pre-tarmac age. The two tracklesses rumbled heavily over the setts and bounced over the limestone ruts and potholes. Although canvas screens were provided on the rear platforms, the clouds of white dust which arose in dry weather obliged the drivers and conductors to chew peanuts to keep their throats moist. On wet days the solid rubber tyres splashed through the sheets of water lying on the sodden roads, redistributing them in the form of mud over unwary passers-by. Passengers were 'jossed' up and down in their seats, and the ensuing oscillation of the overhead wires caused trolley dewirements.

Improved shock absorbers gave some relief, but the problem of keeping the trolleys on the wires caused the manager to resume his travels – firstly to Johnson and Phillips' works at Chelmsford to inspect a Cedes car being built for Rotherham Corporation, then to Milan to sample Dr. Zani's latest Filovia car, and lastly to Bremen to experience the Lloyd-Kohler patent trackless system which involved two wires suspended one above the other, with a two-wheel carriage running along the upper wire and a bow-collector pressing on the lower.

Wisely spurning the Bremen complexities Mr. Spencer persuaded his Committee to borrow the Cedes car before it was delivered to Rotherham. A whole year elapsed before the car was complete; on December 30th, 1912, the manager was authorised to erect Cedes-style overhead equipment in Queen's Road (Manningham Lane to Station Road) on the proposed All Saints' Road – Peel Park route for use by the vehicle.

A merciful Providence then intervened: the Cedes car never appeared, thus sparing Rotherham and Bradford the endless misfortunes which befell Keighley a few years later. The Queen's Road section was duly wired up, apparently in January, 1914, with normal Bradford poles, span wire construction and the makeshift type of hangers used on the Thornbury - Laisterdyke section. As the Midland Railway perversely declined to allow tracklesses to cross the bridge at Manningham Station the desired link with Peel Park could not be made; the steeply-graded Queens's Road section was therefore used for brake-testing purposes only.

Perhaps the manager had already concluded that trackless designs could be greatly improved*, and although the 1910 Act forbade the Corporation to construct tracklesses, there was nothing to prevent him from building the bodies and ordering chassis to his own design. Construction of tramcar bodies at Thornbury Works began in 1912, and on November 13th a 'new railless trolley vehicle body' built there was inspected by the Committee, who then authorised the purchase of a chassis, motors and trolley equipment to the manager's specification. Messrs. David Brown of Huddersfield contracted to build the chassis and Siemens Bros. the electrical equipment. The trolley bases, evidently evolved as a result of trial and error, embodied vertical springs and were described by the late Edgar Oughtibridge as the most successful trolley springs ever invented; adopted by Leeds and Rotherham, they were still in use in the last-named town until about 1949. Trolley dewirements thus ceased to be a major problem.

A Daimler motor-bus was inspected in January, 1913, but the Committee did not trouble to seek Parliamentary powers for the operation of such vehicles. Instead, the R.E.T. Co. were asked to provide

replacements for Nos. 240/1 with appropriate allowances for the two existing cars and reimbursement for the cost of their repairs. Presumably R.E.T. declined these requests, and when later in 1913 tenders were invited for 28 railless chassis, they were not among the successful competitors.

Meanwhile the new trackless vehicle had been completed, and was inspected at Laisterdyke on September 22nd, 1913. As the tramcar fleet had expanded since the opening of the new body shop, tracklesses 240/1 had been re-numbered in a new series matching the Leeds series, i.e., 501/2. The new car was therefore No. 503, and proved so satisfactory in operation that it was loaned to Sheffield for the duration of the Municipal Tramways Association conference there a few weeks later.

Mr. Spencer described his latest brainchild as "much lighter and sweeter running" than its two forerunners, although for several years tracklesses were to be plagued by transmission troubles, as the torque of the motors imposed considerable strain on the drive

Above: No. 503, the first Thornbury-built railless car, equipped with current-measuring apparatus and temporary trolley ropes, seen on its trial run at the bottom of Queen's Road in 1913 – the only railless car ever photographed there. *B.C.T.*

Below: In more familiar surroundings – No. 503 in Sticker Lane, between Laisterdyke and Dudley Hill. *B.C.T.*

* He admitted in 1930 that at times he had "almost despaired"

Children halt their play as No. 505 poses at Oakenshaw terminus, probably soon after the opening day, June 25th 1914, the vehicle being newly in service the following month. This was one of the production batch of Bradford City Tramways-designed buses on chassis built by David Brown.. *B.C.T.*

mechanism, hence the use of twin motors, each of which drove a rear wheel.

The question of enlarging the railless system aroused debate. Bingley U.D.C. when considering the proposed extension of the Bradford tramways from the Boggs, Allerton, to Ling Bob, Wilsden, concluded that as the cost of road widening was as great for tracklesses as trams, they might as well have trams (though in the event they had neither). There was in addition a strong body of feeling that the tracklesses were causing untold damage to the roads, especially those which were unpaved: it was alleged that the cost of road maintenance in Sticker Lane had trebled since 1911.

On the other hand, the residents of Low Moor and Oakenshaw believed that any kind of service was better than none: following two petitions they learned in December, 1913, that work would begin shortly as a means of finding work for the unemployed. The Committee were now dedicated to expansion, the success of the trackless venture having been amply demonstrated.

Accordingly the ambitious tenders for 28 new cars were placed in January, 1914, as follows:- David Brown and Sons Ltd: 28 chassis with spares (£8,736), Siemens Bros: 56 motors and 29 controllers (£3,834), Dick Kerr Ltd: 60 circuit breakers (£123), Brecknell, Munro and Rogers: 28 junction boxes (£30-2-0), Electro-Mechanical Brake Co: 30 resistances (£213-15-0) and C.H. Spencer (the manager's brother*) 58 Bradford

patent trolley bases (£370) – total £13,306-17s. The bodies were to be built at Thornbury Works to the same design as No. 503.

Although the proposed All Saints Road - Peel Park route and a rural service from Thornton via Keelham to Halifax's Causewayfoot tram terminus were deferred, work commenced on two new routes and extensions to the existing one. They were constructed, inspected and opened, without ceremony, in the sequence in which they had been approved: – Odsal to Oakenshaw on June 25th, 1914, Dudley Hill to Bankfoot on July 17th and Laisterdyke to Bolton on October 13th – the day on which the tramways were extended from Bingley to Crossflatts.

Meanwhile European events had intervened in an unexpected way: the heir to the Austro-Hungarian throne had been assassinated at Sarajevo three days after the residents of Oakenshaw had flocked to see their first trackless descend the dusty road from Odsal. On August 4th Britain joined 'the European War', and tramway materials laid out ready for the Baildon extension were hastily retrieved as the men who were to have assembled them marched away to the Western Front. All plans other than those already authorised were postponed indefinitely, and a Leeds offer to take over the last ten of the current contract was accepted.**

*The lowest tenderer having withdrawn.** Presumably the chassis were used for the 1915 routes to Otley and Burley.*

Tenders for the Canal Road route were accepted on October 5th, when a British Mannesmann Tube Co. tender for light poles @ £4-11-0, medium @ £6-8-1 and heavy @ £7-8-7 each was agreed.* By February 22nd, 1915, the route was complete, and when Major Druitt made his formal report on March 15th the service had already been operating for four days – at a fare of 1d any distance.

The three routes were different in character. The Bolton – Bankfoot route (i.e., the original 1911 section extended at both ends in 1914) linked six important tramways at Bolton, Undercliffe, Bradford Moor, Laisterdyke, Dudley Hill and Bankfoot. At Bolton a large clockwise terminal loop had been laid out via Pelham Road, Idle Road, Bolton Road and Undercliffe Road, an awkward arrangement which necessitated two crossings of the Eccleshill tram wires: the arrangement was reversed at a later date. The route was always served from Thornbury Depot, and a frequent service was provided.

The isolated Oakenshaw line was essentially a shuttle-service between the turning circle at Odsal (Cleckheaton Road) and the reversing triangle at South Street, Oakenshaw. Uniquely, in view of the sparse population of the route, and the prevailing half-hour frequency, only one set of overhead wires was provided: Major Pringle's report of his inspection made no mention of passing loops. The southernmost road of Bankfoot tram depot was set aside for the few trackless allocated to the service, but no overhead wire connections were made between the depot, the Odsal terminus or the adjacent Bankfoot trackless terminus: trackless cars entering or leaving service were obliged to travel with the 'positive' trolley on the tram wire and a trailing 'skate' in the groove of the tram rail.

In contrast, the Canal Road route to Bolton Woods and Frizinghall commenced in the city centre, adjacent to the central Forster Square tramway termini. Vehicles travelled outwards direct to Frizinghall, a few yards short of the city boundary at Dumb Mill, returning via Gaisby Lane, Bute Street, Bolton Woods and Stanley Road back into Canal Road. Numerous mills, warehouses and railway sidings flanked this somewhat dismal route, and as early as April, 1915, demands for a more frequent service were made, much to the Chairman's delight.

Less delightful were complaints about dust and damage for which the trackless were held responsible. Killinghall Road residents accused them of shaking foundations, vibrating windows, destroying the macadam road surface and assailing passers-by with 'blinding dust' in dry weather and mud on wet days. The inhabitants of Horton Grange Road petitioned against the now-deferred All Saints' Road - Peel Park service which, they claimed, would depreciate property values: already several houses were empty because of the 'sandstorms' which blew up, and now that the road had been tar-sprayed it was wrong to 'ruin' it.

Rejecting these exaggerated claims the Chairman pointed out that even if the Highways Dept. had had to spend a little more on suburban roads since trackless began, it had benefitted hugely from the tramways

Railless lorry No. 502, originally No. 240, returns empty after a delivery of goods to mills in the Canal Road area. It was converted to this form in May 1916, receiving the registration AK 4516 as shown. *Photographer unknown*

which had been obliged to provide and maintain much of the paving in most of the main roads. If there were to be a 'day of reckoning' the Tramways Dept. would be greatly in credit.

Ultimately, in May 1916, it was agreed that $^3/_8$d per car mile run by the railless cars should be paid to the Highway Department and rubber anti-splash devices were fitted to all the vehicles. Frequent axle breakages were occurring, but David Brown accepted liability for defective steel castings.

As the construction of the new cars (504-520) progressed, the original pair of railless cars fell into disuse, and there is no memory of their use on the extensions to the original route. It is unlikely that they ever visited Oakenshaw or the Canal Road route, and photographs of them as 501/2 are unknown. However, though they were no longer to be privileged to 'joss' the hapless passengers, a new role as goods vehicles awaited them. Number 502 re-appeared as a 'Railless Trolley-Battery Goods Lorry' in May, 1916, its original body being transformed into a lady-conductors' room at Bankfoot Depot (and afterwards into a garden shed at Marshfields). Able to operate on batteries or on the tramway (with its trolley on the tram wire and a rail-skate to complete the circuit), it could carry 50 cwt. (2.5 tons) of goods such as wool or other materials at an economical cost of 13.696d per mile. Trouble-free, it suffered only one 2-hour breakdown in 1919, and from November, 1918, until the early 1920s, it made two daily journeys to Leeds via the tramway. About the same time it acquired a second trolley which allowed it to use trackless wires also.

As the Great War pursued its tragic course, shortages of staff and materials worsened drastically. Lady conductors appeared, and the widely-spaced gas-lamps had their modest output reduced for fear of Zeppelin air-raids.

* *Identical with those bought for the Oakenshaw, Bankfoot and Bolton extensions and the Bingley tramway.*

Catastrophic explosions at the Low Moor chemical works in August 1916 caused widespread damage and injury. Their effect on the nearby Oakenshaw trackless service is not known (apart from the fact that it was suspended for several days) as wartime news was carefully censored, but it is recalled that the shock wave of the first explosion rocked a Bankfoot–Bolton trackless as it meandered along Rooley Lane: the driver, petrified as his vehicle heeled over on two wheels, did not slacken speed until he reached safety.

The little fleet, simple and robust, soldiered faithfully on. Numbers 503/4/10/11 usually served the Oakenshaw route from Bankfoot depot, leaving the rest at the Thornbury 'railless' shed to serve the other two routes. Cars needing overhauls were often out of service for long periods, and the three highest-numbered vehicles (518-520), although built in 1914/5, did not enter service until much later (1916/1919), by which time their still-unsullied paintwork was already darkened by age. Several cars meanwhile had appeared in an unadorned wartime Navy grey and white livery: grey was also the colour of the second trackless lorry, a covered wagon constructed from the remains of 501 in 1918.

'Navy grey' took on a new meaning for Mr. Spencer when he was summoned by the Admiralty to serve as Assistant Director (Labour Division) of the Shipping Labour Department at Chatham naval dockyard in January, 1917. The Rolling-Stock Engineer (Mr. J.W. Dawson) assumed control of the undertaking in daily consultation with the Chairman (Ald. Priestley) until, after urgent appeals, Mr. Spencer was reluctantly released a year later, only to accept the post of Operating Manager of Tramways for the London Underground Group in July, 1918; he left Bradford at the end of September.

His successor, Mr. R.H. Wilkinson, A.M.I.E.E., of Huddersfield Corporation Tramways, was appointed on October 7th, and the War ended one month later, on November 11th, 1918.

With their smooth, solid tyres the early tracklesses were at a disadvantage in icy or slushy conditions. Number 518, one of the final three BCT single-deckers whose entry into service had been delayed, in this case to 1916, seen in R. H. Wilkinson's livery braves the elements at Dudley Hill, circa 1921, by which date these vehicles received registration numbers.

Covered railless lorry No. 501, originally No. 241, waits at the bottom of Leeds Road with its positive trolley on the tram wire, its negative trolley anchored down and a skate in the tram rail for negative return.

Chapter Three
Innovation, Frustration and Vindication

The new General Manager took up his duties at a critical time. Wartime shortages had decimated the entire fleet. Of the 252 tramcars in service four years earlier only 117 were still usable – more than 50 were unsafe and 20 beyond repair. New traction motors ordered in 1915 had not been delivered; many miles of tramway were in urgent need of renewal, and monetary inflation – a hitherto unknown phenomenon – had pushed the price of steel up to unprecedented heights. The whole of the undertaking was grossly overloaded, as it was handling more traffic than ever before with less than half a fleet. Overall the prospect was daunting.

Mr. Wilkinson wasted no time. Even before the Armistice had been signed new proposals were emerging – improved tramcar designs, better destination displays with illuminated route numbers for the trams, and a complete reorganisation of the Canal Road railless route. The last-named, on which outward-bound cars travelled direct to Frizinghall but returned via Bolton Woods, was split into two separate services with different schedules reflecting reduced levels of demand in May 1919. The now-redundant Gaisby Lane section was disconnected at both ends but left in situ, whilst double wires were erected from the Canal Road/Stanley Road junction to the two termini, with a new reversing triangle at Bolton Woods.

It seems that R.H. Wilkinson had already formed a favourable opinion of his small trackless fleet – home-made, battered and neglected but surprisingly durable and trouble-free – and he began to see tracklesses as potential tramcar replacements in the event of wholesale tramway renewal proving financially impossible in the long run. Encouragingly, the newly-formed Ministry of Transport was displaying interest in the railless lorry, No. 502.

Could a Bradford tramcar be constructed in railless form, and would such a vehicle be more economical than a rail vehicle? Mr. Wilkinson thought it could, especially where frequencies of less than three minutes on a double-track tramway and five minutes on a single-track-and-loop tramway were required. By February, 1920, he had obtained Ministry sanction to build an experimental 'two-deck railless trolley vehicle', and as a special concession its weight allowance was increased from a laden to an unladen weight of 5 tons. Construction began immediately at Thornbury, and the car would have been ready for trials in June had a steel shortage not intervened. In July the Committee approved an even more revolutionary design, this time for a one-man operated double-decker, but the startling idea was not pursued.

In an article published by the technical press* Mr. Wilkinson unveiled his vision of a bright future. Hitherto, he said, railless had been seen as a mere adjunct to trams, but he had been very impressed by their

* Tramway and Railway World, July 1920

performance. Numbers 503-520, being 'light and fairly fragile' cars had operating costs of 4d per mile less than the trams, although 51-seaters ascending Bradford's steep gradients would cost 2d more per mile than 50-seat trams because of the higher tractive resistance of solid rubber tyres on granite setts. Railless were less comfortable and reliable than trams and more prone to side-slide in adverse conditions, but were flexible and silent, and could inter-run with trams if required.

The manager could have added that he had already suggested the conversion of one of his tram routes to railless operation. This was the portion of the Birkenshaw route outside the city boundary, i.e., beyond Tong Cemetery; the idea was not formally debated, as the Committee were not ready for such a radical change. As an alternative to track relaying at an estimated £21,480, they chose Sandberg rail-hardening at 27/- per yard, which prolonged its life for a further 15 years.

Railless car No. 521, the first double-deck covered top trackless in the world, was enthusiastically hailed by the press on November 4th, 1920:-

'NEW TYPE OF ELECTRIC TRAMCAR'

'Bradford added one more to her long list of interesting experiments yesterday, when the Tramways Committee had a trip on a new electric car. The vehicle is the first of its kind constructed, and has the unusual quality of being adaptable to a permanent way, although primarily intended for 'trackless' routes. It thus possesses a flexibility that is regarded by many as having a special value. Centred in it is the possibility of a revolution in passenger transport in our great cities.

The heaviest source of expenditure in connnection with tramways is the upkeep of the permanent way. Relaying of important lengths of tramlines is a disorganising and expensive feature which Corporations have to face; £20,000 a mile of single track is the cost of such an undertaking now. Overhead equipment and a double line means £54,000 per mile.

The railless electric cars which have been in existence for nine years are familiar to everybody. The new car differs materially. It is particularly distinctive by reason of its enclosed top deck, the provision of which is made possible by a 7 ft. wheel base (i.e., axle spacing). The sides of the vehicle taper towards the roof, giving quite a graceful effect. The new car has a seating capacity of 51 passengers (26 being accommodated on the upper deck). The ordinary type of electric (tram) car accommodates an average of 60 passengers and the old railless cars only 29.

Early yesterday morning the members of the Tramways Committee had a trial trip from Bolton, via Killinghall Road, Sticker Lane, Rooley Lane and Manchester Road to Town Hall Square. The rubber-tyred vehicle, with its well-sprung seats, fixed traversely – char-a-banc fashion – made a good impression when travelling along paved roads. At Bankfoot .... the negative

Number 521, the world's first double-deck top-covered trackless – every inch a 'railless tramcar' – seen at Killinghall Road on its trial run in November 1920. Despite appearances, there was no access for passengers to the front balcony, where resistances were mounted. The body, built in BCT's Thornbury Works, retained the narrow cab as used on the early single-deckers. The chassis used components supplied by Kirkstall Forge, later to become a large-scale maker of bus and trolleybus axles. In this case, chain drive to a solid rear axle was used.

B.C.T.

trolley was disconnected and fastened down. Contact with the permanent way was effected by fixing an iron shoe to the front of the car. The shoe fits the groove of the rail and is connected by a short rod to the steering axle of the car. It thus serves to steer the car automatically and to provide the earth return*.....The remaining trolley was brought into contact with the single wire, and the car proceeded smoothly along the permanent way."

Four sets of 'steerers' to the design of Mr. Cross, the Rotherham manager, had been bought from R.E.T. in February 1917.

In general appearance No. 521 resembled a balcony-type tram with an open platform, quarter-turn stairs and a centrally placed cab as on Nos. 501-520. For ease of maintenance, standard tram parts were used, including a Dick Kerr 45 h.p. motor and solid rear axle. Entering service on the Bankfoot-Bolton route a few days later, No. 521 was proudly demonstrated to the Lord Mayor of Birmingham. Thus emboldened, Mr. Wilkinson, in January 1921, formally advocated the replacement of the Idle, Thackley and Eccleshill tramcars by a fleet of double-deck tracklesses in order to avoid expenditure of £168,919 on overdue track renewal.

Above: After a few weeks in service No. 521 acquired deeper mudguards and brighter headlamps. She is seen here travelling along the dusty Rooley Lane   *B.C.T.*

Below: Six-wheeler No. 522. Although ungainly to modern eyes it was a tribute to municipal inventiveness and was noticeably longer than No. 521. The scene is Laisterdyke, circa 1922, with the Latimer Street reverser in the background. The concept of using two steering axles on a six-wheeler was not adopted for commercial vehicles of any kind as a production option until the late 'thirties and even then remaining fairly uncommon.   *Keighley News*

'Sow the wind', it is said 'and reap the whirlwind". Mr. Wilkinson was destined to realise the truth of the proverb, as the storm aroused by his proposal was long-lasting and damaging. "Forgive them", prayed Alderman Sowden, "for they know not what they do!" Councillor Hainsworth vowed that the whole of Idle was resolutely opposed to tracklesses, whilst Councillor O'Neill, a former tram driver, accused the Committee of adopting the line of least resistance and imposing "these ugly vehicles" upon the unwilling passengers; in icy weather the 'Noah's Arks' would be positively dangerous on the long gradients. In a more constructive vein – and no doubt recalling that the original Noah's Ark had rescued mankind at a time of even greater difficulty – Councillor Walter Hodgson offered the rural reaches of his native Thornton as proving-grounds for tracklesses.

Cautiously the Committee voted in principle to seek additional operating powers. Three new vehicle designs were promptly unveiled – a four-wheel double-decker weighing not less than 7.5 tons unladen, a six-wheel double-decker 2 tons heavier and a one-man-operated single-decker. Intrigued, the Ministry gave provisional approval, and following an inspection of the new one-man railless at York the Committee sanctioned the construction of six one-man single-deckers @ £1,800 each and a six-wheeler @ £2,200 as replacements of older vehicles.

The Coal Strike of May/June, 1921, brought about a 25% reduction of tramcar and railless services and a suspension of Sunday services until supplies improved. Meanwhile vehicles dependent on neither coal nor electricity were beginning to appear on the highways in

Number 523 was designed for one-man operation and the driver appears to be issuing tickets to Mr. Edgar Oughtibridge and others as they board outside Bradford Moor School soon after the vehicle entered service in 1923. Perhaps the 'conductor' was off-duty travelling to work? This batch of vehicles was based on chassis built by the Associated Equipment Co Ltd (AEC).
Keighley News

the form of petrol char-a-banc and small motor-buses; investigations proved them to be so inferior in performance and operating costs that when Mr. Denby Burnley sought permission for a private bus service from the Lidget Green tram terminus to the village of Clayton, outside the city boundary, permission was readily granted, as the Department did not see itself threatened.

Road Fund licences were first issued to the passenger-carrying tracklesses in March, 1921, superseding the arrangement whereby the Tramways Department contributed a revised payment of $^3/_4$d. per car mile to the Highways Department. The cars were licensed in the City's original 'AK' series.

The six-wheel double-decker, No. 522, emerged from Thornbury Works for inspection in January, 1922. Its design incorporated four-wheel steering with close-coupled wheels on stub axles in an attempt to reduce the burden of the drivers, who claimed that when driving No. 521 they had to stand up and brace themselves against the steering wheel when turning the car at Bankfoot. For the first time a foot-controller was provided, and the seating capacity equalled that of a tramcar. The open platform was later enclosed.

Like its sister vehicle No. 522 was allowed a

trail-blazing journey, this time by courtesy of the tram wires and the 'steerer' from Crossflatts to Bradford Moor via the 1 in 9.5 gradient of Church Bank before joining No. 521 for regular duty on the Bolton-Bankfoot service. Neither of the double-deckers is known to have travelled on the Oakenshaw or Canal Road routes – indeed, their height would have debarred them from the latter route with its arched overbridge. Dubbed 'Chinese Lanterns' or 'Flying Cottage Loaves' by their users, they rumbled heavily over the granite setts and vibrated badly if coaxed beyond their permitted 12 m.p.h. speed limit. Pictures fell from parlour walls as they passed by, and when, in the feeble glow of the gas street lamps, No. 522 passed between a dog (on the lead) and its owner, the animal did not survive.

Despite their experimental nature the two double-deckers performed satisfactorily. Number 521 was more reliable than the six-wheeler which was prone to axle failures. In order to avoid transmission problems both were fitted with chain drive, whose 'sludgy, slushy' noise was added to the dull rumble of the solid rubber tyres and the hiss of the trolley wheels. The resistances were mounted on the balcony above the driver's cab, the original intention of providing balcony seating having been dropped – providentially, perhaps, as the platform staff were once observed throwing handfuls of snow up to the balcony of No. 521 when plumes of smoke were seen arising from the overheated resistances. Nevertheless the 'Chinese Lanterns' lighted the way to important developments in Birmingham and Keighley, where similar vehicles replaced some trams in 1922 and 1924 respectively. They also underwent scrutiny from the London Metropolitan Police who were considering the licensing of covered top double-deck buses in the capital.

A few of the single-deckers were now withdrawn, but most of them were rebuilt, notably No. 513, which received a fully enclosed rear end with rocker panels. Also reconstructed was the overhead line on the Odsal-Oakenshaw section, double wires being provided at last.

Meanwhile, plans for expansion were encountering rough weather. As early as November, 1920, Baildon U.D.C. had received the tempting offer of a direct railless service from Bradford if they would agree to annexation to the city; similarly Denholme U.D.C. learned that a route from Thornton tram terminus to the city boundary at Keelham could be built immediately, with an extension into Denholme within three years of annexation. The councils declined the bait.

Nevertheless, aware that in outlying towns and villages owner-operated motor-bus services were now springing up to connect with the tram and trackless services, Mr. Wilkinson was anxious to extend the municipal network before potential competitors became strong enough to damage it. In a new Provisional Order he sought to:-

(i) extend existing trackless routes from Oakenshaw to Cleckheaton and from Frizinghall to Baildon,

(ii) construct new trackless routes from surburban tram termini to outlying communities, ie, from Lidget Green to Clayton, Greengates to Yeadon and Bailiff Bridge to Brighouse, and

(iii) create a long trackless route from Bradford (Forster Square and Rawson Square) via Manningham Lane, Shipley and Baildon Bridge, to Guiseley (White Cross), where connection would be made with the Leeds Corporation trackless routes from Guiseley to Otley and Burley-in-Wharfedale.

Alas, the timing was inopportune. Baildon, Shipley and Cleckheaton and the other districts were bitterly opposed to the scheme: having recently escaped incorporation into the City they saw Corporation tracklesses as a back-door threat to their independence. Anti-Bradford feeling triumphed, and the ambitious plan was withdrawn in February, 1923.

Meanwhile, in Thornbury Works, the six one-man operated tracklesses authorised in May, 1921, were now approaching completion. At the official inspection of the first complete vehicle, No. 523, on the first day of 1923, the Committee found themselves viewing a neat, compact little car with smoking and non-smoking compartments for 13 and 17 passengers respectively. Unusually, the car body was polished and varnished like contemporary railway carriages, with ivory roof and black wheels and trolley booms; apart from fleet

numerals and Corporation coat of arms they were unornamented. Like double-decker No. 521 they were powered by a single DK31B 45 h.p. tram-type motor, with a hand controller, and the chassis were among the first trackless products of the A.E.C. concern.

A month later No. 523 (and subsequently its fellows, 524-8) was fitted with soft iron trolley skids in place of the normal 6in. brass trolley wheels, Mr. Wilkinson's theory being that his patent device would be cheaper and would cause less wear on the overhead wires. The fallacy of the theory was soon proved when extensive wire renewals became necessary, and there followed a reversion to trolley wheels, albeit of 4in. diameter and a new design.

Another innovation in March, 1923, was a trolley position indicator actuated by the movements of the trolley bases. The position of the trolley booms relative to the vehicle was measured in feet from 0-14 on a semi-circular chart (later by a row of electric bulbs), the object being to dissuade drivers from straying too far from the wires.

One-man operation was the manager's response to repeated losses: the old two-man single-deckers incurred a deficit of 4d. per mile, but if the new cars could be managed by the driver (who would receive a 10% wage increase) a reduction to 1.5d. per mile deficit could be achieved. Ungratefully the Committee deferred the proposal at the urging of Ald. Trotter, a frequent critic of the Department, who contended that tracklesses should be scrapped, not extended. However, as the Alderman's prized municipal baths were distinctly less profitable than tracklesses, his advice was rejected and one-man operation duly began.

The 'one-manners' were confined to the Bolton-Bankfoot and City-Frizinghall services. They were not used on the City-Bolton Woods route because of the need for a conductor to 'pull' the overhead 'frog' at the Stanley Road junction where the two routes diverged, and the Bolton Woods passengers therefore continued to enjoy the spartan comforts of the 1914 cars.

Although Nos. 523-8 were unquestionably superior to their predecessors, the solid rubber tyres continued to provide an uncomfortable ride. A journey over the unyielding granite setts of Canal Road caused teeth to chatter and cheeks to quiver, while the rumble of the wheels and the creak and rattle of the wooden-framed body and the windows drowned all conversation. Small wonder therefore that the public could not be induced to welcome tracklesses in place of trams; no matter that the renewal of the tramway network might be financially impossible, and no matter how uneven the tracks might become, the public determinedly preferred lurching, swaying tramcars to juddering, bone-jarring railless cars.

Undeterred, the manager prepared another Provisional Order to enable (but not compel) the Corporation to substitute tracklesses for trams on all routes inside the City and those outside the boundary which were operated by Bradford. This included the Shipley and Bingley tramways which were leased by Bradford from the respective U.D.C.s. It would be

Above: In the gloomy confines of Canal Road No. 515 of the BCT-built batch, dating from 1914, prepares for another spine-jarring journey over the granite setts to Frizinghall, Circa 1923

Courtesy: Mr. J. A. Pitts, Copyright: Keighley News

Below: The only known photograph taken at Frizinghall: 'one-manner' No. 526 stands in Canal Road ready for its return journey. *Courtesy: Mr. F. Hartley*

necessary for the local councils to obtain their own Provisional Orders if the Corporation could persuade them to do so – which was by no means certain. The problem was a long-term one, and could be allowed to mature.

At this juncture unexpected support came from Clayton U.D.C., who invited Bradford either to extend the Lidget Green tramway to Clayton village or to provide a trackless or motor-bus service. The outcome, in November, 1923, was a Provisional Order for a City-Clayton trackless route as well as the ultimate replacement of all the tramways.

In support of the Order Mr. Wilkinson stated that wholesale conversion to tracklesses would cost £603,320 compared with expenditure of £1,050,000 every 15 years on tram track. Aware of the lack of experience of double-deck tracklesses on hilly routes, he advocated 37-seat single-deckers with standing room for 25 on mountainous routes such as Queensbury. Operating costs were only 84.2% of income with low capital costs, rapid acceleration, flexibility and (relative) comfort. Immediate proposals were therefore:-

(i) trackless wires along the Lidget Green tramway @ £8,615:

(ii) extension of the Oakenshaw-Odsal route to City via the Manchester Road tramway, and 5 tracklesses: £10,739: plus £23,068 at a later date for vehicles and a negative feeder cable when the Lidget Green tram tracks wore out. Vaguer proposals for a Duckworth Lane – Haworth Road bottom route were also made.

Contemplation of future prospects was by no means confined to Bradford: indeed, the relative virtues of tramcars, tracklesses and petrol omnibuses were fast becoming a national issue, especially in areas where competition from private bus operators was beginning to cause concern. Neighbouring Keighley agreed in January 1923 to explore the desirability of a joint 2-mile trackless route to link the two tramway systems at Crossflatts and Stockbridge, the connecting bus service having been discontinued as far back as 1914. Later in the year delegations from St. Helens and Wolverhampton inspected the Bradford tracklesses and returned home suitably impressed.

Long-term aspirations, of course, could not take precedence over the continuing need to maintain regular and reliable services. In September 1923 the Corporation approved an unemployment relief programme which earmarked £205,968 for tramway renewal and £10,800 for six one-man tracklesses to be built at Thornbury, in anticipation of which four obsolete vehicles were offered for sale in December.

Nevertheless the year 1924 brought endless frustration as one by one the manager's recommendations were deferred or referred back by the Estimates Sub-Committee. The Provisional Order (also objected to by the outer districts), the plan to equip the Lidget Green tramway with trackless wires, the purchase of six one-man tracklesses from A.E.C. in lieu of Thornbury-built cars, and a proposal to seek motor-bus operating powers were all thwarted, so that when the year ended all that the manager had to show for his pains was an Act authorising the Clayton trackless route. Late in the day, Leeds were seeking trackless powers for a Baildon Bridge-White Cross route, whilst Bingley U.D.C., serenely unaware of current events, still hankered after an extension of the Crossflatts tramway.

Although enjoying the support of the Tramways Committee, Mr. Wilkinson regularly encountered hostility from the powerful Finance and General Purposes Committee whose chairman, the formidable Ald. Joseph Stringer, represented the Idle area whose love for tracklesses was indiscernible. Additionally he had to endure the public scorn of his professional colleagues, one of whom, Walter Young of Dundee, thundered that "to suggest that tramways can be superseded by trolley omnibuses is unthinkable. The idea of a vehicle seating 37 passengers having a standing capacity of 25 extra passengers as mentioned at Bradford ... does not require comment".

Before the year ended Bradford found itself in sharp dispute with the first of many private bus

Good photographs at Bolton Woods are unknown. This close-up of No. 506 and its staff, circa 1923, omits all details of the terminus. *Courtesy the late Harold Brearley*

operators demanding entry into the city. The ensuing 'bus battle', bitter and protracted, was assisted by the anti-municipal attitude of the West Riding County Council, the deficiencies of statute law and the effects of the 1926 General Strike. The chief losers were the tramways and the Rate Fund, but Mr. Wilkinson's ambition for the total replacement of tramcars by railless vehicles was also among the victims.

Dutifully persevering, the manager next recommended the renewal of part of the Allerton tramway (Four Lane Ends – Chapel Lane) @ £31,350; simultaneously, however, he once again urged the replacement of the Idle and Thackley trams by tracklesses on grounds of cost, i.e., whereas it would cost £43,493 to relay the track from Bolton as far as Five Lane Ends (where the two routes diverged), it would cost only £51,049 (including the purchase of 12 tracklesses and removal of tram tracks) to convert the entire Idle and Thackley routes. Emphasising that motor-buses, though independent of rails and wires, had operating costs 25% higher than trackless costs, he estimated that over a 15 year period the losses on the lightly-trafficked Idle/Thackley routes would be: tramcars £8,411, motor-buses £7,494 and tracklesses £4,191.

In the ensuing uproar Ald. Stringer said, "You would not get one vote for tracklesses in the whole of Idle – they are called an abomination!" His motion to relay the Bolton-Five Lane Ends section and to reconsider the Idle/Thackley question at a later date was carried 44-16 on April 7th, 1925.

Promptly referred back by the Council in May, a mammoth debate followed on June 9th when the Tramways Committee chairman (Ald. Priestley) after describing tracklesses as "very beneficial" and trams as "a boon and a blessing", significantly abstained from voting. The "big, ugly, gormless" tracklesses were condemned by Coun. Nutton who had collected 1,000 signatures in defence of the trams; Ald. Gadie viewed the prospect of traffic congestion with evident alarm, while Ald. Guy declared himself opposed to the trackless system "because he knew something about it!" He had been part of the 1909 deputation which had returned from the Continent favouring railless but now "wished they had never attempted such foolery!"

The anti-trackless move failed by a 33-32 vote, but battle resumed only a month later. On the previous day (July 13th) a Garrett demonstration trackless had been taken over the Idle tramway by the usual expedient of a trolley on the tram wire and a skate in the groove of the decaying tram track; unfortunately on the return journey the skate had come adrift near Springfield, and a coping-stone had to be thrust under the rear wheel to prevent the car from running backwards.

Criticisms of this attempt to 'cajole' the Council helped to defeat the Idle/Thackley trackless proposal 35-27. The matter therefore disappeared entirely from Council agenda for three years.

Quietly confident that the ever-worsening state of the Idle and Thackley tram tracks would eventually force the Council's hand, Mr. Wilkinson pursued his quest for improved railless rolling stock. The Garrett demonstrator, UM 1755, which had previously been tried at Keighley, was sent on its travels, and an A.E.C. one-man-operated single-decker – fitted this time with Westinghouse brakes, presumably of air-pressure type – was hired for a month's trial in October, 1925, when it operated in service on the Bolton-Bankfoot service (and no doubt elsewhere). Comfort arrived at last with the introduction of pneumatic tyres: one of the 'one-manners' (523-8) was equipped with an experimental set about November, 1925, followed by the other five in April 1926 to the immense relief of the sorely-jarred Canal Road passengers.

Perseverance received its due reward: authorisation was given in November 1925 for the purchase of three A.E.C. tracklesses @ £4913-8-6d and 3 Garretts @ £5040, the specifications to be similar to those of the recent demonstrators. Moreover, Ministry of Transport loan sanction had been received for the construction of the route to Clayton.

Signs were not wanting, however, that other battles were looming. Alarmed for some time by the distinct possibility of invasion by private buses, the Corporation had sought Parliamentary sanction for the operation of motor-buses inside and outside the City. At the insistence of the West Riding County Council – an implacable opponent of all forms of municipal expansion – Parliament had restricted the Corporation's bus operating powers to the City itself, whereupon the Tramways Department had immediately ordered 10 A.E.C. motor-buses as well as three front-entrance A.E.C. type 603 trackless cars. Then, increasingly disturbed by the urgency of the situation, they immediately sought leave to purchase no less than 24 petrol buses – a request unhesitatingly approved by the Estimates Sub-Committee, thus proving that their opposition to tracklesses stemmed from motives other than the financial considerations which should have been their sole criteria.

A sad occurrence at this juncture was the accidental death of Ald. Enoch Priestley, aged 72, on February 2nd, 1926. As Chairman of North Bierley U.D.C. he had compelled Bradford Corporation to promise a new highway and tramway to Wibsey as the price of his District's incorporation into the City; the highway was duly named St. Enoch's Road in his honour. And when he began his long career as Tramways Committee

Photographed at Bankfoot about 1927 but still in its Keighly livery, No. 536, the original Garrett demonstrator, had previously shown the advantages of tracklesses to the reluctant residents of Idle. Its Leeds registration number was a momento of a spell in that city's fleet, and it had also run in its maker's home town of Ipswich. This was a type S, predecessor of the more successful type O, the body being built by Roe, as on subsequent Garrett vehicles for Bradford.   *B.C.T.*

Above and below: Framed in trees A.D.C. No. 531 and Garrett No. 534, both new in September 1926 stand opposite the 'Black Bull', Clayton. The location is the foot of 'The Avenue' constructed several years later. The taller build of the A.D.C 607 as compared to the Garrett O is evident. The A.D.C vehicles had bodywork by Strachan & Brown, a frequent choice for A.E.C. and A.D.C. vehicles of the period.

B.C.T.

Chairman he decreed that Wibsey should become route No. 1! A shrewd but genial man – by trade a butter factor living modestly at 'Hollybank', Wibsey – he achieved the unusual distinction of an obituary in national transport journals. Even more remarkably, he can still be glimpsed in the *Daily Telegraph's* literary legend, the 'crag-visaged' Alderman Foodbotham, perpetual chairman of the 'Tramways and Fine Arts Committee' (a highly appropriate juxtaposition) brooding in his Gothic mansion on Cleckheaton Moor (a place which right-minded Bradfordians, of course, would refuse to know).

It could reasonably be said that the Clayton route marked 'the end of the beginning' for Bradford's trolleybuses. Whereas almost all the districts outside Bradford (and some of the city fathers inside!) were resolutely opposed to municipal tracklesses, Clayton U.D.C. had specifically requested a trackless service, thus providing Mr. Wilkinson with a welcome opportunity to buy a number of up-to-date commercially produced tracklesses and demonstrate their efficiency. When therefore Messrs. Blythe and Berwick, whose Lidget Green-Clayton petrol bus service was to bear the brunt of trackless competition, sought permission to extend their service into Bradford, they received a prompt refusal.

The first of the Corporation's own petrol bus fleet arrived in April 1926 being placed immediately in experimental service on the Bankfoot-Bolton route whose passengers waited to sample them in preference to the customary tracklesses. But before the novelty had worn off, the outbreak of the General Strike paralysed all Corporation services. The effect was drastic, damaging – and permanent. Messrs. Blythe and Berwick immediately ran their Clayton buses into Bradford, and every Corporation route was swamped by a motley assortment of piratical privateers eager for the rich pickings so long denied. And even when the Strike was over, competition remained firmly entrenched on almost all the major roads into the city.

The future of the trams was publicly brought into question for the first time, but secure in their greater carrying capacity and their ability to survive on cut-throat fare levels, they weathered the initial onslaught and received the benefit of a modernisation programme. Nevertheless the protagonists of trolley vehicles and motor omnibuses redoubled their efforts whenever the question of track renewals arose.

The Clayton route – the first new trackless route for eleven years – opened on September 4th 1926 when the Tramways Committee and the Clayton Urban District Council enjoyed an afternoon excursion on two of the new A.D.C. 'trolley-buses', led by No. 529.

From the city centre to Lidget Green the tracklesses shared the overhead wires with the tramcars as well as a common loading point in Thornton Road (New Inn). Beyond lay new territory – a newly developing Corporation housing estate, a railway bridge under which only single-deck vehicles could squeeze, a narrow country lane and then, across the city boundary, the outlying suburbia and winding village streets of Clayton.

The terminus was at Bull Hill (otherwise known as Town End or 'the Wells'), a 4d. ride from Bradford. Here the official party alighted to stretch their legs and pose for photographs while venerable Claytonians stared in wonder at vehicles 'which needed clothes-props to make them go!' This suggestion that 'Clayton fowk' never left their native village was presently reinforced by the Chairman of Clayton Council (Coun. W. Hindle) and his Chairman of Highways (Coun. E. Foulds), who in praising 'the Rolls-Royce standard of comfort' which the new tracklesses had brought to the ordinary public, added that they could well remember when a trip to Bradford was a rare treat!

In this quiet backwater the new tracklesses were therefore something of a revelation. Mounted confidently on large pneumatic tyres, with deep, well-sprung leather-upholstered seats and powerful motors supplemented by 'power boosters' in the form of weak-field control, they were more than a match for Blythe and Berwicks' buses. Battle was soon fiercely joined with no quarter asked and none received. In the narrow lanes vehicles jostled and jousted in the contests to reach the terminus first. Scraped paint, broken rear-view mirrors and de-wired trolley booms were the inevitable outcome of these exhilarating races. Even the more sedate tramcars which shared the overhead wires between City and Lidget Green were infected with the new competitive fever: when the Department began to rewind the tramcar motors to increase their power, the resulting 'high-speed' cars were promptly placed in service on the Lidget Green section so that the trams 'did not get in the way of the tracklesses!'

The weak-field control referred to above was designed to provide economical fast running on level ground, and was applied by the final notch of the power pedal, but if used on a rising gradient, such as on Scar Hill, Killinghall Road (between the Golf House and Pollard Lane), the speed fell away until 'full field' on the penultimate notch was restored.

The three vehicles (529-531) ordered from A.E.C. were actually delivered by A.D.C. (Associated Daimler Co.), a short-lived marketing partnership between A.E.C. and Daimler; they comprised A.D.C. type 607 chassis with 55 h.p. Bull motors and centre-entrance Strachan bodies. The slightly more elegant Roe-bodied Garretts, (532-4) were powered by 50 h.p. B.T.H. motors. A month later the manager was authorised to buy 'the A.E.C. spare railless trolley vehicle and also the similar Garrett demonstration vehicle'. The Garrett, RT 1345, joined the fleet as No. 535, being easily distinguished by its brighter blue livery and its concentrically-mounted Estler trolley booms. In contrast, the A.D.C. vehicle, which had actually been built to B.C.T. specifications, sported a bright red livery and was naturally dubbed 'the fire engine'; it carried a Strachan centre-entrance 37-seat body and a 50 h.p. Bull motor. A cheque for £1,425 was duly posted to A.D.C. in December 1926 when the trackless, KW 200, joined the fleet as No. 540.

Meanwhile seven further tracklesses had entered service, and in view of the close watch kept on railless expenditure by the Estimates Sub-Committee, it is curious that the new acquisitions apparently escaped entry in the Minutes. They comprised the original Garrett demonstrator, UM 1755, star of the ill-fated journey to Idle in 1925, which now ceased its wanderings and took up a settled existence as No. 536, still in its plum and cream livery, for which reason it was known as 'the Keighley trolley'; Nos. 537-9 (KW 204-6) which were replicas of Garretts 532-4, and three A.D.C. type 603 Strachan-bodied trackless (541-3, KW 201-3), which were smaller versions of No. 540 but with front entrance – the first in the fleet – intended for one-man operation.

The long-disused Gaisby Lane wires and the little-used Queen's Road brake-testing circuit, relics of an earlier, pioneering age, were dismantled in 1926 and the poles lifted for use elsewhere. Simultaneously the whole of the overhead fittings were re-designed to Municipal Tramways Association specifications: composition insulators gave way to porcelain, and spacing between the positive and negative wires was increased from 1ft. 1in. to 1ft. 6in. as on the Clayton route.

The four trackless routes had always existed in isolation from each other. The Clayton and Frizinghall/Bolton Woods services operated from different parts of

The short wheelbase of A.D.C. 603-type Nos. 540-3 (the first front-entrance trackless in Bradford) caused them to pitch and see-saw on uneven roads, but they were in regular use on all the pre-1929 routes. No. 541 was photographed at Rooley Lane (Birch Lane) in 1927.   *B.C.T.*

the city centre and used the tram track and tramway overhead wires for depot journeys to and from Thornbury – to the discomfiture of a policeman on point-duty at the end of Well Street who kicked an erring 'skate' back into the groove of the tram rail and received a shock which unceremoniously threw him flat on his back. The Odsal-Oakenshaw cars were similarly isolated from Bankfoot depot: only the Bolton-Bankfoot cars enjoyed a proper depot connection. Perhaps the spectacle of new trackless using outmoded methods may have impressed itself upon the Estimates Committee: in February, 1927, they voted £729 for negative trolley wires from Laisterdyke to the city centre (Thornton Road), thus enabling the Clayton trackless to travel to and from the depot in

a dignified manner. A few hundred yards of extra wiring would have conferred a similar benefit on the Canal Road trackless, but no connection was ever made.

A similar form of segregation existed in the vehicle fleet. The new A.D.C.s and Garretts did not stray from the Clayton and Bolton-Bankfoot routes, whilst the Canal Road route continued to be served by the Frizinghall 'one-manners' (523-8) now mercifully running on pneumatic tyres, and the Bolton Woods 'crew' vehicles of the 504-520 class in all their solid-tyred discomfort. The Odsal-Oakenshaw route saw no vehicles other than the latter.

The flood of private buses now swamping the City brought these anachronisms to an end. Yorkshire (Woollen District) buses operating into Bradford from Cleckheaton and beyond imperilled the Odsal-Oakenshaw trackless so seriously that their replacement by a Corporation motor-bus service from the city centre was considered. Instead, in March 1927 it was decided that 'a through service of railless electric trolley vehicles be instituted between Oakenshaw and the centre of the city', necessitating the outlay of £2,500 for new wiring on the span-wire system between Odsal and City. This was obviously a future investment, as when the Manchester Road tramcars were eventually superseded by trackless, no further expenditure would be needed on the most heavily-trafficked section of the route. Such a change-over obviously lay in the distant future, as the Corporation were actually negotiating to extend the tramcar service to Brighouse, which would have strengthened the Manchester Road tram services considerably.

The old Odsal-Oakenshaw 'boneshakers' performed their last duties on October 23rd 1927 when possibly for the first and last time they used the new Manchester Road wires for a final journey to Thornbury Works and the scrapyard. Next morning a fleet of new English Electric/Leyland single-deck trackless inaugurated the new City-Oakenshaw service from a loading-point in Town Hall Street. Part of a batch of ten vehicles ordered in April at a cost of £14,012-10-0d, they were numbered in the series 544-553, and a significant sign of changing times was that whereas the early trackless had incorporated as many tramcar parts as possible for ease of maintenance, the new vehicles were based on Leyland 'Lion' bus chassis with a view to the exchange of spare parts with the growing motor-bus fleet. Four vehicles took up residence at Bankfoot depot and the remainder at Thornbury. The old Odsal turning-circle was dismantled.

A few weeks later the manager was authorised to link the Oakenshaw and Clayton routes as a cross-city service. Although the link was established shortly afterwards, (March 14th, 1928) its advantages were unclear and its disadvantages many, as no less than nine new sets of overhead 'frogs' and crossings with their attendant 'dead sections' were needed in the Town Hall Square area. These additional pitfalls for the unwary in a complex and heavily-used hub of the tramways were an unfortunate source of dewirement, damage and delay.

Above: Number 548, seen here at Killinghall Road in 1927, was one of ten vehicles marketed by English Electric but based on Leyland 'Lion' PLSC chassis with E.E. body and electrical equipment. *B.C.T./W.Y.P.T.E./W.Y.A.S.*

Left: The second batch of English Electric/Leyland tracklesses had plainer front panels, giving a hint of later trends in appearance. Number 554 stands at 'the back of the Town Hall', a few yards away from the Oakenshaw route *B.C.T.*

Equally serious it was found that delays on one section of the cross-city route caused disruption on the other, as the tracklesses shared the overhead wire with the trams between Odsal and Lidget Green. After a few years, the through service was discontinued, to the relief of tram and trackless drivers. Indeed, their motor-bus counterparts were accustomed to poking gentle fun at them: when incoming buses from Brighouse and Huddersfield reached the foot of Manchester Road their conductors sometimes alighted, pretended to 'pull' the overhead frog for Clayton and blew their whistle as a starting-signal, greatly to the mystification of the point-duty policeman, who wondered where the trolley booms had disappeared to! Throughout its existence the through service was maintained by Garretts, A.D.C.s and the later English Electric single-deckers as well as Leylands from Thornbury and Bankfoot depots.

Attention now turned to the Allerton tramway, for which track renewals (including a section on a centrally-placed sleeper track from Crow Tree Lane to Yew Tree Lane) had been agreed early in 1925. But the unexpected emergence of motor-buses had raised doubts as to the whole future of transport in Bradford, and immediately after the General Strike it was resolved that buses should replace the Allerton trams. The now familiar game of municipal shuttlecock began. The Council referred the decision back to the Tramways Committee, who promptly reaffirmed it, only to relent a fortnight later in favour of 'such means of transport other than tramways'. A firm proposal to instal tracklesses at a cost of £37,650 including removal of the tram rails and reinstatement of the carriageway was approved in February 1927 only to be reduced to £29,560 despite lengthy harangues by the Mananger, Chairman, Deputy Chairman and City Engineer. The economies were to be made in the fixed installations, with the result that the 1902-vintage tram standards were retained as far as Four Lane Ends, and the tracks were left untouched until the mid-1930s except where the reservation was to have been. The ensuing Provisional Order was unsuccessfully opposed by its intended beneficiaries, the Allerton residents!

In April 1928 the Manager was authorised to buy six new railless cars (554-559) to replace the remaining 1914 cars; the contract again went to the E.E.C. Co. for similar vehicles. A few days later, however, Mr. Wilkinson recommended that in view of road widening in Harrogate Road the Greengates tramway beyond Undercliffe should be replaced by double-deck motor-buses with the possibility of tracklesses in about four years' time (presumably when the Undercliffe trams were withdrawn). The closure – the first tramway abandonment – took place in November, after which tram standards removed during road-widening were replaced by new and heavier standards bearing electric street lighting of the type which in 1927/8 replaced gas lighting on all tram and trackless routes in the city and the Clayton, Queensbury and Shipley urban districts.

Meanwhile, no doubt bracing himself for the anticipated storm, the manager had mentioned the fateful word "Thackley", whose tramway, he said, was now in such a dangerous condition that the conversion of both the Thackley and Allerton routes should be carried out forthwith so that they were ready for use as soon as the Provisional Order became an Act. Permission to anticipate parliamentary approval did not materialise, but neither did the storm: all the sound and fury of previous years had been drowned by the clatter of the unfortunate tramcars staggering over the outworn tracks. Local councillors were now complaining of shock, bruising and impending disaster, thus enabling the Tramways Committee Deputy Chairman (Coun. W. Hodgson) to observe that but for interference by the Estimates Committee headed by Ald. Stringer and his Idle colleagues ('a clannish lot') they would already have 'a trolley-bus service which would delight them'. So Mr. Wilkinson's ruse had worked: the projects were approved unanimously.

Detailed planning could now begin. For the Allerton route a central terminus in Tyrrel Street, between Bridge Street and Ivegate, was selected in face of fierce opposition from dispossessed taxi drivers. Shipley U.D.C. finally agreed to accept tracklesses and to sell the Thackley-Nab Wood tramway overhead equipment to Bradford, who would erect new equipment in its place. Plans to buy fourteen more E.E.C./Leyland 36-seat single-deckers were dropped, however, as better prospects were now in view.

The success of a pioneer Guy Motors six-wheel double-deck trackless at Wolverhampton in 1926 had spurred on competition within the industry, and the English Electric Company's entry into the field was warmly welcomed by Bradford, as the company's products had always given complete satisfaction: indeed, its traction motors were actually manufactured at Phoenix Works, Thornbury. Contracts worth £14,351-16-6d were therefore placed with the company in March 1929 for half-a-dozen six-wheel (ie three-axle) double-deckers with air brakes and upper deck rear emergency windows – a recognition of the increased weight of the new vehicles and the arduous nature of the routes they were destined to encounter. In Allerton's steep main street, prophesied Mr. Wilkinson, fully-laden petrol buses would face severe problems, but tracklesses would ascend and descend with ease ("And shake the buildings down!" interjected Coun. Guy – a remark which earned him a rebuke from the Chairman, Coun. Irvine Smith, who emphasised the tremendous improvements made since the advent of the 'Flying Cottage Loaves', recently withdrawn). Eleven 34-seat single-deckers were simultaneously ordered from English Electric for general use.

Meanwhile a further trackless had been acquired – a Leyland/English Electric single-decker, No. 560 (CK 3898), which had seen service in the North since mid-1927 including six months regular use at Ashton where it had carried loads of up to 65 miners without a single breakdown. Following service at Maidstone (from July 25th, 1928) it found a permanent home in Bradford; basically similar to Nos. 544-559, it boasted modern rheostatic braking.

The official inspection of the Allerton route took place on November 25th, 1929. Between City and Four Lane Ends the overhead wires were shared with the Thornton tramcars, and an intermediate turning-circle was provided at Chapel Lane, plans for a similar facility at Squire Lane having been discarded. At Thornbury part of the tram depot (the 'Far West') was ceded to the trackless fleet which had now outgrown and forsaken its 1915 corrugated-iron 'Railless Shed', more popularly known as 'The Tin Shed'.

In preparation for the conversion of the Thackley tramway the order for six double-deckers was increased to thirteen, and vehicles of the first part of the order (572/3/7) arrived at the same time as some of the second part (578-581). No. 572 had been photographed in August at the E.E. Company's Preston works and was probably the vehicle which travelled over the Preston tramways for demonstration purposes.

The electrical equipment embodied series/parallel control actuated by pedals with notch regulators, ie ratchet devices to prevent excessive acceleration. These produced a staccato 'ter-cumpa-ter-cumpa' sound as the drivers pedalled to attain full power, after which the gentle whine of the transmission took over. Release of the pedals opened the contacts with a noise like a falling cashbox: the air brake resembled a genteel sneeze. From the rear platform the heat from the tyres could be felt (and smelled) as the laden vehicles hurried up the hills. After a full shift at the controls the drivers claimed that they 'paddled' in their sleep; inevitably their steeds were dubbed 'the Paddlers'.

Bradfordians who glimpsed a rear view of the gleaming new vehicles – the city's first commercially produced double-deck tracklesses – were considerably impressed, though their aesthetic tastes were somewhat jarred when No. 572 and its fellows ventured outside the depot, as their appearance was marred by an unhandsome projecting cab. The design was influenced by the need to achieve a seating capacity similar to that of the tramcars within the existing weight regulations.

For Mr. Wilkinson much was at stake: his credibility and reputation which had sustained so many rebuffs and reverses rested on the success of the new venture. The civic opening of the Allerton route on November 29th 1929 and the commencement of the public service on December 1st was therefore deeply satisfying to him. The comfort and speed of the well-sprung, deeply-upholstered tracklesses was enthusiastically welcomed by the Chairman as well as by the members of the Yorkshire, Lancashire and Derbyshire section of the Municipal Tramways Association who rode over the route on two special tracklesses described as 'the finest vehicles of their type ever built'.

Determined to display his proteges to their best advantage the manager allocated high-speed tramcars to the Thornton route to avoid delays on the common section of wiring and imposed a 2½d. minimum trackless fare on outward journeys to discourage short-distance passengers between City and Four Lane Ends. More spectacularly, in February 1930, he organised a race between a petrol bus and a trackless:

Seen at the end of its days, No. 560 had on a varied career not only in Bradford but also at Ashton and elsewhere. Effectively, it had been the prototype for the batches of Leyland-based English Electric single-deckers of 1928 and 1929, having been built in 1927 and the only one officially acknowledged as a Leyland, though its Preston registration number, CK 3898, reflects the English Electric origin of the body, built in that town *F. Hartley*

the trackless emerged victorious, although the Rotherham manager alleged that the bus was deliberately held back when the trackless suffered a dewirement at Chapel Lane!

Thus vindicated and emboldened, the manager and City Engineer raised once again the future of the Idle tramway – the cause of so much sound and fury – with the recommendation that tracklesses be instituted and the route extended to Greengates at a total cost of £15,580 including vehicles. Also, neatly circumventing the Council's earlier refusal to sanction the full cost of the Allerton conversion they reported that as the tram rails were to be partly removed, a new negative feeder cable costing £6,250 would be needed. Unable to deny the obvious success of the Allerton service, the Council meekly agreed.

Alas: triumph and euphoria were shortlived. All too soon it became apparent that the 'Paddlers' were not performing properly. One by one they suffered burnt-out motors and had to be ignominiously replaced by the hitherto unnoticed new E.E.C. single-deckers, Nos. 561-9, whose 34-seat capacity caused great overcrowding and loud complaints. Even louder was the condemnation in the Council chamber where all the old doubts and dislikes were revived. If the manager was doing his best, said members, his best was insufficient and his appointment should be terminated.

It was disclosed, however, that the responsibility lay with the manufacturers, who were already rectifying it at their own expense: the fault lay in the gear ratio, which had been quickly exposed by the taxing climb through Allerton village.

Temporarily silenced, the critics retired, but the rumblings continued all year. The reign of the single-deckers on the Allerton route was fairly brief, and the revitalised double-deckers gave no further trouble. But rapid wear on the overhead line ears on the side-running sections gave cause for concern, though

Imposing English Electric six-wheeler No. 581 was bought in 1929 for the Allerton service but is seen here in Dudley Hill Road in 1930. Although among the earlier vehicles to arrive, in December 1929, this was one of the second half of the first batch of twelve vehicles (572-583) based on English Electric E11 chassis, more truly an 'own-make' venture by that firm, even though components were bought out from specialist firms such as Kirkstall for axles and Rubery Owen for the frames. The body design showed signs of emerging English Electric standards, notably at the rear, where the enclosed staircase was very up-to-date. At the front, the set-back upper deck was more conservative and the cab design did not marry-up too happily with it. These were 'the Paddlers'.

B.C.T.

the problem was solved by reversing the ears so that the impact of the trolley wheel was1 against their "hard" side.

Much more serious were rumours of financial irregularities in the conversion of the Thackley tramway, now in hand. Apparently unable to keep costs within the approved estimates, the manager (rumour said) had in desperation bought new equipment under the guise of routine maintenance expendituure, and sensing the imminence of discovery had turned to Holy Writ for guidance.

Chief guest at the cermonial opening of the Saltaire (via Thackley) route on March 29th 1930 was Mr. Spencer (manager, 1898-1918) who was so impressed by the transformation wrought by the latest trackless venture that he prophesied even more futuristic developments such as electric vehicles powered by radio beams.

Public service began on March 30th, and the reaction was wholly favourable. Unable in the excitement of the moment to decide on a name for the new conveyances, a press report declared the 'vehicles' to be '.... infinitely superior to the old tramcars, being luxuriously appointed, roomier and much more comfortable to ride in. In fact a ride on one of the new cars strikes one as a lightning change from ancient to modern. They are speedier and brook no delay on the part of intending passengers. You must keep dead time or you miss the bus, for it steals swiftly and silently upon you, and a second later it is off again. One feels inclined to express some doubt whether the agitation worked up in Idle against railless some time ago was well founded.'

Mr. Wilkinson must have relished that comment.

The long, tortuous and demanding nature of the new route earned it the title of 'The Long Drag' – a name reputedly shared with an even longer railway not many miles distant. Involving a journey time of 30 minutes, it diverged from the Eccleshill tramway at Bolton Junction and the Idle tramway at Five Lane Ends before squeezing through the constrictions of upper Idle to Thackley, where a complete turning-circle existed for use by 'Thackley nobbuts', ie vehicles working between Thackley and Saltaire only. Shipley was reached via a long descent and a low, awkward railway bridge at Windhill; in Shipley town centre, where power supplied by the U.D.C. was fed in, the City-Baildon Bridge tramway was crossed at right-angles. A tight turning-circle had been erected at the top of Saltaire Road, well clear of the City-Manningham Lane-Saltaire-Bingley-Crossflatts tramway. In the interests of economy, sound tram standards were retained, although those in Shipley were hurriedly deprived of their massive pear-shaped finials in case the vibrations set up by the fast-moving tracklesses dislodged them.

Depot accommodation was provided at Thornbury with access via Well Street and Forster Square as well as a one-way connection at Bolton Junction. No connection was made with the Canal Road wires with which the Saltaire route shared a few traction poles at the foot of Balme Street.

For the Canal Road trackless passengers the contrast between the 'Paddlers' and their own antiquated conveyances was all too painful. Although the 1914- vintage cars (504-520) were now a memory, the remaining 'one-manners' (526-7) which continued to provide the service along with one or two newer single deckers compared poorly with the relatively comfortable private buses now roaring past them on their way to Baildon, Shipley and beyond. Nevertheless the service was a homely one: the staff often delayed the departure of the last trackless from City until known 'regulars' – frequenters of the 'White Lion' in Kirkgate – were safely aboard. On one remembered occasion a

morning trackless overshot the Frizinghall turning-circle and was stranded there until workers at nearby Dumb Mills emerged for their mid-day break and pushed it back under the wires; its absence from the route had not been noticed!

Preparations for the replacement of the Idle tramcars began in May 1930 when an English Electric tender for 12 'double-deck railless electric trolley vehicles' @£27,000 was accepted without demur. Serious opposition to the tracklesses had finally been overcome by the unqualified success of the Saltaire (via Thackley) service. Equally important, Royal Assent was given on August 1st to the Provisional Order for the wholesale replacement by tracklesses of tramcars inside and outside the City boundary*, the only disappointments being the deletion at the insistence of the unfriendly West Riding County Council of three sections in the County area, i.e., Tong Cemetery – Birkenshaw, Gain Lane – Stanningley and Baildon Bridge – Baildon Green, on grounds of hypothetical 'unsuitability' – though Hunsworth U.D.C. was keen to see tracklesses at Birkenshaw.

It was therefore ironic and sad that Mr. Wilkinson, now assured of a future for the tracklesses he had championed so long and at such a personal cost, was not allowed to reap the rewards of his forthright perseverance. On September 15th, 1930, he notified the Town Clerk that he had been advised to retire on grounds of ill-health; his attendances at Committee, infrequent of late, never resumed, and he retired on superannuation on December 31st. Happily he saw the full and entire vindication of his theories, as he survived until 1943, long after his detractors had been finally confounded.

at an estimated cost of £494,571 compared with £916,000 for the renewal of tramways.

English Electric No. 567 passes the 'Five Lane Ends Hotel' en route for Saltaire, circa 1930. The gleaming tramlines were used by the Idle trams for a further year. This batch of vehicles, ordered at the same time as the first six-wheel double-deckers, were also 'English Electric' in chassis make, though still using Leyland parts. This vehicle entered service on the same days as the double-decker shown on the opposite page, December 3rd 1929. B.C.T.

Chapter Four
Triumph of the Trolleybus

There was no time to lose. Severely affected by the flood of private buses which had clung, leech-like, to the Corporation's main routes since the General Strike, and suffering now from loss of patronage as a consequence of national and local trade depression, the Department was at a low ebb.

Within days of the announcement of Mr. Wilkinson's retirement Lord Ashfield, chairman of London's company tramways, agreed to allow Mr. Spencer to carry out an investigation of the Department. The ensuing report, promptly and thoroughly produced, revealed that Bradford's operating costs were higher than London's in every instance except for the repainting of traction poles which in Bradford received a three-yearly one-coat treatment. Running costs per vehicle mile were: tramcars 1s. 6.5d, motor buses 1s. 2.5d, tracklesses 1s. 2d. Compared with its London equivalent, Thornbury Works employed one third more staff but achieved only half the output. The 'outward and visible signs' of the Corporation's acceptance of the

report included decreased wages, a reduction of 100 in the workforce, an investigation into motor-bus deficits and the possibilities of diesel engines in place of petrol machines, confirmation of the trolleybus policy and a simplified fleet livery with minimum gilding and lining-out: only the 'Clarendon'-type fleet numerals introduced in 1919 survived as reminders of a more splendid age.

On December 13th 1930 a new team was appointed – C.R.Tattam, M.Inst.T., General Manager; H.J. Troughton, A.M.I.C.E., Rolling Stock Engineer, and Norman A. Scurrah (works superintendent) Car Works Superintendent, the appointments dating from February 1st 1931. Charles Richard Tattam, manager of the Balfour Beatty Group since 1920, had sound experience of all three types of transport through the Group's ownership of the Mansfield and Llanelly undertakings, and saw trams as victims of the Great War.

His first public appearance was on March 20th

Magnificent but sombre in gold-lined Prussian blue and ivory, No. 595 is proudly displayed at the English Electric works in Preston in 1931. This was numerically the last of the second dozen E11 six-wheelers, the 'Tripplers', with modified frontal design, more aesthetically satisfactory than the 1929-30 order. Forward vision for the driver when negotiating in traffic must have been difficult, however. This was one of ten of these vehicles sold to Newcastle Corporation in 1942, though this one was used for spares only. *English Electric Co., courtesy B.C.T.*

Soon to become B.C.T. No. 596 this English Electric demonstrator combines the body style of the 'Paddlers' (though with a 'modernised' profile) with the more advanced equipment of the 'Tripplers'. The moulding above the cab advertised for many years the merits of Hammonds' Ales. The vehicle dated from 1929, having been an exhibit at the Commercial Motor Show that year, but was made redundant as a demonstrator by the agreement between A.E.C. and English Electric to market trolleybuses as a joint venture, though not taken into stock in Bradford until March 1932.

English Electric Co. Courtesy B.C.T.

1931 at the formal opening of the Greengates (via Idle) trackless route, successor not only to the Idle tramway but also to a Greengates (via Swain House Road) bus service introduced to fend off private competition. The tracklesses, which began to operate the public service on March 22nd, ran beyond the old tram terminus to Albion Road, a short distance from the Greengates (via Undercliffe) bus terminus. Although the name 'Idle' appeared on destination blinds, no terminal facilities were provided there, but a circle was erected at Five Lane Ends, precipitating the abandonment of the tramway track to that point, relaid at such cost only six years earlier.

For the Saltaire (via Thackley) route the balance of the 1929 order for single and double-deckers had been delivered; numbered 570/1 and 574-6, 582-3 they were of course identical with those purchased for the Allerton service. In body style and technical refinement the twelve six-wheel double-deckers (584-595) delivered in February/March, 1931, for the Greengates conversion were superior to their predecessors. With their 100 h.p. English Electric motors and easily-manipulated contactor control they gained instant popularity with the drivers, who nevertheless had to remember to 'trip'

a small foot pedal after each brake application, a peculiarity which inevitably earned the soubriquet of 'Tripplers' for the new vehicles. The 'Tripplers' represented the end of an era as well as the beginning of a new: they emerged in the last, undiminished magnificence of the Wilkinson livery and were the last six-wheelers and all-English Electric vehicles ordered by Bradford.

An interesting feature of the Bradford undertaking in the 1930s was the partial segregation of vehicle types between the 'old' fleet ordered before the first tram-to-trackless conversion (Allerton) and the 'new' fleet which was now no longer regarded as experimental. The 'one-manners' (523-8), the Garretts and A.D.C.s (529-543) and Leylands (544-560) continued to ply their accustomed paths. Only once did an 'old' trackless venture on a 'new' route: one afternoon front-entrance A.D.C. single-decker 543 was drafted from the Bolton-Bankfoot service for a journey to Saltaire and back. Fearful that the patent 'eddy' brake might be inadequate for the long descent from Thackley to Windhill the driver applied the handbrake continuously, filling the saloon with smoke. By this time the oldest vehicles – the railless lorries – had vanished into history, and No. 511, last of the 1914 cars serving as winter gritting wagons, had retired after being photographed as late as January 5th, 1930.

The 'Roaring Twenties' with their tumults and contentions were over: the increasingly uneasy Thirties were beginning. Trade depression continued to cast dark shadows, but long-term planning continued in the belief that all would come right in the end. For the Tramways Department the period 1932-3 was one of consolidation and evaluation; the finances of the undertaking were taking a favourable turn, and the trials with diesel engines were proving successful.

One further six-wheel trolley vehicle entered service – No. 596, similar in appearance to 572-583 but with the more modern equipment of 584-595. An English Electric demonstrator, its travels had been cut short by the announcement that the English Electric (E.E.C.) and A.E.C. companies had joined forces to produce a new breed of trolleybus chassis, types 661T-662T and 663T, based on the popular A.E.C. Regent, Regal and Renown designs.

Meanwhile the wildest excesses of private bus competition had been curbed by the 1930 Road Traffic Act, though the challenge remained. Since November 1929 tracklesses had not operated on the Frizinghall service between 9 a.m. and midday, to the annoyance of would-be passengers who were thereby obliged to pay the higher protective fares applicable to all private buses within the City boundary. Then, on October 13th 1931 it was agreed that for a trial period the Frizinghall and Bolton Woods services should be worked by Corporation motor-buses as a means of recovering traffic lost to the West Yorkshire Road Car Co. Motor-buses operated from September 25th (prior to the decision!) until December 8th when the tracklesses surprisingly returned – not the obsolete 'one-manners' but the front-entrance A.D.C.s (541-3) and others of their generation. Two months later the company offered to withdraw their competition on the Clayton route if the Corporation would terminate 'their service of railless trolley vehicles on the Frizinghall and Bolton Woods Section'; Mr. Tattam estimated that the closure would save £2,000 per year. Despite objections by Coun. T.I. Clough the agreement was concluded, and the final day of the Corporation service was April 30th, 1932. No significance was attached to this first abandonment of a trackless route (even though a part of the city was left without municipal transport), as the Corporation had other plans in mind.

When proposals for an express motor-bus service to Crossflatts in place of the loss-making trams beyond Bingley suffered unexpected defeat following strenuous opposition from the West Yorkshire Road Car Co., the County Council and Keighley Corporation, Mr. Tattam concluded that in order to recover lost ground on this key route he would have to play his trump card, the 1930 Trolley Vehicle Act, whose implementation the protestors could not prevent. As from May 1932 the lease of the Bingley tramways was accordingly renewed on a year-to-year basis only, and a universal 1d.

any-distance tram and trackless fare was applied outside peak hours, Mondays to Thursdays, on all routes within the City, thus effectively undercutting the independent operators.

Meanwhile the old Bolton tram depot, built in 1898, had been adapted for tracklesses at a cost of £1,200 in the summer of 1931. The incoming six-wheelers and single-deckers naturally served the Saltaire (via Thackley) and Greengates (via Idle) routes and shared the depot with the remaining handful of Eccleshill tramcars, a new open-air siding having been laid alongside the depot to accommodate extra trams serving Peel Park at holiday times. Between City and Bolton Junction trams and tracklesses used separate overhead wires, an unusual feature which imposed considerable stresses on the many Edwardian tram standards but also enabled sporting passengers to lay bets as to which 'steed' would be 'first past the post'. Regrettably an accident induced the Ministry to order the removal of the tram wires to prevent overtaking.

Two tales of Bolton Depot are worth recounting. Descending Idle Road at speed one day a six-wheeler suffered the dewirement of one trolley which, flailing about, caught the live wire and pulled it taut as piano wire as the vehicle braked. Unable to free it, the conductor reported the mishap to the depot foreman, Mr. Fisher, who angrily took a ladder and climbed to the roof of the trackless, from which vantage-point he unwisely sheared the wire with cutters. Up flew the trolley boom, released from tension; the trolley head catapulted away out of sight while the severed wire fell to the road. The driver, hearing shouts of "Get this bl— dy thing in the shed!" instantly released his handbrake: the ladder clattered to the ground, and the depot staff, hearing a crescendo of oaths as the trolley-bus rolled towards them with Mr. Fisher clinging grimly to the roof, discreetly vanished into the inspection pits.

Another day a trackless was backed out of the depot and allowed to coast down Bolton Road at gathering speed. Not until he touched the rheostatic brake pedal at Peel Park did the driver remember that the master controller was still in the 'reverse' position: the trackless stopped dead and the conductor with his cash and tickets was hurled the full length of the saloon. Suggestions that this accidentally-discovered form of deceleration might be adopted as an emergency brake were rejected for fear of even worse emergencies, not least insurance claims from bruised and buffetted passengers.

Important future developments were foreshadowed at the end of 1933. Adopting modern terminology the Committee resolved to replace tramcars by 'trolley buses' in the Eccleshill, Lidget Green and Thornton routes.

In the autumn of 1931 an A.E.C/E.E.C 663T six-wheeler had given demonstration runs in Bradford and London before being exhibited at the Commercial Motor Show. Painted green and cream, it bore an English Electric body with half-cab and dummy 'bonnet' (like the Notts. and Derby four-wheelers built a year or two later), forward entrance with folding door and twin staircases; power was provided by an 80 h.p. D.K.130A motor. Although the novel vehicle found favour with Southend-on-Sea (it became their fleet No. 116), for the new Bradford routes tenders worth £50,640 were sought for 21 double-deck four-wheelers and overhead equipment. The three proposed routes required vehicles able to provide fast, intensive services; the A.E.C. and E.E.C. designers believed they had the answer.

Bradford, hovering uncertainly between prosperity and commercial depression, was a city of granite-paved streets, dignified Victorian warehouses, well-built stone residences and back-to-back cottages all blackened by the sooty outpourings of a thousand chimneys: a bustling, homely, friendly city nevertheless, in whose lively thoroughfares horse-drawn wool wagons, coal carts and milk floats easily held their own with the motor-cars which for most people were an unattainable dream.

Into that world came Queenie – a vision in pale cream and pastel green, sleek, luxurious, gleaming with bright chrome and polish, a foretaste of a future in which everything would be new and functional yet well-designed and pleasing to behold. In comparison with her the other trolley-buses and motor-buses appeared as sombre, ugly relics of the Twenties – as indeed most of them were; the neat tramcars had to admit to feeling outdated, and even No. 393, Queenie's petrol-powered twin, was dismissed as a mere 'Juggernaut'.

To the statistician – that unfortunate being to whom beauty is an intangible, unclassifiable irrelevance – Queenie was an experimental front-entrance trolley-bus with an A.E.C. 'Q' type 761T four-wheel chassis and E.E.C. 63-seat body and electrical equipment. But to the press she was a creation 'as fair as a lily' as she brightened the drab streets in her 'cheerful colours'; for a 2¹/₂ year old boy who chanced to be at Allerton one summer morning that year, Queenie's unexpected arrival on the scene created an instant impression which remains forever fresh.

Alas: Queenie was ahead of her time. As two-axle vehicles were limited to an overall length of 26 ft, her front-entrance design deprived her of an overhang behind the single-tyred rear wheels. Consequently her unusual weight distribution brought problems in icy conditions, and the lack of platform doors made her even chillier than the other trolley-buses in the totally unheated fleet: the conductor's cheerful cry of "Front door today, luv – we've a fire in t' parlour!" was doubly ironic. Long after her trials were completed and her bright colours dimmed to match her standard-liveried petrol-driven twin, she officially joined the fleet as No. 633. No further 'Q' vehicles were ordered: for the new routes the increasingly popular AEC 661T chassis had been specified from the outset.

The Eccleshill tramcars performed their last duties on May 29th 1934 being replaced next day by a mixture of Bolton Depot's six-wheelers and single-deckers – mostly the latter. Taking advantage of good-quality materials offered for sale by defunct tramways, the Department had erected ex-Accrington poles with ex-Dearne District finials, but the overhead equipment set a new standard, being suspended from stylish Brecknell Willis hangers (the Thornbury brass-foundry which had produced the traditional unequal-arm hangers had closed during the 1931 economy drive). A triangular reverser was erected at the entrance to Moorside Road, being superseded by a tight-radius turning-circle outside the 'Mechanics' Institute' in 1941.

Route numbers, used by the trams since 1919, were theoretically applied to the rest of the fleet about 1930, the series 40-59 being allocated to the trolleybuses and the higher numbers to the motor-buses. By 1931 the

Representatives from the Transport Department, the Committee, English Electric and A.E.C. admire the sleek line of the 'Queenie', the AEC/EEC 'Q' trolleybus, as she reflects the spring sunshine at Thackley Corner in 1934. The vehicle had been produced for display on the English Electric stand at the 1933 Commercial Motor Show, and receiving the registration KY 6210 on entering service as a demonstrator in Bradford in February 1934. After being taken into stock she was given the number 633, after the first two batches of A.E.C. 661T.

trolleybus series was:- 40 Allerton, 41 Chapel Lane, 42 Bolton-Bankfoot, 47 Clayton, 48 Pasture Lane, 49 Oakenshaw, 50 Saltaire, 51 Thackley, 52 Greengates and 53 Five Lane Ends; as the sequence was roughly alphabetical the Bolton Woods and Frizinghall routes were presumably 43/44. Realising, however, that the tramway abandonment programme would cause the disappearance of familiar numbers, the Department decided to retain existing numbers when trolleybuses took over. Thus the Eccleshill route remained No. 33, and the other routes were renumbered:- Allerton/Chapel Lane 31/32; Bolton-Bankfoot 34, Clayton/Pasture Lane 37/38, Oakenshaw 39 and Saltaire/Thackley/Greengates/Five Lane Ends 40-43.

The long Thornton route was appropriately opened on November 20th, 1934, by the Lord Mayor, Ald. Walter Hodgson, who was a native of Thornton and had served as Tramways Committee Chairman since 1930. Travelling over the new route in No. 604, one of the new A.E.C./E.E.C.s, he bade an official farewell to the 'rocking-horse' tram service which ceased the same night.*

From the new City terminus in Victoria Square to the bottom of Listerhills Road and between City Road end and Four Lane Ends the Thornton trolleybuses shared the Clayton and Allerton wires respectively; much of lower Thornton Road had never previously been served by Corporation transport and, like the new extension beyond the former tram terminus (Ashfield Road) to Thornton cemetery it was still gas-lit. The extra-wide carriageway between Fairweather Green and Spring Head Road, mostly constructed in 1923 as an unemployment relief measure, posed problems for the overhead line staff, who adopted the Nottingham style of catenary suspension to counteract the sagging effect of long runs of span wire. At the widest parts (Bell Dean Road and Hoyle Ings Road) extra-tall poles succeeded (but only just) in retaining the wires at an acceptable height, and strings of 'fairy lights' were strung up at these points to guide drivers in foggy weather.** Once again many ex-Accrington poles with Dearne District finials were used on the wide sections, with new or relocated poles elsewhere.

The 21 English Electric-bodied A.E.C 661Ts bought for the Thornton and Lidget Green routes closely resembled London Transport No. 63 (and later Ashton Leylands 48/52/55) and were numbered 597-617. A high seating capacity of 60 was achieved by the expedient of confining the driver to a half-cab and housing the contactor equipment in a waterproof cabinet attached to the offside chassis frame (as on the Q), thus releasing space over the nearside front wheel for a double longitudinal seat – a popular feature for small boys. Like 'Queenie', they had all-metal bodies in which the customary traction lighting (fed direct from the overhead line) was prohibited: low-tension lighting was therefore supplied from a motor generator; this emitted a continuous buzz when in use, but if the trolleys were removed from the wires a battery cut in to supply the side and tail lamps and reduced-voltage lighting elsewhere. English Electric type 405 80 h.p. regenerative motors powered the rear axle via double-reduction gearing.

The trolleybuses were painted in the now standard livery – Prussian blue panels with ivory bands, black beading, plain gold leaf lining, dark grey roof and Gill Sans letters and numerals. The interiors were equally serviceable – cream-painted ceilings, dark oak polished woodwork, brown-leathercloth-covered lining panels, tubular framed seats with Listers' latest blue-patterned moquette upholstery (lower saloon) and brown hide upstairs); vertical stanchions and ceiling rails (from

*although a few trams reputedly supplemented the trolleybus service next day.

** similar lights existed at the wide junction of Rooley Lane, Rooley Avenue and Mayo Avenue, Bank Foot.

Smart, businesslike and efficient AEC/EEC No. 601 in Rooley Lane in 1934 - the start of a new era of travel. This was one of the first dozen of the initial batch of 661T models, all of which entered service on 21st November for the Thornton route. The English Electric metal-framed body was to a new standard design, of up-to-date outline, similar to a prototype vehicle for London Transport delivered in August of that year, though the latter undertaking decided on six-wheelers just as Bradford took an opposite view.
B.C.T./W.Y.P.T.E./W.Y.A.S.

which brown-enamelled handgrips hung for the convenience of standing passengers) were covered in black Doverite.

They were fast. On the long, gradual ascent to Thornton they maintained a good speed at all times; on the return journey they flew like avenging furies. The loud hum of the double-reduction gears increased rapidly in pitch as they accelerated; the trolley-wheels hissed sharply, and at speeds of 35-40 m.p.h. (e.g. from Spring Head Road to School Green) the combination of transmission noise, reverberation from the trolley gantry and the vibration of the all-metal body rendered conversation on the upper deck not worth attempting. Driving them was a special skill, as power and electric braking were on the same (left) foot pedal. To decelerate, the driver slowly released pressure on the pedal; to coast, he removed his foot altogether, and to brake after coasting he applied power quickly and then released pressure, bringing the vehicle to rest with the right foot air-brake pedal. Wrongly used, the system could stop

Left: **Numbers 597 and 609 at Four Lane Ends, November 1934. The trolley gantry was a prominent feature of this generation of vehicles – later designs gradually evolved into a tidier style with the structure built into the roof.** *Transport World*

Below: **The lower saloon of No. 601 showing the continuous bell-push strip in the polished wood cornice and the extra seats over the front wheel which were later removed and the cab extended to full-width reducing the seating capacity to 58 – the contactor equipment on the offside had proved difficult to maintain and was moved into the extended cab, though another factor may have been problems with reflections and excessive internal light at night. Note the absence of grabrails or seat handles.**
B.C.T./WYMPTE,WYAS

the bus violently, with resulting passenger discomfort and complaints – accusations of trolleybus 'jerkiness' dated from this period.

The patent regenerative braking fed power back into the overhead line, thus reducing power costs but occasionally creating spectacular side-effects: descending Leeds Road from Thornbury Depot the new trolleybuses could explode the light bulbs in the Hall Ings tramway shelter; venturing on to the Bolton-Bankfoot route they encouraged the Wakefield Road trams to climb hills like spring lambs.

Hard on the heels of the Thornton conversion came the closure of the Lidget Green tramway. No new installations were required other than the redesigning of the Lidget Green turning-circle, the original of which, installed for emergency use when the Clayton route first opened, appeared to be virtually unusable: its only recorded use was during the spectacular 1933 snowstorm (which confined tracklesses to depot from February 25th until March 2nd) when single decker tracklesses operated the Lidget Green journeys on the morning of Saturday, March 4th, in place of the tramcars – a unique substitution. The new trolleybus service (No.4 as in tram days) began on December 12th, 1934, with a miscellany of Thornbury-based vehicles – single-deckers, six-wheelers, 'Queenie' and new A.E.C/E.E.Cs* as far as Lidget Green and the usual singledeckers to Clayton, from where all other vehicles were debarred by the low railway bridge.

On the demise of the Eccleshill trams a turning-circle had been provided at the foot of Lister Lane to cater for circuses, pageants and other attractions in the park; the destination 'Peel Park' therefore existed on trolleybus indicator blinds until 1948 when it was physically cut out and re-used in motor-buses providing a daily service to the Otley Road entrance to the park – trolleybuses thenceforth displayed 'Park Gates', a name normally applied to a Manningham Lane short-working. In 1935 the original Laisterdyke reversing triangle in Latimer Street, whose use necessitated the manual swinging of trolley booms and a certain amount of 'fly-shunting' when vehicles entered or came out of service, was replaced by a new triangle in Greenhill Lane, usable in either direction, with a double curve from Leeds Road into Killinghall Road.

The pace of tramway abandonment was quickening now. Between April, 1934, and February, 1935, no less than five routes were earmarked for closure, although four of them were deemed unsuitable for trolleybuses by reason of low frequencies or an excess of sharp corners. For the fifth route – the intensively served Duckworth Lane tramway – great changes lay ahead. Until early 1934 the Department had intended to renew the tram track in White Abbey Road and use the high-speed trams shortly to be displaced from the Thornton route; when pressed to instal trolleybuses the Chairman had demurred on the grounds that it was the best tram route and that it would be 'a pity to risk anything there when the trams are giving satisfaction'. However, his hand was forced when the Highways department decided to double the width of White Abbey Road, which would have necessitated the complete re-siting of the tracks.

Conversion to trolleybuses was therefore approved in September, 1934, at a cost of £38,500 for 15 double-deck vehicles, overhead equipment (including a few ex-Burnley poles) and an extension beyond the existing tram terminus along Pearson Lane to connect with the Allerton route which, together with Thornton, could then be served from Duckworth Lane Depot as in tramway days. The Pearson Lane project was dropped when residents of that exclusive area petitioned against it, and pending the completion of a new Royal Infirmary at the top of Squire Lane a terminal loop was provided around the depot, via Toller Lane and Little Lane. Motor-buses performed tramcar duties for a few evenings to facilitate the completion of the overhead wiring layouts, and commenting on the departure of the last trams the press solemnly pronounced that 'Ichabod** was written upon their walls'.

For the opening of the new route, No. 8, on October 2nd, 1935, fifteen additional A.E.C/E.E.Cs (identical with 597-617 except that the upper deck rear roof domes were painted ivory instead of grey) were placed in service as 618-632. On this, the busiest of all Bradford's routes, their success was spectacular and immediate. Although the demise of the trams had evoked regretful nostalgia, first-day passengers were 'in the mood of children with a new toy' as they took out their watches to time the trolleybuses. Popular fears as to the steep ascents and descents of Godwin Street and Whetley Hill were stilled as the powerful vehicles hummed busily up and down the granite-setted gradients.

Their rapid, determined acceleration was a great asset, as the many stopping-places on the densely-populated route were closely spaced, and the banshee wail of the regenerative brake acting on the double-reduction rear axle was soon a familiar sound in the area. Unfortunately their speed when compared with the more leisurely pace of the Siemens-motored trams (which despite promises had not been replaced by the high-speed tramcars displaced from the Thornton route) created tremendous difficulties for the conductors, who were often unable to cope with 60 seated and 12 standing passengers on a route only 3,275 yards long where passengers were beginning to alight only three stops out of the city centre. Not until T.I.M. ticket machines replaced the traditional bell-punches and additional hanging straps were provided for standing passengers was the problem alleviated; missed fares were common, and the author once beheld a frustrated conductor alighting at Whetley Street to (successfully) pursue a passenger who had left without paying his fare.

Now served from Duckworth Lane Depot the Duckworth Lane, Thornton and Allerton routes enjoyed the benefits of an all-new fleet. The six-wheelers

---

including perhaps No. 614, which entered service that day.

**'Thy glory is departed'.*

A typical 1937 Bradford scene - granite and stone setts, the Prudential Assurance Buildings at the city terminus of the Duckworth Lane and Allerton routes, an Austin motor car, Newby's (greengrocery and game), Harrison Parkinson (chemists) and smartly dressed ladies alighting from No. 630, one of the batch of fifteen A.E.C. 661T models with English Electric bodywork that were virtually identical with the original batch but dated from the latter part of 1935 – most entered service in October for use on the new No. 8 route, as in this case. The three-letter registrations were a novelty at the time, Bradford having completed its two-letter series with the final KY marks earlier in the year.   *G.H.F. Atkins*

which had maintained the Allerton service almost exclusively until 1934 and had occasionally visited Thornton were now seen only as Thornbury-based extras to Bell Dean Road and Chapel Lane.

Meanwhile the little fleet of Garretts had quietly faded away. Number 536 had actually preceded its former Keighley stablemates to the scrapyard in 1931, whereas fellow-demonstrator 535 had survived its old Leeds colleagues by seven years. Modifications were made to the new A.E.C/E.E.Cs whose roof-mounted circuit breakers had posed unusual problems: the long Bowden cables had stretched with use, so that when the circuit breakers blew, drivers were unable to reset them.

They were therefore re-positiioned in the cab above the driver's head, being hurriedly moved a few feet sideways following a unique but disastrous double short-circuit on six-wheeler 588 which dropped molten rubber on the driver's head and caused a frantic swerve which wrecked the vehicle. Also, the contactor equipment, accessible only via hinged panels on the offside of the A.E.C/E.E.Cs, was difficult to maintain; the driver's cab was therefore extended to full width to accommodate it, thereby depriving small boys of their previously mentioned favourite 'ringside' seat and

reducing the seating capacity of the vehicle to 58.

The extension of the Duckworth Lane route to the new Royal Infirmary opened on April 20th, 1936, after which the Little Lane circle was used only by depot vehicles. The extension required a tight turning circle and the building of a high retaining wall and was constructed to the new 2ft. 0in. overhead wire spacing being advocated by the Ministry of Transport. The positive and negative line hangers were attached to each other by a metal bar coupled to a porcelain insulator. All subsequent routes conformed to the new specification, but routes already constructed to the 1ft. 6in. spacing were not converted until 1946-1952.

Another form of overhead line improvement had been introduced to the city on November 24th 1935 when electrically-operated 'frogs' had been installed at Bolton junction. Conductors of Eccleshill trolleybuses were now spared the need to alight, pull a trigger to switch the frog and wait until the trolleys were on the Eccleshill wires: in future drivers applied two power notches as the trolleys passed beneath a 'skate' on the positive wire, thereby activating a solenoid which switched the frog to the Eccleshill direction, and a second skate reset the mechanism afterwards. Over a period of years this useful invention was extended to many well-used junctions where it was safe to do so: coloured signal lights informed drivers when the frog had been set and reset.

It has sometimes been alleged that the conversion of Bradford's tramways to other forms of transport was carried out in a haphazard, unplanned way, whereas in fact it was governed by the life-expectancy of the permanent way, the imminence of major highway schemes and the influence of the Finance Committee. The routes converted to motor-buses in 1933-5 were, in general, those which did not merit the expense of trolleybus installations, though it is significant that the loss of cheap fares associated with electric traction led to calls for trolley-buses to Shelf and to Haworth Road via Duckworth Lane and Heights Lane with the aim of reducing fares from 3.5d. to 2.5d.

Two examples of official intransigence occurred in October 1936 when requests for a trolleybus service to Horsfall Playing Fields (by the Parks Dept.) and passenger shelters outside the Town Hall (by the Transport Manager) were smugly dismissed as 'not feasible', which in reality meant that it could be done, but those responsible did not want it!

The triumphant progress of the trolleybuses was momentarily halted on February 24th 1936 when a fire at the Corporation Electricity Works plunged the city into darkness. Trams and trolleybuses were immobilised (except in the independently-supplied Shipley and Bingley areas) until a limited traction supply was restored next day. Borrowed motor-buses temporarily filled the gap, but the incident was not permitted to inhibit trolleybus expansion: after all, householders did not revert to gas lighting simply because their electric lights had failed once!

The conversion of the Crossflatts tramway, foreshadowed four years earlier, was agreed on December 18th 1936 at an estimated cost of £115,303. An important, prestigious route, five of whose seven miles were outside the city boundary, it required an intensive service as far as Saltaire and was subjected to determined competition from the West Yorkshire Road Car Co. In the interests of high-speed operation the overhead equipment was to be designed to ultra-modern specifications – 2ft. 0in. separation with hickory-wood spacer bars, grooved 'cottage-loaf' section cadmium copper wire and flush-fitting mechanical ears to provide an uninterrupted path for the trolley wheel, extra-short line ears on straight sections, easy curves with equally spaced pull-offs to minimise dewirements, frogs and crossings incorporating brass runner bars for rigidity, reduced pole spacings (necessitating the replacement or resiting of almost every pole) and augmented power supplies. Negotiations with Bingley and Shipley U.D.C.s and the West Riding County Council (the highway authority outside the city) were well in hand by May 1937 but the process and preparations were inevitably lengthy and complex.

Meanwhile attention had been drawn to the Wakefield Road setion where it was claimed that between Dudley Hill and the Tong Cemetery terminus the track was so bad that passengers were liable to be

Repainted in C.R. Tattam's later style of livery, six-wheeler No. 594 of the 1931 batch of English Electric vehicles hastens up Highfield Road on a return journey from Saltaire and Thackley, about 1937. *Courtesy D.M. Bentley*

thrown through tramcar windows or even pitched overboard – a piece of hyperbole which doubtless drew smiles from Bradford's hardy tramcar travellers. Replacemnent by trolleybuses at a cost of £49,400 including road reinstatement was accepted in February 1937.

English Electric Leyland single-decker 547 achieved unique fame when it overturned in Pasture Lane on October 28th 1936; the days of the Clayton single-deckers had long been numbered, however. Plans to increase the headroom under Pasture Lane railway bridge had been explored in January 1935 and accepted eighteen months later. The trolleybus service was suspended on August 15th 1937 a motor-bus service via Bradford Road being provided next day as a temporary measure; normal trolleybus journeys to Lidget Green (with peak-hour extras to Pasture Lane) operated as usual. The road underneath the bridge was lowered, creating a steep gradient at either side; the wires were strung closely together under the crown of the arch, and drivers were warned against trying to pass other vehicles. The route number 37, hitherto confined to timetables, was displayed for the first time on November 24th, when double-deck trolleybuses made their triumphal debut at Clayton.

A revised service pattern was then introduced with alternate Clayton and Lidget Green workings and peak-hour extras to Pasture Lane, although for a further year Leyland and E.E.C. single-deckers continued to be seen at Clayton as frequently as 'Queenie' and the A.E.C./E.E.C.s.

The fleet now numbered 96 vehicles – A.D.C.s 529-531 and 540-543; E.E.C.s/Leyland 544-560; E.E.C.

single-deckers 561-571; E.E.C. six-wheel double-deckers 572-596; A.E.C./E.E.C. 661Ts 597-632 and A.E.C./E.E.C. 761T 633. The A.D.C.s shared the Bolton-Bankfoot service; the Oakenshaw route now saw only EEC/ Leylands based at Bankfoot depot, whilst the single-deckers and six-wheelers appeared on most of the routes served by Bolton and Thornbury depots. The A.E.C./E.E.C.s were virtually ubiquitous except that they were never allowed to venture up Manchester Road, and were let loose on the long reaches of the Saltaire (via Thackley) route only at Bank Holidays when there were sufficient vehicles to absorb their regenerated current.

Even better things were in store now. The progress of trolleybus design and development never slackened throughout the 1930s, and thanks to cordial co-operation between the Transport Department and the English Electric Company's Bradford factory at Phoenix Works, new equipment designed by the company was tested in service by the Corporation, who in turn suggested practical improvements on the basis of practical experience.

The first fruit of this beneficial partnership was trolleybus 634. Like its immediate predecessors this stylish vehicle was based on the highly-successful A.E.C. 661T chassis, but in place of the noisy double-reduction rear axle allied to E.E.405 motors and regenerative braking the design incorporated normal worm-drive and newly-evolved E.E.406 lightweight compound-wound motor with series-dynamic braking, which provided mild regeneration without the inconvenience of large current surges. A few weeks of trials in daily service sufficed: a contract for 57 similar vehicles was placed with English Electric in July 1937 at a cost of £125,884-10-0, No. 634 being bought for £1727 in November.

Public support continued to grow. In June 1937 Cllr. Arthur Smith enquired whether the conversion of the motor-bus routes as well as the tramways was contemplated; more prosaically Ald. Louis Smith requested that alternate Duckworth Lane trolleybuses should terminate at Little Lane instead of the Infirmary. In reply the Chairman (Ald. Hodgson) confidently forecast that 'they would have two or three projects in view with regard to trolleybuses' when the Crossflatts conversion was complete. One of these was a trolleybus replacement of the Heaton motor-bus service, which would comprise a branch from the Crossflatts route to Little Lane, connecting with the Duckworth Lane service and the Little Horton motor-bus service which since 1935 had formed an extension of the Heaton route.

Slowly the traces of abandoned tramways were

Number 634, though outwardly similar in most major respects to the two batches of A.E.C. 661T models with English Electric bodies and equipment already in service incorporated fresh ideas to give new levels of refinement. It had just been completed at the English Electric bodybuilding works in Preston when seen here in January 1937. Series-dynamic control gave mild regeneration without the large current surges and this in turn allowed A.E.C. to revert to the quiet-running worm drive axle.

B.C.T./E.E.C.

submerged beneath a carpet of tarmacadam, 'special work' suitable for re-use having first been recovered. The Thornton and Allerton routes received this treatment in 1936/7, and the Bolton Road passengers escaped at last from the 'atrocious' road surface of which they had complained for so long.

These improvements, however, brought into the open a question now beginning to trouble men's minds. In October 1936 Coun. Harrison queried whether "in view of the imminence of another war" it was wise to cover tram track which could otherwise be salvaged for munitions. Ominous events across the Channel, beginning with the occupation of the Rhineland in March 1936, were creating an atmosphere of unease.

"Coming events", it is said, "cast their shadows before". In July 1937 it was suggested that as trade was rapidly improving because of the Government's rearmament programme it might be advantageous to defer the contract for 57 trolleybuses until prices fell. The Chairman, however, sounded a note of urgency: the cost of the contract was already higher than six months previously, and would be much higher if they waited another six months – possibly they might be unable to obtain the trolleybuses for a very long while if they deferred the purchase. Indeed, the cost rose by £186-10-0 per vehicle before the year was out.

Trolleybus 635, first of the new delivery, entered service on January 7th 1938; its semi-streamlined body, though basically similar to that of 634, resembled the E.E.C. bodies fitted to Daimler motor-buses 446-455. Floor-mounted contactor cabinets in the driver's cab gave the passengers a much better forward view than had hitherto been possible, and interior and exterior finishes were neat, attractive and serviceable. The lightweight all-metal body construction was slightly overplayed – the rumble of the trolley-wheels under line ears and junctions was intrusive on the upper deck – but otherwise the performance was quiet, and trials indicated new standards of passenger comfort.

The conversion of the Crossflatts tramway, delayed by a dispute with Shipley U.D.C., was overtaken by work on the Tong Cemetery route, which opened on July 6th 1938. The route climbed increasingly steeply as far as Dudley Hill, where a short-working loop and connection with the Bolton-Bankfoot route was provided in Mulcott Road; in the city centre the convenient tramway loading-point in Norfolk Street was discarded in favour of new facilities in Union Street, with separate loading points and overhead sidings for Tong Cemetery (18) and Dudley Hill (19) vehicles. A low railway bridge, known locally as 'marble arch' was encountered at Bowling, beneath which curious metallic resonances were created by the trolley wheels of approaching and departing trolleybuses.

The new service was provided from Thornbury Depot, as Bowling tram depot had been quietly turned over to the A.R.P.* unit – this was the year of Munich – although until the following May trams were driven or towed there for scrapping. Overhead equipment on the route was designed to the high-speed standards evolved for the Crossflatts conversion.

Trolleybuses 636-651/3/5 arrived from Preston

in time for the inauguration, being joined by 652/4-660 before the end of the year. Nos. 634-9 were then exchanged for a few of Duckworth Lane's 1935 regenerative vehicles (618-632 series) which began to appear on all services worked from Thornbury Depot.

The contract for 57 trolleybuses awarded to the comapny English Electric had been subdivided at Mr. Tattam's request to comprise 42 A.E.C. 661Ts with E.E.C. bodies and 15 Karriers with Weymann bodies, E.E.C. electrical equipment being of course fitted to both types. Nos. 677-9 therefore emerged in September, 1938, as Karrier E4s, a make previously unknown in Bradford, bearing sleek Weymann bodies similar to those fitted to motor-buses 456-465.

The quaint A.D.C.s and a few of the Leylands now took their leave, although A.D.C. 529 and Leylands 549/550 survived as grit-wagons for winter use. The fleet livery for all vehicles, previously Prussian blue and ivory, was subtly altered to Ultramarine (a blue-black similar to Belfast's 'Princess Blue') with pale cream – a particularly pleasing combination. The alteration went unnoticed by the technical press who, reviewing the latest acquisitions, commented appreciatively that, 'The new vehicles with their blue and white livery possess a smartness which will make them prominent in Bradford, and their comfort, mobility and silent operation will enhance the popularity already gained by trolleybuses in this progressive Yorkshire city.'

Minor route number changes also occurred: Lidget Green changed from 4 to 39 to conform with the other numbers (37/38) on the same route, and Oakenshaw switched from 39 to 35, but plans for a short-working service 36 to Hollingwood Lane (between Lidget Green and Pasture Lane) were not pursued.

Bradford was changing. Under the impetus of the increasingly urgent re-armament programme the combs, spindles and looms of the myriad worsted mills quickened their pace, and the 'dole' queues of the earlier 'thirties melted away. More motor cars were seen in the streets; bright new houses and schools were springing up beyond the reach of the smoke canopy, and life was becoming a little easier than before.

The conversion of the Crossflatts tramway commenced at the outer terminus on May 25th 1938 adding to the prevailing air of modernity. Wisely eschewing the lurid glare of sodium vapour street lighting then on trial in Canal Road, the Corporation Electricity Department and its colleagues in Shipley and Bingley agreed to equip the new, prestigious trolleybus route with mercury-arc vapour lighting for which extra-tall poles were required; consequently every alternate pole was 6ft. higher than its neighbours and bore neat, modern lighting units. The customary short bracket arms, being unnecessary, were therefore omitted and span wires were attached direct to the poles by plain or multiple straps. As on all routes since 1934 Nottingham-type catenary suspension was used, substituted by 'dropper' suspension on the 80ft.

* *"Air Raid Precautions"*

Left: A.E.C./E.E.C. No. 657, new in October 1938, on 'the Golden Mile' in May 1939. The neat turning-circle at Bingley Church was manufactured and erected by the Ohio Brass Co., new in October 1938. This type of English Electric body proved more durable than its predecessor and this vehicle was quite typical in running over 17 years unrebodied – several did over 20. *Keighley News*

Right: More streamlined than No. 634 (see page 41) but with a lower seating capacity - a weight-saving measure – No. 635, seen shortly before delivery, entered service in January 1938 and was the prototype for the 636-676 series of A.E.C. 661T with English Electric bodywork. *B.C.T./E.E.C.*

Below: Streamlined Weymann elegance in 1938. Karrier E4 No. 677, specially posed in Rooley Lane, is journeying neither to Allerton (31) or Clayton (37) *B.C.T./WYMPTE/WYAS*

Below Right: A.E.C./E.E.C. No. 650 seen in Bingley Main Street on a trial run in April 1939.

Telegraph & Argus, courtesy A. Whitaker

carriageway north of Cottingley Bridge. Between Poplar House, Bingley, and Harold Street, Crossflatts, ultra-neat Ohio Brass overhead fittings* were used in place of the well-tried Brecknell Willis components; the trial section proved so trouble-free that it was dubbed 'the Golden Mile'.

About 800 new or resited poles were planted and 28 miles of copper wire strung; new substations for the increased demand were constructed at strategic places. Every available tower-wagon and crew was pressed into action, and for several weeks horse-drawn wagons were stabled overnight at Saltaire Depot whilst their motive power grazed in fields at Nab Wood.

Originally scheduled for February 1939, the change-over was delayed by the construction of a traffic roundabout at Saltaire (the first in the area) and the revision of loading facilities in Forster Square, where trams had used the central island as an anti-clockwise loading-point. A path was cut through the island to allow trolleybuses to share one side of the glass-roofed loading barriers used by the Bradford Moor and Undercliffe trams – a temporary expedient to be replaced by a one-way scheme as soon as the Bradford Moor trams ceased, the real goal being a bus station in the vicinity within seven years.

In this fast-changing scene Ald. Titterington's forecast that within seven years they might decide to 'cut out' trolleybuses altogether was not considered worthy of a reply, and a request for the cost of operating the Crossflatts route by motor-buses instead of trolley-buses received nothing more than an oblique comment that the Tong Cemetery conversion had increased revenues by £151 per month.

On April 17th 1939 trolleybus 650 was seen in Bingley Main Street on an expeditionary journey. Like succeeding test vehicles it encountered stretches where the new wiring could not be completed until the trams ceased, and a member of the depot staff had to sit on the rear platform controlling a new version of the old 'skate' – a trolley wheel running in the groove of the tram rail and attached to the anchored-down negative trolley boom by an insulated cable taped to a hand-held pole. Similarly, a member of the overhead line staff travelled on the upper deck, leaning out of the rear emergency window to check the behaviour of the trolleys on the new wiring and recommend adjustments where necessary.

Around the partly-completed Saltaire island an overhead circle was erected for joint use by the new service and the existing Saltaire (via Thackley) vehicles, a reversing triangle being provided for the latter in Dove Street while the alterations were in progress. Another circle and layby were provided at Bingley Church. In the city centre connections were made with the Duckworth Lane route (via North Parade, Upper Piccadilly and John Street), with the Bolton Road routes (in Forster Square) and to Thornbury Depot (via the existing Well Street and Leeds Road wiring).

The Crossflatts route and its various shortworkings were inspected and approved by Col. Trench of the Ministry of Transport on May 3rd, the trial vehicle being driven by Chief Inspector Lister Wilkinson and occupied by Bradford, Bingley and Shipley representatives. The inspection was obviously a final formality, as the tramcar service ceased only three nights later, on Saturday, May 6th 1939. In a night of feverish activity redundant tram wires were cut down, a truncated tramway siding was connected up at the Bradford Moor loading-point in Forster Square, and all obstacles to a successful inauguration were swept away wherever possible. Inside Saltaire Depot gleaming A.E.C./E.E.C.s of the 653-676 series awaited a new day; others were parked in the Forster Square loading bay ready for an early start.

Next morning's debut was inauspicious. Unnerved by the anticipatory presence of Mr. Tattam the driver of specially-selected trolleybus 666** suffered a damaging dewirement when negotiating the Saltaire roundabout, and another vehicle had to be brought out of the depot for the first journey, from Saltaire to Crossflatts. But as soon as additional turning-circles at Nab Wood and Park Gates had been completed and the last lengths of tram wire removed, the success of the venture was assured.

Service frequencies were generous: intending passengers no longer sprinted to catch a vehicle, as the next one was usually in sight, between City and Saltaire at least. 'The trolleybuses provide an extremely comfortable journey which only those who used the trams on this route can appreciate to the full', reported the press, who nevertheless queried 'whether the retention of so many stops is really a necessity. They are tantalisingly numerous to the suburban rider in a hurry'. Fortunately, however, the service speeds were impressive: the normally quiet, pleasant hum of the A.E.C. transmission rose to a high-pitched whine (marked by the frantic hiss of the trolley wheels) as the trolleybus sped along under the meticulously-planned overhead wiring.

Basic services were from Forster Square to Crossflatts (24) with alternate journeys to Bingley (24) and a very frequent service to Saltaire (25); one or two morning peak-hour extras reversed at Nab Wood (25), whilst football and Bank Holiday extras used the Park Gates circle (un-numbered). Plans for peak-hour extras to Branch (26) were dropped when Shipley U.D.C. declined to allow the construction of turning facilities outside the Branch Hotel or at the entrance to Northcliffe Playing Fields.

The balance of the Karrier E4 contract (680-691) was assigned to Bolton Depot, whose allocation of six-wheelers and single-deckers had not altered since 1931. The advent of modernity was, unfortunately, a

---

an unsuccessful attempt was made by the Department to manufacture its own form of twin-hanger with composite spacer bars; a solitary example was in use for a few years outside Bolton Depot.

**despite being startlingly dubbed 'The Beast' by well-educated scholars of Bradford Moor School (Revelations Ch.13 v.18), 666 and its fellows gave long, faithful and reliable service.

The A.E.C./English Electric trolleybuses bought for the Bradford-Crossflatts route conversion had only a short time in which to display their clean lines and pleasing livery. Within four months of the conversion in May 1939 blackout masks and white paint on trolley booms, mudguards and lower panels marred their appearance. Number 654, which had entered service in July 1938 (working elsewhere at first), approaches Nab Wood while, in the background, the new Bingley street lighting languishes disused and partly dismantled. *Keighley News*

mixed blessing, as the steeply-cambered roads in the Bolton area caused the lightly-sprung Karriers to sway and roll unpleasantly until the suspensions were adjusted: their performance on the tortuous Clayton route caused them to be barred from that route in later years. A few more Leyland single-deckers (558-560) were withdrawn, leaving Eccleshill and Oakenshaw as the only routes regularly served by single-deckers.

In the warm summer of 1939 Bradford Corporation's passenger fleet presented a smart, efficient picture. The almost wholly double-deck motor-bus fleet comprised modern A.E.C.s and Daimlers plus a few older Leyland Titans, whilst the timeless tramcars, reduced to a mere 112 but still a match for most vehicles on Bradford's gradients, were all high-speed, well-upholstered cars. In the eyes of the public, however, the future lay with trolleybuses, and the "two or three projects" hinted at by Ald. Hodgson were confidently awaited.

But what were they? Although the final tramway abandonment was expected within three years, no long-term plans had been announced. Bradford had always maintained a route-by-route approach to future

developments, but trolleybus conversions needed time, forethought and capital commitment. The next tramway due for closure was the Wibsey route, whose long gradients and intensive services were ideal for trolleybuses - indeed, many corroded standards in St. Enoch's Road and Fair Road had been replaced by trolleybus poles. Yet, curiously, the Department had no plans for Wibsey trolleybuses: in January they had commenced a supplementary motor-bus service to Moore Avenue via Canterbury Avenue, and in July resolved without debate to replace the Wibsey trams with motor-buses at a cost of £39,000.

What had happened? Why, only a few weeks after the spectacular success of the Crossflatts trolleybuses, should an equally major route be destined for motor-buses? No doubt several factors influenced the change of mood – the proved success of diesel engines since 1932, a reluctance to 'put all the eggs in one basket' after the Electricity Works breakdown, and difficulties in obtaining copper wire because of re-armament.

It could be conjectured that of the remaining tramways Queensbury, Stanningley, Wyke and Bowling Old Lane would become motor-bus routes, leaving

Bradford Moor (30) and Thornbury (9) for trolley-buses. The future of the Odsal (15) route was problematical: 1927-vintage trolleybus equipment existed over its entire length and could be modernised (together, possibly, with the Oakenshaw extension) but the presence of parallel bus services to Wyke, Brighouse, Huddersfield and Shelf made it less attractive.* The third of the 'two or three possibilities' could, however, have been the promised City-Heaton-Little Lane route, where a substation, already supplying the Crossflatts section, had just been opened in Wilmer Road.

The outbreak of the Second World War on September 3rd, after weeks of mounting tension, abruptly set aside all such considerations. Motor-bus services were quickly curtailed to conserve fuel supplies, and with the resumption of the Undercliffe tram service it became apparent that electric traction was to be a valuable asset in the 'War Effort'. Out went the new street lights (and the old); the freshly-painted two-tone green traction standards received three white bands (or one solid band at stopping places) as an aid to pedestrians and drivers; white paint was applied also to mudguards, platform edges, the bottom of lower deck panels and the tips of trolley-booms.

Vehicle lighting was cut to the minimum. Headlamps, never brilliant at any time, were reduced to a masked slit, and 'cats-eye' reflectors had to be embedded in the carriageway beneath section breakers. Front destination screens (and, uniquely, the rear screen on 634) were screened by a cowl; route numbers and rear destinations were unlighted. Interior lampholders were quickly replaced by conical masks made of 'blackout paper'; the bulbs were coated with blue paint, but the effect was so eerie that red paint was substituted until grey-painted canisters masking clear bulbs were devised to provide dim interior lighting.

For trolleybus drivers great vigilance was needed to avoid causing arcing at junctions, crossings and breakers; blackout shields resembling upturned loaf-tins were placed over 'frogs' and crossings, without much success, as the blue flashes inevitably caused by trolleybuses negotiating complex depot yard wiring could be seen over a wide area. Clinch ears on round-section wire were a minor source of sparks; for several evenings motor-buses were used on the Duckworth Lane route while new grooved wire with flush-fitting mechanical ears was strung up (although no more round wire was bought after 1937, it was not eliminated for many years).

By the end of 1939 the blackout had caused several pedestrian fatalities and a weekly drop of £850 in traffic revenue.

*however, the existence of the name and number on trolleybus destination blinds may have been a pointer.

Standing passengers (as many as the lower deck gangway could accommodate) were a familiar feature of trolleybus travel as the war got under way. Conductresses began to replace men who were called up. The interior furnishings of this AEC/EEC (640,650,660 or 670) include grey wool repp seat backs, silk cut-moquette seats, cream-painted ceilings, dark oak woodwork and grey blackout masks covering the lights.
B.C.T./WYMPTE/WYAS

Chapter Five
War and Austerity

Although the severe problems encountered by Bradford's transport in the First World War were not repeated in the Second, demands on the services were great. Queues formed at most stops – in Forster Square they spilled into the roadway – and vehicles carried a full standing load: indeed, in the Oakenshaw single-deckers the seating was rearranged peripherally to accommodate 'crush loads'. Fortunately the trolleybus and tram services were allowed to operate at almost pre-war frequencies, whereas their motor-bus counterparts, dependent on imported fuel, ceased at 9 p.m. and did not run on Sunday mornings.

Similarly the dilapidation of the previous war did not recur. Unlike municipalities such as St. Helens, Sheffield and South Shields whose vehicles suffered greatly from air raids and associated problems, the Bradford trolleybus, tram and motor-bus fleet enjoyed pre-war standards of maintenance throughout: boarded-up windows and battered paintwork did not occur. Minor economies were made: stops were reduced slightly; copper sleeves were used on the underside of line ears to prolong their life; yellow paint lining replaced gold leaf, and time-table booklets were not published, but these were insignificant sacrifices in comparison with those suffered elsewhere.

A Karrier E4 demonstration trolleybus entered service in January 1940: offered for sale @ £2,455, it was formally purchased as No. 692 in March. Whether it had ever operated outside Bradford is doubtful, as it was painted in the standard Bradford colours and was identical with 677-691 apart from minor details, i.e., the route-number display was alongside the destination aperture (as on the newest motor-buses); the headlamps were mounted differently, and the outward flare of the lower-deck panels (a typical 1939-1953 Weymann feature) imparted an elegant appearance. In June the manager was authorised to buy a number of poles on offer to Bradford, but the source and type are unknown.

An unexpected move was the closure of the Oakenshaw trolleybus route on July 31st, 1940. The official reason was 'the bad condition of the overhead equipment and the cost of replacing it'; some of the wiring beyond Odsal dated form 1915 and (in the words of drivers) 'hung down like yards of clothes-line', i.e., slackly, and in blackout conditions the triangular reverser at the terminus and inadequate wiring at the depot entrance posed problems. Additionally, the absence of any negative feeder point past Odsal prevented the use of all-metal bodied trolleybuses, but there were plenty of composite bodies in the fleet. In the breathless interval between Dunkirk and the Battle of Britain the disappearance of a minor route evoked neither comment nor opposition. The remaining Leylands (552-557) were replaced by motor-buses, but the 1927 wiring in Manchester Road (Croft Street to Odsal) was retained with interruptions at junctions and other places; bonded to the tramway positive wire it provided a useful power booster until the end of tramways in 1950.

The imminence of the threatened German invasion and intensification of air raids on South-East England induced Southend-on-Sea Corporation Transport to seek safer homes for its newest trolleybuses. Bradford agreed to hire six A.E.C./E.E.C.s @ £20 per vehicle per month; the order was later modified, and four (124-7) migrated at the height of the crisis to their refuge at Saltaire Depot for almost exclusive use on the Manningham Lane routes (displacing 653-656). Their pale (powder) blue and off-white livery with mid-grey roof earned them the instant name of 'Bluebirds'; drivers liked the smoother acceleration provided by their extra resistance notch, but depot staff cursed their traction (high-tension) lighting, made possible by the composite construction of their Strachans bodies. Bradford afterwards claimed that the 'evacuees' had benefitted from their Yorkshire holiday, whereas Southend claimed they had been 'ruined'!

Southend trolleybus No. 124, AEC/EEC No. 668 and Undercliffe tramcar No. 232 share the covered queue barriers in Forster Square, 1941 *Modern Transport*

Steel helmets and respirators (gas-masks) were bought for the traffic staff in October, 1940; miraculously, however, the need for them had already passed. Bradford was fortunate to suffer only one air-raid, the Luftwaffe otherwise overflying the city on route to Manchester and Liverpool. Air-raid sirens therefore sounded frequently, and on September 1st there was a five-hour raid which (inter alia) dislodged trolleybus wires in Tyrrel Street and peppered with shrapnel nos. 610, 620 and 639 parked nearby. No other B.C.P.T. vehicles suffered wartime damage, and the temporary canvas patches on 639 were so effectively treated that the vehicle did not need a full repaint for years.

A turning-circle was erected at Springhead Road as a fuel economy measure, and until the end of the war trolleybuses ran to that point (6) and Thornton (7) alternately.

Increasing patronage and the obsolescence of the six-wheelers inspired a request to the Ministry of War Transport in July, 1941, for permission to buy ten trolleybuses. Doubtless hoping for replicas of the A.E.C./E.E.C.s recently delivered to the Notts. & Derby company, Mr. Tattam was disappointed to learn that they had been allocated ten 'utility' vehicles, part of a batch of Sunbeam MF2 chassis ordered by Johannesburg in 1939 but detained in England because of shortage of wartime shipping space.

Like Nottingham Corporation's allocation of 'Jo'burgs' (the remainder went to St. Helens) the Bradford contingent was fitted with Weymann austerity-specification bodies (the first seen in the city) incorporating hardwood and pitch-pine frames, steel panels in place of aluminium, sliding windows in place of the preferred half-drop type, and only one destination aperture. Their B.T.H. electrical equipment embodied the unpopular regenerative braking, but the vehicles were 8ft. wide, i.e., 6 inches wider than the British standard, thus permitting wider gangways which were much appreciated by the tightly-packed standing passengers.

Unprepared for their arrival, observers were baffled to see un-numbered, un-named and unattractive trolleybuses in an unfamiliar light blue and primrose livery undergoing trials on trade plates; assuming them to be someone else's trolleybuses they were surprised to detect Bradford fleet numbers inside. At the insistence of the Ministry they were despatched to Saltaire Depot (displacing 653-662) where their extra width would not conflict with narrow roads and tramcars. Numbered 693-702, they arrived individually between June and October 1942.

Newly-repainted trolleybuses and tramcars immediately began to sport the new colours, unlike the motor-buses, most of which were unwillingly camouflaged in drab khaki-grey paint. Officially termed 'Bradford blue and broken white' but popularly known as 'South Sea blue and primrose', the new colours are believed to have been inspired by the paler hues of the recently-returned Southend vehicles, although the blue is stated to have been a gloss version of the undercoat used beneath the now-superseded ultramarine. Apart from colour changes the livery design remained unaltered, with the usual yellow and black lining, gold lettering and grey roof – a cheerful sight in the drab depths of wartime life.

The single-deckers and six-wheelers began to sport the new colours also, but by decree of the Ministry several of the latter (573/9, 580/4/5/6, 591/2/4/5) were sold for £2,000 to Newcastle Corporation, who were desperate for extra rolling stock. Earlier in the year South Shields' ex-Bradford manager H.J. Troughton had happily welcomed 'Queenie' into his fleet and put her to good use, but the enthusiasm of his Tyneside neighbours was conspicuously muted, as their acquisitions were years older than the 'native' fleet.

Apart from the changes referred to Depot allocations were unaffected by the war; Nos. 663-676 and 693-702 resided at Saltaire, single-deckers,

With anti-blast netting covering its side windows 'Jo'burg' No. 694 negotiates Nab Wood turning circle when brand new in July 1942. The Sunbeam MF2 chassis had been intended for Johannesburg and were of 8ft. width, requiring the Weymann utility bodies to this dimension – special permission was needed for their operation in Britain at that date, for 7ft. 6in. was the maximum in force at the time.
B.C.T./WYPTE/WYAS

New 8ft-wide 'Johannesburg' Sunbeam No. 694 and the first trolleybus to be repainted into the new South Sea blue 7ft. 6in. wide AEC/EEC, No. 671 of 1939, seen at Nab Wood boundary. Immediately behind the vehicles a section insulator divides the Shipley and Bingley power supplies; the Bingley pole (right) displays two white 'blackout' bands while the Shipley pole (left) shows three.

B.C.T./WYPTE/WYAS

six-wheelers and Karriers at Bolton, most of the 597-632 'regens.' plus 634-9 at Duckworth Lane and the remainder – a mixed bag of all types except 'Jo'burgs' at Thornbury. The Thornbury contingent served the Bolton-Bankfoot, Tong Cemetery and Clayton routes and their shortworkings as well as providing peak-hour extras to Bell Dean Road and Chapel Lane and 'changeovers' to other depots. A Bolton single-decker and six-wheeler ran from Saltaire to City via Manningham Lane at 8.40 a.m. each weekday, and a Karrier or a single-decker plied along Manningham Lane as far as Saltaire most Saturday afternoons, though it is likely that no single-decker ever reached Bingley or Tong Cemetery; six-wheelers were similarly unknown at Crossflatts or Clayton.

Bank Holidays however provided 'treats' for trolleybuses as well as humans. The attractions of Bingley, Shipley Glen and Lister Park placed such demands on the Manningham Lane services that other depots had to assist Saltaire. Thus, Bolton's elegant Karriers stole out of Bolton Road to load at the Forster Square barriers, and Duckworth Lane's regenerative vehicles joined the fun by way of the little-used John Street link. At the insistence of Shipley U.D.C. Bradford paid for modifications to Shipley's rectifiers as an insurance against excess regenerated current. Bingley, on the other hand, suffered from a deficiency of current, so that in the event of abnormal loads staff had to be on duty at the substation to reset the overload switches whenever they blew out. One intended function of the Nab Wood turning-circle was its use in emergencies if the Bingley power failed, but as the Shipley/Bingley boundary lay on the Bradford side of the circle, Bingley U.D.C. with deplorable municipal perversity insisted that the insulators dividing the two sources of supply should coincide with the boundary, thus limiting the usefulness of the circle. Nationalisation of electricity in 1948 quickly solved the impasse.

Like most large undertakings Bradford was a valuable training ground for ambitious staff who subsequently obtained leading positions elsewhere. Messrs. H. Muscroft and H.J. Troughton had progressed to South Shields, taking Bradford ideas with them; E.B. Baxter became manager at Stockport, whilst his contemporary R.E. Cox attained eminence at St. Helens and Walsall – but not before he had obtained an M.Sc. degree for a thesis on trolleybus acceleration and the economy of power consumption. Since 1938 all new overhead wiring in Bradford had been suitable for use by carbon-insert sliding trolley-heads (pioneered in London a few years earlier), and in 1942 experimental heads designed by Mr. Cox were fitted to Saltaire-based A.E.C./E.E.C. 666, followed by 667/8. Following modifications the new device spread to the other Saltaire vehicles beginning with No. 673, and gradually to the other depots, but none of the single-deckers, six-wheelers or tramcars received them. The development was timely, as trolley-wheels revolving at speeds up to 40 m.p.h. had worn out the Manningham Lane wiring in little over three years.

By 1943 the bodies of the 1934 A.E.C./E.E.C. 'regens.' were also worn out. Among the first all-metal bodies in the fleet, they had not withstood the vibration of the double-reduction drive, and fractured welds were common. Ministry sanction was procured in June for nine replacement bodies at £1,000 each, and these materialised a year later as Brush 'utility' (austerity specification) bodies with wooden frames and steel panels mounted on the chassis of 599-601, 605/6, 608/9 and 612/3. The original seats were re-used, as were the roof gantries for the trolley bases, retaining the old 1ft. 6in. separation. Before return to Duckworth Lane depot regen. braking was converted to series-dynamic.

As 1944 dawned the Ministries of Supply and War Transport approved the purchase of twelve new vehicles as replacements for the obsolete stock. The tenders,

Above: The first re-bodied trolleybus: AEC/EEC No. 605 displays its new composite body with fully-lined out livery at Brush Coachworks, Loughborough. A shortage of aluminium necessitated the use of steel panels which rusted after periods of condensation.

B.C.T./WYPTE/WYAS

Left: Durability took precedence over comfort when 'utility' Karrier Ws superseded the single-deckers and six-wheelers. Roe-bodied, wooden-seated No. 712, dating from July 1945, reverses out of Balme Street into Bolton Road following the Forster Square fire in 1950. From 1942, the only type of trolleybus chassis available in Britain was the W-type produced in the Wolverhampton factory used by Sunbeam and Karrier and sold under either name, previous Karrier users like Bradford thus receiving their vehicles with Karrier nameplates.

J. Copland

from Karrier, C.H. Roe and Metrovick, costing £33,000, were a formality, as allocations of new vehicles were made by the Ministry of War Transport in the later stages of the war; English Electric were fully engaged on war work.

Shipley U.D.C. approved plans in March, 1944, for a turning-circle at Ashfield Avenue, Frizinghall, for peak-hour shortworkings on the Saltaire (via Manningham Lane) route. This was a substitute for the proposed Branch (26) shortworking referred to above, and the former tram number (27) was inserted into the blinds. Numeral blinds now bore the series 4-9, 15, 18-19, 24-27 and 31-59, of which 4 was obsolete, 9 and 15 were tram routes, 35 (never displayed) had represented Oakenshaw, 36 had been for Hollingwood Lane and 44-59 were relics of the pre-1934 numbering.

Following the success of Allied landings in Normandy some of the more stringent wartime controls were relaxed. Vehicle lighting was brightened slightly, and in July the 5-year old decision to replace the Wibsey trams by motor-buses was re-confirmed at a much increased cost of £46,000. But whereas the 1939 decision had passed without comment, its reiteration aroused a storm. 'We know the track is bad', wrote one resident, 'We also know that trolleybuses are the future policy for Bradford, and that our electricity station is second to none. Why waste this supply and spend £46,000 on a temporary measure?'

The manager's reply that neither vehicles nor overhead equipment were obtainable was only partly accurate: three months later he was allowed to order 25 more trolleybuses for an estimated £75,000 and 12 replacement bodies @ £1,200 each. Nevertheless motor-buses replaced the Wibsey trams in January, 1945, and a few of the heavier poles were removed for use elsewhere.

The imminence of peace brought not only war-weariness and an impatience to shake off wartime controls but also unprecedented truculence towards authority. In December, 1944, the City Council learned that staff were 'asking for their cards' if complaints were made against them, and a reported sickness rate of 212 on January 8th, 1945, clearly concealed substantial absenteeism. Jobs were in plentiful supply, and the newly-coined phrase, "I couldn't care less!" was to bedevil relations between management and staff for years to come, though there was always a solid core of devoted, reliable staff to act as an inspiration to the rest. A maximum load of eight standing passengers was imposed on union insistence.

Delivery of the 'austerity' trolleybuses began in May, 1945. First arrivals were the Roe-bodied Karriers ordered in January, 1944; numbered 703-714 they were spartan, unprepossessing vehicles whose only attractive features were that they were new, electrically-propelled and painted in the full Bradford Corporation Transport livery. The wooden-slat seating and an apparent absence of springs in the W-type chassis ensured a rough ride for the Bolton Road passengers to whose service they were assigned.

Mercifully, although no less than 28 wooden seated motor-buses were already in service, in the trolleybus fleet Nos. 703-714 remained unique. Normally upholstered Karrier Ws 715-719 followed at the end of the year with Park Royal bodies and, happily, English Electric equipment and low-voltage lighting. Numbers. 720-733 were identical except that, as 703-714, they had high-tension lighting and Metrovick equipment. Material shortages obliged 703-733 to use trolley wheels for some time, although most of the fleet now used skids. The last of the Karrier Ws, 734-739, were fitted with skids from the outset, and with their Roe bodies, more stylish than their predecessors, heralded a slow return to normal conditions.

By this time the blackout was a memory; vehicles and streets were brightly illuminated again, and pole-painting resumed after an interval of five years.

All pre-1934 trolleybuses now retired - single-deckers, grit-wagons and six-wheelers, a few of the later migrating to South Shields and others becoming caravans. Civic leaders retired also: following political changes at the Town Hall Coun. B.W. Berry replaced Ald. Hodgson who had presided over the passenger transport scene since the days of R.H. Wilkinson, and the spectre of nationalisation darkened the scene.

Established policies continued nevertheless. The 1946/7 Capital Programme included £50,000 for the conversion of the Bradford Moor tramway to trolleybuses (still referrred to in the index of minutes as 'railless'). The delivery dates of materials and vehicles were, unfortunately, matters of conjecture. Thus, although orders were placed in September, 1946, with A.E.C. Ltd. for 12 chassis (£22,771-4-0) and with Weymann for matching bodies (£26,400), delivery was to be long delayed.

Work on the Bradford Moor route began nevertheless. Conventional traction poles being unobtainable, a 'job lot' of unusual fluted 'B' and 'C' poles was planted between Stott Hill and Hawthorne Street with 'A' and 'B' types in Harris Street, supplemented by heavier poles ex stock where required. The fluted poles were about a foot shorter than normal, and lengths of tram line had to be cemented into the base to provide the necessary height: apart from two dozen planted afterwards in Squire Lane, the rest were sold, reputedly finding their way to India by mistake!

After a long interval trolleybus wires were strung up from the 'Cock and Bottle' to Hawthorne Street with a right-angled crossing of the Bolton-Bankfoot wires at Killinghall Road. Wiseman and Co. twin-hanger suspension (without catenary) was used, the Bingley 'Golden Mile' having proved its worth. However, the trams were destined to use the new wires for a long time, as vehicle builders were in no position to fulfil their contracts: indeed, Weymann (a favoured supplier) sought release from their obligations and were replaced by Roe. Meanwhile the chassis manufacturers, A.E.C., had entered into a trolleybus partnership with Leyland under the name of British United Traction (B.U.T.) which, in the appropriate guise of 'Bradford's Untiring Trolleys' was advertised in the 1947 timetable, the first to appear since May, 1939.

Widespread renovation of the overhead lines now began. The Bolton Road group of routes, Manningham Lane (as far as Saltaire), Duckworth Lane, Thornton, Lidget Green and Tong Cemetery all received new wiring suspended from 'extruded rod' line ears. Existing tramway-type hangers were retained, but on the pre-1936 routes the spacing was increased from 1ft. 6in. to 2ft. 0in. with wooden spacer bars, the process being mostly complete by 1951. Most of the 'Nottingham' catenary was gradually removed, with the notable exception of the wide sections of Thornton Road and Bingley.

Inter-route connections received attention too. Squire Lane between Duckworth Lane and Allerton Road was wired up and a complete turning-circle was

Above: More stylish and better-appointed than the earlier Roe-bodied Karrier Ws, Nos. 734-9, dating from spring 1946, foreshadowed a return to normal standards. Number 737, seen in Rooley Lane (the B.C.T. photographer's favourite location), was later modernised and re-bodied and now resides in Bradford Industrial Museum.

Above and right: B.C.T./WYPTE/WYAS

Right: Re-painted in the South sea blue and primrose colours, 1939 Karrier/Weymann No. 690 passes through the bottleneck in Town Lane, Idle, on a return journey from Saltaire and Thackley in 1946. The 1927 style street lamp and 1930 vintage overhead equipment were modernised shortly afterwards and No. 690 received carbon-insert skids.

Below: Park-Royal-bodied Karrier W No. 733 of April 1946 rests at the Clayton terminus; its upholstered seats provided some protection against the hard suspension.   *J. Copland*

installed at Four Lane Ends to permit depot access for Allerton and Thornton trolleybuses without traversing the city centre; the Squire Lane equipment comprised partly-worn wire and the remaining stock of tramway-type hangers. The Four Lane Ends work brought forth the indignation of residents, as the inevitable hammering and clattering took place at night. Similarly the Thornbury route was upgraded: trolleybus wires were erected in Hall Ings to allow depot-bound trolleybuses to pick up passengers at the Thornbury tramcar loading point; between Hall Ings and Harris Street new poles and wires were provided (partly as adjuncts to the Bradford Moor route), and from Laisterdyke to the depot the old side-brackets were superseded by new span-wire equipment. Only the central portion of the route (Harris Street-Laisterdyke) retained its 1902 tram poles and 1927 wiring used by trams and trolleybuses alike.

Sporting facilities also received a share of attention: the combined attractions of rugby and speedway at Odsal Stadium induced the Department to devise an overhead turning-circle with sidings for each direction at Birch Lane near Bankfoot terminus, for the storage of 'sports specials' during the matches.

The remaining 1934/5 English Electric bodies were now at the end of their days; nine had already been rebodied by Brush in 1944, and the manager was authorised to rebody a further eighteen at his discretion. In the event all 27 old bodies were eliminated over a 2-year period, the overhauled chassis being despatched one by one to Northern Coachbuilders at Newcastle. The six 'Mark I' bodies received first were the last to be fitted with trolley wheels; the more elegant Mark II version closely resembled contemporary Bradford motor-buses as well as new South Shields, Newcastle and Maidstone trolleybuses. Being of composite (wooden frame, aluminium panels) construction they absorbed the transmission vibration much more efficiently than the original all-metal bodies, and it was unfortunate that the retention of the double-reduction

AEC/EEC No. 622, new in 1935, proudly displays its second body - a composite Northern Coachbuilders Mark I – at the 'New Inn', Thornton Road in 1946. This body design had distinct echoes of London practice in the cab area; the bodybuilder had a rebodying contract for LPTB in 1945-6.

J.A. Pitts

gearing condemned vehicles of such an up-to-date appearance to emit an out-of-date noise.

When Bradford's 'blitz victim', No. 639, was thoroughly overhauled and repainted in 1948, an era died, as it had been the last trolleybus in the pre-1942 ultramarine and cream livery and the last with trolley-wheels. Until the advent of carbon-insert trolley-heads the approach of a trolley bus had been heralded by a hissing, swishing noise which (except in the case of the 'regens.') drowned all other sounds, but now the quiet hum and whine of the transmission could be heard. Bradford's 'silent service' had arrived. Silence was not the only advantage: carbon inserts lengthened the life of the wires tremendously and permitted higher speeds at curves and junctions. For the next two decades the Overhead Line Department progressively improved wire alignments which, predictably, were exploited to the full by speed-loving drivers.

Contemplating the future of the Undercliffe

The crew of Northern Coachbuilders Mark II re-bodied No. 627 admire the panorama of Ilkley Moor obtainable from Allerton terminus where the old tramway waiting room and 1929 overhead equipment are still in use. The A.E.C. chassis was also from the 1935 batch and the 1948 body enabled it to live on to 1960. The Mark I and II distinction was a Bradford means of identifying the two body types.

C.W. Routh

tramway the Committee voted in February 1947, to set aside £50,000 for its conversion to trolleybuses. Initial plans for a 'trolleybus-only' road through the northern part of the Forster Square island similar to the one created in 1939 on the opposite side were discarded in the interests of traffic flow; the future Undercliffe and Bradford Moor loading-points were therefore to be kerbside locations in the north-eastern corner of the Square with the Manningham Lane services removed to the southern side. Contracts were placed with B.U.T., English Electric and Weymann for eight trolleybuses and with J. Spencer for the Undercliffe traction poles which were delivered unpainted, red lead or oxide primers being unobtainable.

In June 1948 the dwindling band of tramcars at Thornbury exchanged places with the trolleybuses, which then occupied the whole of the more modern east wing.

Interesting prospects were offered by a 1948 Parliamentary Bill (emerging ultimately as the Bradford Corporation Act, 1949) which created 'powers to enter into working and other agreements with neighbouring trolley vehicle operators'. This alluded, of course, to joint working with Huddersfield, whose trolleybuses operated to Brighouse, only a few miles from Odsal where the remnants of the old Oakenshaw wiring still provided power for the trams. Such a long-term project clearly depended on factors such as possible nationalisation of electricity and transport and the quest for new trolley- and motor-buses to supersede the remaining tramcars.

By June 1948, the Bradford Moor route was complete except at the inner and outer termini, and to avoid possible conflict between the intended trolleybuses and the Undercliffe trams the latter were replaced by motor-buses as a temporary measure. The Thornbury workshops were busily inserting 'Bradford Moor (30)', 'Chelmsford Road' and 'Undercliffe' into destination blinds, and at least one trolleybus (634) could also display '20' for Undercliffe.

At last, early in 1949, the twelve B.U.T.s ordered in September, 1946, arrived at Thornbury where they were stored in two vacant 'roads' exhibiting the meaningless display, '47, Reserved'. The interminable hiatus had allowed B.C.P.T. to benefit from the latest Ministry regulations authorising increased vehicle widths of 8ft. 0in. Resplendent in their light blue and primrose livery with pre-war style gold leaf lining, the dimensions of the B.U.T.s (740-751) were emphasised by the broad primrose waistbands and deep windscreens; their spacious interiors, large platforms and luxurious suspension provided new standards of comfort. For purposes of driver familiarisation No. 740 was licensed in May for exclusive use on the Bolton-Bankfoot route where it could not conflict with tramcars (except on depot runs between Thornbury and Laisterdyke); no such restrictions applied to 7ft. 6in. vehicles.

The tramcar service between Forster Square and Bradford Moor operated for the last time on July 23rd 1949, and a temporary motor-bus service (89) commenced. As soon as a roundabout had been built at the outer terminus (junction of Leeds Road and Leeds Old Road) overhead equipment with Wiseman's hangers was erected from Thornbury Depot and around the roundabout to connect with the Leeds Old Road wires installed two years earlier. Similar construction took place between the 'Cock and Bottle' and Forster Square with additional wires at the North side of the Square where the trolleybuses were to load; modified access from Bolton Road was provided at the end of Canal Road, where a few of the old Bolton Woods/Frizinghall poles were brought back into use. New wires in Harris Street provided an emergency connection between Leeds Road and Barkerend Road, and a turning-circle at Chelmsford Road replaced the former Killinghall Road tram short-working.

When the finishing touches had been applied - poles painted and tram-stop signs replaced by trolleybus signs - Karrier trolleybus 729 performed a test run from Bradford Moor to City and back on October 13th: its acceleration up mountainous Church Bank reputedly caused a policeman on point-duty to lose his helmet. The shuddering austerity motor-buses retired unmourned and unphotographed on Saturday December 3rd, and Sabbath calm returned to the nearby

The last Karrier E4 to be purchased, No 692, of 1940, was never photographed in its original colours. This 1948 view shows it in fully-lined postwar livery outside the Corporation Gas Department Head Office in Britannia House. Compare its design with that of No. 690 on page 48. The Weymann body was basically similar, but the outswept skirt panels were a characteristic feature favoured by this bodybuilder not hitherto seen in the fleet. The headlamps, though still of the small type favoured by B.C.T. were mounted slightly higher.   *J. Copland*

Top: Long awaited and warmly welcomed, Roe-bodied B.U.T. No. 748 inaugurates the Bradford Moor service on December 4th 1949. The 9611T chassis was equivalent to the A.E.C. Regent III bus model. The departure point was outside the Commercial Cable offices, Midland Buildings, Forster Square. *J.A. Pitts*

Left: The destruction of Midland Buildings by fire in June 1950 prevented trolleybuses from using Forster Square for many weeks. Bradford Moor passengers had to board their vehicles in Hall Ings, where No. 747 is seen opposite the 'Telegraph & Argus' office and St. George's Hall, which was then in use as a cinema. *Author*

Cathedral precincts when the new B.U.T. trolleybuses took possession of the route next morning.

Historical continuity was preserved: the old tramcar route number (30) returned, and the first trolleybus (748) recalled the last tram (248). But all else was new: Church Bank had been resurfaced, and the performance of the new 120 h.p. vehicles was a revelation - they soared up the 1 in $9^1/_2$ incline, accelerating as they did so. The arduous routine of the busy route was taken in their stride as the endless procession of silk-smooth, all-conquering B.U.Ts swept triumphantly up and down, circling Forster Square with a flourish.

The island loading station was abandoned on December 5th by the Manningham Lane services (Crossflatts, Bingley, Saltaire and Frizinghall) in favour of kerbside loading on the South side of the Square. This facilitated the commencement on January 1st 1950, of a through service between Bradford Moor and Saltaire/Bingley/Crossflatts as in tramcar days; vehicles were provided by both Thornbury and Saltaire depots. Teatime and Saturday morning extras shuttled between

*Left:*The pre-war Weymann bodies of several Karrier E4s were reconditioned by the Samlesbury Engineering concern in 1950. The provision of sliding vents in place of half-drop windows and trimming of the louvre above them altered the appearance considerably as seen by number 681 passing the Transport Department offices at 11 Forster Square.

R.F. Mack

Chelmsford Road and Frizinghall, displaying No. 27, as the Chelmsford Road number (29) did not appear on the blinds!

By this time it was evident that the trolleybus undertaking had reached its peak. Costs had risen rapidly; the electricity supply had been nationalised, and motor-buses were easier to obtain. The Thornbury tram route, already wired from end to end for trolleybus depot journeys and therefore available for trolleybus operation at a moment's notice, was destined for motorbuses: on the central portion (Harris Street-Laisterdyke) the tram poles and 1927-vintage overhead equipment remained. The Undercliffe project was cancelled and attempts (fortunately without success) were made to cancel the order for eight further B.U.T.s; the poles, however, were already in stock.

Forebodings were confirmed on January 25th, 1950, when the Chairman stated regretfully that although trolleybuses were 'clearly the best vehicle for a hilly city' they now cost 1.5d per mile more to run than motor-buses, and economics would eventually make the latter predominant. Thoughts of trolleybuses to Huddersfield had long since vanished like morning mist, and when the last tram ran on May 6th the remnants of the Oakenshaw wires came down at last.

Excitement and ingenuity reigned when a fierce fire on June 8th rendered Forster Square and lower Bolton Road unusable; the new wires hung down in festoons. The Bradford Moor service was instantly diverted via Harris Street to a central terminus in Hall Ings, whilst Bolton Road trolleybuses turned by gravity at Wapping Road for a few days before venturing back as far as Balme Street and reversing thence into Bolton Road. Many and varied were the improvisations devised by Manningham Lane drivers: some ran their vehicles

into North Parade and coasted back into Manor Row in front of the Yorkshire Penny Bank; others travelled the full length of North Parade and coasted down Upper Piccadilly to Manor Row, while others doggedly kept their trolleys on the wires by the expedient of running into Rawson Square via North Parade and reversing down Upper Piccadilly to Manor Row. Prefabricated curve segments (the first in Bradford) were installed overnight at both ends of Upper Piccadilly to allow vehicles to circumnavigate the block under wires, but the cross-city service was suspended until the Square reopened fully on August 6th.

In the prevailing atmosphere the arrival of the eight Weymann B.U.T.s (752-759), originally destined for Undercliffe, was almost nostalgic: it was hard to believe that these superb vehicles were to be the last all-new purchases.

However, it was evident that even if the undertaking faced ultimate decline, the process would be unhurried, as the fleet was quite modern and represented a large capital investment. When, therefore, the bodies of some of the 1938/9 A.E.C./E.E.C.s were reported as decrepit, the Committee unhesitatingly agreed that the chassis should be renovated and the bodies rebuilt or replaced. Accordingly in February, 1950, the Samlesbury Engineering Co. had agreed to reconstruct four Weymann bodies on reconditioned Karrier E4 chassis: trolleybuses 679, 681, 687 and 689 returned to service in the autumn. In November sanction was given for 12 new bodies for A.E.C./E.E.C.s and Karrier E4s, but an offer by C.H. Roe to supply 7ft. 6in. wide bodies at a cost lower than those supplied for 740-751 was rejected by the City Council, who insisted on competitive tenders; the successful bidders were Crossley Motors of Stockport @ £2,125 each.

Upholstered seats salvaged from motor-buses 456-465 (and others) replaced the less-than-popular wooden slatted seats in Karrier Ws 703-714. Minor economies were made: yellow lining was omitted when vehicles were repainted, and pole bases were no longer painted in a darker (bottle) green.

Rumour was now rife: the 'grapevine' asserted that the Bolton Road routes and the section beyond Bingley Church were to close, and the atmosphere was heightened by a decision to institute a Clayton motor-bus service along the old route used by the private buses which the 'tracklesses' had superseded. But the 20-year reign of Mr. Tattam was ending, and only eight days after the Clayton decision Mr. C.T. Humpidge, manager at Rochdale, was appointed to succeed him. Judgement was thereupon suspended in knowledgeable circles.

Top: The last all-new trolleybuses bought by Bradford were Weymann-bodied B.U.Ts Nos. 752-9 No. 758, seen here on the first enthusiasts' tour on July 29th 1951, explores new territory at Bowling Bridge, Wakefield Road. Though derived from shapely contemporary Weymann motor bus body designs, these vehicles achieved a new standard of neat finish with the incorporation of the trolley gantry within the double skin of the roof. *J.B. Copland*

Bottom: Crossley bodies were fitted in 1952 to five 1938/9 AEC/EECs. No. 636 was photographed at Bingley in 1954. Here again there was an affinity to contemporary Crossley bus bodies, also represented among B.C.T.'s fleet at the time. *R.B. Parr*

Chapter six
Silk Purses and Full Coffers

The decade of Chaceley Thornton Humpidge marked Bradford out as a city possessing certain distinctive features – not least its trolleybuses. Widely experienced in electric traction in Nottingham, Portsmouth and Liverpool, he took a keen interest in them from the outset, and when advised that the Odsal, Thornbury, Wibsey and Greengates (via Undercliffe) routes would be suitable for trolleybuses he studied them closely. Greengates was discounted because of cross-city links with Haworth Road, and Odsal because there were too many competing motor-bus services on the route, but the other seeds bore fruit. A decade of ingenious development began, and no more was heard of Clayton motor-buses.

The new policy held out a prospect of the electrification of routes (exclusive of 'spurs' or branches) which warranted a basic 10 minutes frequency, on the basis that the capital outlay would be recovered within a reasonable time. Critical scrutiny centred on the Yorkshire Electricity Board's scale of tariffs by which Bradford paid 1.89d. per unit compared with the Yorkshire average of 0.8d.; it was officially declared that if charges could be equalised, trolleybus services would be extended on major roads.

An enthusiasts' tour – the first of an annual series for the next twenty years – occurred on July 29th 1951, when B.U.T. 758 was seen at Allerton, Clayton, Duckworth Lane and other places where no 8ft. 0in. wide vehicle had ventured previously. These congenial events enabled little-used wiring to be given an airing, new vehicles to be sampled and old favourites to receive due appreciation.

By this time the new B.U.T. fleet (740-759) had migrated to Saltaire Depot, displacing the 'Jo'burgs' and some A.E.C./E.E.C.s; their speed showed to good advantage on the long cross-city link to Bradford Moor. However, when roadworks and raised manholes caused damage to the underslung tubes which housed their 'trolley sticks' they were temporarily exiled to the Wakefield Road services while the slightly higher-mounted Karrier E4s deputised for them.

In July the contract for 12 Crossley bodies was extended at a cost of £2,215 to include a Karrier E4 which had suffered collision damage. But the fleet had been too large for current needs ever since the delivery of Nos. 752-9, and Mr. Humpidge espied a neat way of using surplus trolleybuses to supersede austerity motor-buses. On February 19th, 1952, the Council were persuaded that as overhead wires already existed over the entire Thornbury route, trolleybuses should take over the passenger service which motor-buses had inherited from the trams two years earlier. In anticipation of this decision the manager had (three months previously!) renewed the overhead equipment between Harris Street and Laisterdyke, a process which caused the old tram poles to wilt so visibly that one hundred J. Spencer replacements were ordered for installation when opportunity permitted.

Motor-buses therefore ended their brief tenure of Thornbury Depot's 'Far West' on March 1st, 1952, and trolleybuses took over the Thornbury service next morning. The City loading-point was in Hall Ings (the old tramway waiting room), while at the outer terminus the vehicles shared the Bradford Moor turning-circle. An emergency connection with the latter route also existed in Harris Street, and the Bolton-Bankfoot route was crossed at Laisterdyke. The former motor-bus route number (89) was inserted into trolleybus number blinds, as it matched the number (90) of the Stanningley motor-buses which shared the route. Initially Thornbury was served exclusively by the 13 trolleybuses newly rebodied by Crossley – A.E.C./E.E.C.s 635/6/7, 640 and 652 and Karrier E4s 677/8, 682/4/5/8, 691 and 692. With 7ft. 6in. wide bodies and 59 seats the 'Crossleys' embodied new features such as side destination screens and twin-track number blinds at front and rear, the latter replacing the rear destination blinds.

The 'Crossleys' also bore the name of 'Bradford City Transport' in place of 'Bradford Corporation Passenger Transport' which had superseded 'Bradford City Tramways' in 1936. Livery modifications had also occurred: No. 683 had emerged from Thornbury paintshops in June, 1951, without the usual primrose band beneath the lower saloon windows; subsequent vehicles had no primrose bands beneath the upstairs windows either (the Weymann B.U.T.s, Roe-bodied Karriers and the 'Jo'burgs' had never had any). Simultaneously the poles bought for Undercliffe were used as replacements at Windhill, Oak Lane and St. Mary's Road.

A gyratory traffic scheme was instituted in Town Hall Square early in April, 1952, when trolleybuses entering service via Tyrrel Street were diverted around it; from August the Thornton Road services (5-7, 37-39) used Town Hall Square as a turning-point in preference to the New Victoria Street and Victoria Square wiring which was therefore disconnected (and dismantled a year later). The Thornton service had used Victoria Square as a terminus (with an overhead siding to allow Clayton trolleybuses to pass) from 1934 to 1942, when the loading-point had transferred to the New Victoria cinema (later 'Gaumont' and 'Odeons 1 and 2') in Thornton Road.

Following the introduction of mercury-arc and sodium vapour street lighting units which were affixed to the traction poles independently of the traditional short (span-wire) bracket arms, the gradual removal of the latter began in July, although the process was never completed.

Purchase of new 'Autoticket' machines in addition to the T.I.M. equipment in use since 1936 spelled doom for the time-honoured 'Barker' bell punches and ticket

The balance of the contract for Crossley bodies was assigned to 1938-40 Karrier E4 Chassis, the newest of which, No. 692, is seen turning from Idle Road into Pelham Road in 1958. *Author*

racks used since the early years of the century, but the old-type 'Autoticket' of Oller Ltd. issues occasionally appeared in emergencies or for special events.

Well-timed confirmation of the shrewdness of the manager's policy came when diesel fuel tax increases costing Bradford £27,775 coincided with the standardisation of traction current charges thoughout Yorkshire which reduced Bradford's costs by £30,000. Although the latter helped to prejudice the future of trams in Sheffield and Leeds, in Bradford the effect was literally 'electrifying'. ' Wibsey Trolleys as Economy Measure', trumpeted the Press, and Mr. Humpidge judged that so long as trolleybus costs could be kept lower than motor-bus costs, electric traction would be secure. The beginnings of trolleybus abandonment elsewhere – in West Hartlepool, St. Helens, Darlington, Notts. & Derby and Llanelly – were not seen as deterrents: acting on the principle that 'one man's meat is another man's poison', the manager resolved to take advantage of good-quality modern equipment which would obviously become available on the second-hand market, thus eliminating the need for heavy capital expenditure for years to come.

The first coup was a contract signed in September, 1952, for the purchase of the entire Nottinghamshire and Derbyshire Traction Company fleet of 32 trolleybuses at a cost of £52,500 for 15 1949 B.U.T.s, £9,000 for 10 1941/2 A.E.C./E.E.C.s and £1,000 for 7 1937 A.E.C./ E.E.C.s. From South Wales Transport (Llanelly and District Traction Co.) 10 Karrier W. chassis were acquired for £4,100 for reconstruction and rebodying. The 'Notts.

& Derby' vehicles were to act initially as a 'float' pending the rebodying of the 10 'Jo'burgs', 10 of the 1938/9 A.E.C./E.E.C.s and the 10 'Llanellies' by East Lancashire Coachworks at a cost of £76,470. Before being rebodied all chassis (except of course the 'Jo'burgs') were to receive new 8ft. 0in. front axles and to be modified for bodies of increased dimensions, i.e., 27ft. 0in. long and 8ft. 0in. wide.

Post-war redevelopment of the City centre was slowly beginning; smooth tarmacadam and new alignments were obliterating tram-lines and granite setts, and with the abolition of petrol rationing increased motor traffic was envisaged. In plans for the Wibsey route Mr. Humpidge proposed a central terminus at the rear of the Town Hall with connecting wires from Bridge Street to Town Hall Square via Union Street and Town Hall Street, the intention being to relieve traffic congestion in Tyrrel Street which the Wibsey service had always used as its loading-point. However, in view of the narrow bottleneck then existing at the Hall Ings/ Bridge Street/Union Street intersection, the manager was persuaded to retain the Wibsey service in Tyrrel Street – with new cross-city wiring to Forster Square via Broadway – and, instead, to remove various motor-bus services to the rear of the Town Hall.

Great was the Committee's fury when an essential link in the chain – new wires in front of the Town Hall – was rejected on grounds of cost: the Chairman (Coun. A.S. Downey) threatened to resign, but when a ratepayer shrewdly contrasted the Council's approval of £412 for

Above: Ex Notts. and Derby B.U.T. No. 760, still in its original owners' colours (judged to be sufficiently similar to B.C.T. livery to be acceptable temporarily), waits at the Dudley Hill barrier in Union Street while Crossley AEC/EEC No. 637 pulls into the Tong Cemetery barrier. Typically of the period, No. 760 is displaying an incorrect number blind – 18 instead of 19. Apart from being 76ft. 6in. wide, this batch of vehicles dating from 1949 was directly comparable with Bradford's newest vehicles with their 120 h.p. English Electric motors and Weymann bodywork.   *J.A. Pitts*

Below: In 1954 the Broadway link between Forster Square and Leeds Road was officially inaugurated by ex Notts. & Derby No. 588. Although dating from 1941 and based on A.E.C. 661T chassis this batch of vehicles had Weymann bodies very like the post-war style.   *R.F. Mack*

two grand pianos for schools with its disapproval of a mere £1,774 for the public's wider benefit, the Council was shamed into compliance.

The cost of the Wibsey route was estimated at £28,855 plus £15,548-2-0 for two substations, rectifiers and D.C. meters, with a further £3,000 for the cross-city link to the Eccleshill route, via Broadway and Forster Square. Subsequently £9,800 was voted for a spur from the Wibsey route to the new Buttershaw housing estate via Wibsey Park Avenue, Reevy Road (as yet unpaved) and Reevy Road West to a terminus at Cooper Lane roundabout.

Pole-planting began on April 9th, 1953, all city centre poles being painted silver with red and blue bands for the Queen's Coronation. Good-quality 1937-vintage Wibsey tram poles were retained and supplemented by a mixture of Undercliffe poles, new Stewarts and Lloyds purchases, a few from Sunderland and some of the stock of 238 bought from Notts. & Derby. Erection of overhead equipment was economically contrived, being undertaken by the overhead lines staff at night when not engaged in repairs elsewhere.

Aware that successful trolleybus operation depended upon first-class overhead equipment, Mr. Humpidge wisely invested in new, high-quality materials: indeed, the cadmium-copper wire bought for the Wibsey installation had a breaking-strain of 30 tons p.s.i., and was virtually unworn when ultimately dismantled. B.I.C.C. twin-hangers, initially with galvanised steel separators but later with wooden bar separators were bought from mid-1950 onwards to the virtual exclusion of other types. Prevailing prices per unit were: a pole £30, trailing ('wayward' or converging) frog £70, pull (manually operated diverging) frog £90, automatic frog £110.

The Notts. & Derby fleet arrived at Thornbury after performing final duties for its original owners in April, 1953. The B.U.T.s, now numbered 760-774, entered service almost immediately, as did three of the 1941/2 A.E.C./E.E.C.s, 587/8 and 596, whereas the remainder followed at intervals after overhaul and renovation. The A.E.C./E.E.C.s, being virtually contemporary with 'native' vehicles of the same make, were fitted into a gap conveniently existing between the motor-bus and trolleybus series (580-596). Four of the new recruits (586/7, 595/6) had been painted in full Bradford livery whilst still operating in the Midlands; conversely No. 588 and most of the B.U.T.s operated in Bradford for a year or two in their old colours – a deeper blue and ivory. B.U.T.s 764/9 entered service in a special powder-blue and off-white Coronation livery.

Although the 'Notts. & Derbys' were of the now-obsolescent 7ft. 6in. width, they were comfortable, well-sprung vehicles. For a time they retained their auxiliary traction batteries, a feature which once proved useful when a power failure isolated the hilly Allerton route beyond Chapel Lane: an enterprising driver succeeded in coaxing his ageing A.E.C./E.E.C. to the terminus at 4 m.p.h., and then drastically boosting his batteries by a fast cityward descent!* Two 'Notts. and Derby' features left a permanent mark: vehicle roofs were in future painted in the fleet blue instead of grey, and where appropriate mid-blue paint replaced brown for interior use.

New and unprecedented ways of overcoming the persistent shortage of labour for 'unsocial' jobs in local industry were now being tried. Employers were looking further afield than previously, and when a trickle of immigrants from India and Pakistan began, Bradfordians had to accustom themselves to the hitherto unknown sight of coloured conductors and subsequently coloured drivers, whose knowledge of local geography understandably fell short of normal requirements. As early as January, 1953, the Committee emphasised that there would be no colour bar.

The unwillingness to accept discipline noted in 1944 continued to cause problems; destination displays were often incorrect, and when incautious drivers attempted to adjust them while the vehicle was moving, vehicles sometimes overturned with disastrous results.

*an experiment with battery propulsion had been tried in Bradford in June 1937 when batteries of 30 lead-acid cells weighing 400 lb. had propelled a trolleybus (unladen weight 7 tons 4.5 cwt.) plus 13 cwt. of passengers for 4.25 miles at 4.1 miles per hour.

Town Hall Square was one of the hubs of the network. Ex-Notts. & Derby No. 586, a Weymann-bodied A.E.C. already 21 years old, passes through on a journey to Springhead Road in 1958. A Leyland bus of the Leeds independent operator, Samuel Ledgard is visible in the background.
Author

Staff turnover was high, and the 'old-timers'' grumble that "They're always changing!" was regrettably correct. Newly-qualified drivers gained experience on trolleybuses with their simple controls before graduating to the more complex motor-buses, a factor which did nothing for the standard of trolleybus driving; impatient acceleration and fierce braking became prevalent, and the sensible benefits of coasting and progressive electric/air braking were ignored. Automatic acceleration devices were therefore introduced as a means of avoiding excessive power consumption, following earlier multi-notch-control experiments with No. 637.

Continuous financial inflation coupled with economic expansion led to ever-rising costs. Regular wage and fare increases impelled the Transport Department to apply economy measures: external cleanliness was an early victim, and the interval between repaints lengthened to 100,000 miles. After the abolition of petrol rationing in 1952 the number of passengers carried on the trolleybuses began to decline (motor-buses were of course affected equally). Nevertheless a proposal to reduce the Crossflatts service beyond Bingley to peak-hour operation only, in return for 'protection' within the city boundary from competing West Yorkshire buses, raised so much criticism that the

plan was withdrawn and timetables adjusted. No attention was given to suggestions that the rival services should have an equal number of stops: the proportion remained unfavourable at three trolleybus stops to two West Yorkshire stops, so that trolleybus journey times were inevtitably longer, and income remained at 2.84d. per mile below average.

The new cross-city link between Forster Square, Town Hall Square and Victoria Square, via Broadway, completed on November 7th, 1953, was inaugurated by trolleybus 588, on hire to the Trolleybus Society, on June 20th, 1954, but plans to extend the Eccleshill service to Victoria Square were vetoed by the police on grounds of congestion at the proposed terminus. And, frustratingly, the Corporation had decided to lay new sewers beneath Broadway, so that after the new wiring had been used by a few Peel Park circus 'specials' it had to be temporarily dismantled.

By this time the Wibsey route was nearing completion. A trial run as far as Little Horton was successfully accomplished by B.U.T. 754 (borrowed from Saltaire Depot for the occasion) on July 18th, 1954, and a Little Horton peak-hour service using two vehicles began on November 8th. Shortly afterwards the Duckworth Lane 'school' (driver-training) trolleybus managed to climb to St. Enoch's Road Top despite a

The Transport Committee and senior civic leaders rode on B.U.T. No. 754 when it was used to open the Wilsey route. Amongst the group in Tyrrel Street are C.T. Humpbridge (second from left), Alderman Downey, Alderman H.K. Watson (in trilby hat), Alderman E Newby (centre of group, hand in pocket), Alderman J. Shee (centre in Homburg hat),L.L. Christie (under the first 'A' in 'Boardman'), J.R. Hanchett (behind Mr. Christie), N.A. Scurrah (in belted overcoat) and E.E. Robinsom (overhead lines superintendent, far right). Behind Alderman Shee is H. Carr, former General Manager of the City's Electricity Department.

Telegraph & Argus

considerable voltage drop.

As soon as necessary substations at Spicer Street and Ormond Street had been commissioned, the whole of the Wibsey installations were inspected by Brigadier Langley on behalf of the Ministry of Transport on March 15th, 1955. Minor realignments of kerb edges in Little Horton Lane having been attended to, the Transport Committee sallied forth triumphantly over the new route on April 19th, No. 754 having again been commandeered on both occasions.

Public services to Wibsey (45) and its regular shortworking to St. Enoch's Road Top (44) finally opened on April 24th, using vehicles from Thornbury Depot. Crossley/Karrier 685 made the first early morning ascent to St. Enoch's Road Top, following which a herd of cows which had apparently been enjoying a Sunday morning 'lie-in' unintentionally delayed the first Wibsey trolleybus, No. 677, at Brownroyd Hill. Otherwise the new service – the second motor-bus to trolleybus conversion – was instantly successful. Fume-laden Tyrrel Street breathed again, and the laboured ascents of the long gradients by even the most modern motor-buses were forgotten – that is, by everyone except the ex-bus drivers who feared that faster journeys would lead to adjusted schedules. It was noticeable that as soon as reassurances had been given, trolleybus speeds increased remarkably!

Other plans were evolving: a new Provisional Order sanctioned an extension of the Eccleshill route into the new Thorpe Edge estate, a diversion of the Greengates route via Old Park Road and a supplementary service to Clayton (The Avenue) via Bradford Road. Less fortunate was a proposed 1,375 yard enlargement of the Chapel Lane turning-circle by way of Grange Road, Dog Lane, Ley Top Lane and Greenbank Road, which was deferred and not revived. And the transfer to the Street Lighting Department of 222 poles in Croft Street and Manchester Road confirmed that trolleybuses would never again run to Odsal.

Following the Wibsey conversion and preparations for the rebodying programme there was a temporary shortage of vehicles, and a few withdrawn Karrier E4s were briefly reinstated. Ten surplus single-deck Karrier E4s and Ws had been bought from Darlington Corporation as a source of cheap spares (£50 per vehicle), and it was observed that when they arrived at Thornbury two (GHN 403/4) were not dismantled: indeed, they were overhauled, partly painted (Darlington colours were similar to Bradford's), assigned the temporary fleet numbers T403/4 and allowed test runs to Bierley Church before returning to store in March, 1955. However, by then the last of the ' Notts. & Derbys' (the 1937-vintage A.E.C./E.E.C.s) were entering service following thorough overhauls: T404 was therefore eventually disposed of, but T403 lingered on.

It should not be imagined, of course, that the purchase by the proud city of Bradford of other people's 'cast-offs' was entirely without its critics – 'Second-hand vehicles, second-hand city!' wrote one shocked observer – but in general the rate-paying public appreciated the determined efforts being made on their behalf, especially as the non-Bradford origins of the acquisitions were not always evident.

The dismantling of some of the pre-war trolleybuses and the resulting abundance of spare parts encouraged the enterprising Assistant Rolling Stock Engineer (J.R. Hanchett) to experiment, with interesting and varied results. Single-reduction rear axles, prop-shafts and E.E. 406 motors salvaged from 1938/ 9 vehicles replaced the older, noisier equipment under 1934/5 A.E.C./E.E.C.s, although 618/627 received a temporary ill-matched combination of equipment which made them the slowest vehicles in the fleet.

A.E.C./E.E.C.s 602/610 with ex-Newcastle Metrovick motors and B.C.T. single-reduction rear axles performed so silently that they were dubbed 'the Rolls-Royces'. Utility Karriers 715-9 acquired ex-Newcastle E.E. 409 motors which increased their power. Uniquely No. 639 (the 'Blitz' victim) received the Northern Coachbuilders body of No. 618 in an attempt to 'marry' sound bodies to newer chassis, but the experiment was too costly, and no more pre-war chassis were allocated for rebodying.

At the same time most vehicles had their seating capacity increased from 56 to 58 or 59; in most cases there was adequate space on the upper deck for extra seating, but the 'Notts. and Derby' B.U.T.s became excessively cramped, to the discomfort of long-legged passengers.

Rear destination blinds were gradually superseded by number blinds from May, 1955, as a consequence of which the Bingley service which had always shared the Crossflatts number (24) received the vacant number 26. The unused numbers 49-59 were cut out and re-sewn into motor-bus blinds.

An improved type of trolley head was designed, incorporating a continuous rim which prevented the head from becoming entangled if a dewirement occurred; known as the 'Bradford' head, it was adopted by the Mexborough and Rotherham systems also. A set of Teesside-type Anti-Attrition heads was tested briefly, producing a dry, scraping sound under 'frogs' in place of the crisp click-click of the 'native' heads.

Increasing traffic flows necessitated the construction of a roundabout at the junction of Duckworth Lane and Toller Lane; overhead wires were duly altered and were first used on December 11th 1955. Nine days later an early, determined snowfall caused disruption in Bradford's Pennine foothills: the first trolleybus to Dudley Hill took 1 1/2 hours to complete the outward journey; the Clayton service terminated at Pasture Lane, and Bradford Moor trolleybuses were diverted via Well Street and Harris Street to avoid Church Bank.

New Year's Day 1956, brought a 'new look' to the Wibsey route in the form of the 'Jo'burgs' returning to service with gleaming new East Lancashire Coach Builders bodies unlike anything seen previously. Gone were the traditional polished woodwork, brown hide upholstery and brown leather-cloth lining panels, replaced by modern Formica, stainless steel and blue leather; an enamel badge bearing the civic arms adorned the vehicles' front panels. The spacious rear platforms were designed to accommodate platform doors if

Top: The public service to Wibsey opened on April 24th 1955, when Crossley-bodied Karrier No. 677 was photographed at the terminus

J. Copland

Above left: The only car in sight when No. 754 descended St. Enoch's Road on its return from Wibsey was the manager's stately pre-war Austin saloon.

Telegraph & Argus

Above right: The first trolleybus to Buttershaw on April 8th 1956, was 'Llanelly' No. 784, representation of the new formular of using reconditioned chassis purchased from other undertakings as a basis for new bodywork. This was one of the ten Karrier W chassis dating from 1945-6 purchased from the Llanelly & District Traction Co. and fitted with East Lancashire bodywork before entry into service with B.C.T. in 1956.

Author

Wintry weather prevailed when 'Jo'burg' No. 701 performed its first exploratory journey to Buttershaw. Mr. Christie, in scarf, hat, gloves and Wellington boots, is taking no chances but Mr. Humpbridge and the Chief Inspector believe that the new platform doors will combat the cold. Although this photograph was taken in Forster Square, Buttershaw trolleybuses always operated from Tyrrel Street. In this case the Sunbeam MF2 chassis was already 8ft. wide – the rebodied vehicle had been in service a week when carrying out this duty in Januarty 1956. Note the B.C.T. A.E.C. Regent III bus with Weymann body visible behind.

Telegraph & Argus

required, but the only vehicle so fitted was 701, which entered service later than the others, being used for a trial run from Forster Square over the new Buttershaw route on January 11th with its doors firmly closed against the wintry blasts.

Overhead installations on the new 'spur', from St. Enoch's Road Top to Cooper Lane, were ready before the highway was fit for use; pleas for completion of the unmade connection between Reevy Road and Reevy Road West fell on deaf ears until Mr. Humpidge threatened to open the service whether the road was finished or not. Only a few hours after the hurriedly-supplied tarmacadam had cooled, the service was opened on April 8th by the highest-numbered trolleybus 'Llanelly' 784. Thenceforth the Little Horton Lane services – St. Enoch's Road Top (44), Wibsey (45) and Buttershaw (46) – ran alternately from the city terminus in Tyrrel Street, supplemented by peak-hour extras to Little Horton (numbered 47 -unofficially at first).

The 'Llanelly' trolleybuses on their enlarged and renovated chassis had followed hard on the heels of the 'Jo'burgs' with identical bodies. Nos. 775-778 had B.T.H. equipment and 779-784 Metrovick; their good riding qualities proved that even Karrier W chassis could be tamed by the experts at Thornbury Works! In June came the last ten of the thirty vehicles rebodied by East Lancs. under the 1953 contract – these, the first A.E.C./ E.E.C.s ever to bear 8ft. 0in. bodies – were 634/8, 651/ 4/5/9, 664/6 and 674/5, of which all except 634 were identifiable by the wire-mesh grille inserted into the front inspection panel for extra motor ventilation.

On their arrival the 'Jo'burgs' were despatched to Duckworth Lane Depot where their 100 h.p. motors helped to accelerate the service without significantly increasing power consumption.

Meanwhile the old permanent-way yard adjoining Bowling motor-bus depot had been adapted for use by the driving school. A single set of overhead wires, fed from but not connected to the Wakefield Road wires, led up Foundry Lane to form a complete circle in the yard. A spur allowed vehicles to enter a new high-pressure steam-operated chassis washing plant; No. 749 was the first trolleybus to use the plant on May 3rd. Not surprisingly the traction motors and associated cables became saturated in the process, and in future trolleybuses were towed to and from the plant.

Although the spur itself was later removed, driver-training continued in the yard, and the overhead layout was considerably enlarged in 1962 to include a reversing triangle (usable in either direction) and a section-breaker on a steep gradient.

Long-discussed alterations to the Clayton service now materialised. Although the Ministry refused to permit the installation of trolleybus wires in Bradford Road until it was widened, a more acceptable extension from 'Bull Hill' up The Avenue to a specially constructed turning-circle at the junction with Clayton Lane was now ready for use. A pleasant, quiet ascent flanked by modern houses, cow pastures and a cricket field, The Avenue's official first trolleybus on July 15th, 1956, was unspectacular old A.E.C./E.E.C. 605 with its 22-year old chassis and leaky 'utility' body. Providentially the shabby sight was cloaked by a discreet mist – the lingering remnant of a dense fog under whose cover a normal service vehicle had clandestinely traversed the new section a few days earlier!

A miniscule contraction of the network occured in May when the long-disused wires outside the 1915 Railless Shed at Thornbury were cut down (inside the shed the wires survived until 1974); a few weeks later poles appeared in the Bank, Eccleshill, as heralds of the long-term project to extend the Eccleshill service to Thorpe Edge. Good second-hand material continued to be acquired when opportunity arose: St. Helens had contributed a rectifier and circuit breaker in 1953; in 1956 the dwindling Leeds tramways sold two rectifiers, a new D.C. switchboard and a tower-wagon, while the closure of Edinburgh's tramways released a further rectifier (new in 1951, handed over in 1958).

International events now intervened again. The Suez oil crisis obliged the Department to reduce motor-bus services by 5% for three months and raise all its 3d. fares to 4d. to meet the increased cost of oil. Pausing only to impress on H.M. government the strategic advantage of electric traction, Mr. Humpidge made maximum use of trolleybuses for football, cricket, hospital and special journeys, thus bringing about (for instance) the rare sight of a Saltaire B.U.T. at St. Luke's Hospital, Little Horton. The Park Avenue sports ground was soon provided with a 'spur' from Little Horton Lane to the park gates, using reclaimed tram standards as well as new poles and opening on May 6th, 1957, in time for a Yorkshire county cricket match. Also, two overhead 'sidings', one for each direction, were installed in Manningham Lane for the Valley Parade football 'specials'.

Four years earlier a curve had been installed from Rooley Lane into Wakefield Road as part of a proposed trial extension of the City to Dudley Hill (19) service to Bierley Church; the trial had not actually taken place, but Suez provided an ideal opportunity for the idea to be revived. Accordingly the entire overhead layout at Dudley Hill was remodelled, reducing the number of frogs and crossings from 22 to 18, and vehicles travelling from Bolton to Bankfoot (including the City Circle motor-bus service introduced in 1954 and superimposed on the trolleybus service) were re-routed via Mulcott Road. The Bierley Church circle was renewed with grooved wire and modern fittings, and the service from City began on December 31st, 1956, not as an extension of the Dudley Hill service but as a peak-hour augmentation of the reduced Bierley bus service. Two vehicles sufficed, and the City terminus was the Bierley loading point in Union Street.

Another whim was realised also: the surviving single-decker, T403, could now be pressed into service on the Bierley Church service, to the amusement of staff who promptly named it 'The Pup' and the astonishment of the public, many of whom had never seen a single-decker trolleybus. Special driving skills were needed, as the extreme elevation of the trolley booms prevented 'The Pup' from deviating from the overhead line as far as double-deckers could, and the additional

Left: 'Llanelly' No. 782 circles the roundabout at Buttershaw with its route indication already displaying '45' for its next journey, from Wibsey to City.   *Author*

Right: Proudly exhibiting its sliding doors No. 701, the only rebodied 'J'burg' to have this feature, passes the 'Pack Horse Hotel' in Westgate on a fast run to Duckworth Lane in August, 1956.
Author

Below: 'Llanelly' No. 777 squeezes under the Pasture Lane railway bridge en route for Clayton while in the background a Northern Coachbuilders AEC/EEC rests at Pasture Lane turning circle, September 1956. Note the 'second mand' seated on the nearside of the Karrer's cab, a not uncommon sight when duty or circumstances made it useful.   *C. W. Routh*

tension on the trolley springs could lift conductors from the ground! (The normal trolley pressure for double-decker was 38 lb.) With its lightweight body and 80 h.p. motor it possessed a good turn of speed and was used twice for private tours, when its unexpected appearancces at Eccleshill, Buttershaw, Clayton, Saltaire and Thackley drew startled attention. Householders abandoned Sunday teas to rush to the window; elderly ladies leaped like gazelles when 'The Pup's' trolley-heads arced noisily on the little used North Parade wires, and top-deck passengers of a Bradford Moor trolleybus spontaneously jumped to their feet as the little vehicle crossed their path at Killinghall Road.

By this time the major sewerage excavations had progressed from Broadway to Leeds Road, necessitating the temprorary closure of the lower part of the latter thoroughfare. A turning-circle for the Thornbury service was constructed in George Street, West Street and Vicar Lane, and the Broadway wires were reinstated to allow vehicles on depot journeys from or to Clayton, Wibsey, etc., to travel via Broadway, Forster Square and Well Street. These diversions lasted from April 13th to August 11th, 1957, after which the West Street circle was retained for emergency use.

The reopening of Broadway allowed the much-deferred cross-city trolleybus service to materialise, and on November 3rd trolleybus 654 performed the first journey from Eccleshill (33) to St. Enoch's Road Top (44) and back. Service schedules were adjusted to provide a combined basic five minutes frequency from Tyrrel Street to St. Enoch's Road Top and from Bolton Road bottom to Bolton Junction; on the former section services 33/44, 45 and 46 ran in rotation, with extras to Little Horton (47), whilst in Bolton Road vehicles ran in sequence on services 33/44, 40 and 42. Peak-hour extras ran to and from City only. Passengers appreciated the new facility, although drivers disliked the added overhead complexities in the city centre.

A new phase of the rebodying programme began at the end of 1957, when 25 vehicles returned from East Lancashire Coach Builders. Karriers 715-9 shed their rickety 'utility' bodies and, like butterflies emerging from an ugly chrysalis, displayed handsome new bodies similar to the previous year's model, but with a double platform step which gave an uninterrupted floor level from the platform to the lower saloon. The two-section sliding doors on 'Jo'burg' 701 having proved much too slow in operation, the new bodies featured quicker-acting one-piece sliding doors, interlocked with the power pedal to prevent the vehicles from starting until the doors had closed. Unfortunately this lengthened journey times disastrously; the interlock was removed

Visiting the former haunts of Bradford single-deckers, ex-Darlington T403, 'The Pup', halts briefly in Pasture Lane on Februry 7th 1957. The embankment on the left formed part of the Bradford-Clayton-Queensbury-Halifax and Keighley Railway. The Brush body was only readily recognisable as a 'utility' design from the rear. The longer wheelbase of this version of the Karrier W proved useful as the basis for vehicles just under 29ft. long when rebodied as double-deckers.

Author

Trolleybus in trouble: although the complexities of large-scale sewer excavations in 1957 finally allowed trolleybuses to use Broadway in regular service, persistant 'pitfalls for the unwary' continued to appear. A breakdown gang backed up by a tower-waggon (left) and A.E.C. Matador (right) rescue No. 691, one of the Karrier E4 models that had been rebodied by Crossley, from a perilous position.

Telegraph & Argus

and the doors then saw little use except in winter, when electric 'Panelec' saloon heating provided gentle background warmth and helped to prevent body corrosion (as a side-effect the automatic 'frog' equipment had to be adjusted so that the current drawn by the heaters did not spontaneously activate the 'frogs'). Ex-'Notts. & Derby' 587-596, identically rebodied except for front ventilation grilles, returned to Duckworth Lane Depot. Karriers 720/2/3/4/7 surprisingly retained their traction (110v. d.c.) lighting, with the result that their bodies had to be of composite construction in deference to safety regulations; like 715-9 they worked from Thornbury.

A gradual decline in patronage having been noted, the Thornton schedules were adjusted so that more vehicles terminated at Spring Head Road, but this did not discourage bolder-than-usual plans for the future.

A new Provisional Order authorised trolleybus routes to Bierley (via Bierley Lane, Burnham Avenue, Ferrand Avenue and Shetcliffe Lane) and to the new Holme Wood estate (via Fenby Avenue, Knowles Lane and Broadstone Way). Even bolder was the Capital Expenditure Programme for the period 1958-1963:-

1958/9	28 new trolleybuses @ £6,500;	
	9 bodies @ £3,500	£213,500
1959/60	21 bodies @ £3,500	73,500
1960/1	20 new trolleybuses @ £6,500	130,000
		£417,000
	Plus 69 motor-buses 1959-19063	379,500
		£796,500

Alas for ambition! Raising its head after many years, the Finance and General Purposes Committee refused to sanction more than £136,700 in the first year and pointedly suggested a fares increase to avoid raids on the city rates. In the event 15 badly-needed motor-buses were ordered @ £82,500, and the 48 hoped-for trolleybuses receded into a problematical future. Conceivably, in view of Mr. Humpidge's later desire for a trolleybus version of the new Leyland 'Atlantean' motor-bus, they might have been double-deck developments of Glasgow's B.U.T. R.E.T.B.1s, and would doubtless have received fleet numbers 804-851.

Forays into the second-hand market therefore resumed. Following the closure of the Darlington system the remaining eight Karrier Ws had been bought for £70 each for modernisation and rebodying; a month later (October, 1957) the St. Helens 8ft. 0in. wide B.U.T. fleet was inspected and subsequently purchased in July 1958 @ £1.500 per vehicle. When Brighton Corporation Transport telephoned to offer their two English Electric-equipped B.U.T.s, Mr. Humpidge, not really wanting 7ft. 6in. wide vehicles unripe for rebodying, offered a mere £500 for the pair. To his surprise the bid was accepted!

The long reign of 'utility' Karriers on the Saltaire (via Thackley) and Greengates routes ended on November 2nd 1958 when Bolton Depot closed and all duties were transferred to Thornbury. A small, homely establishment with a coke stove quietly glowing in the corner, it could not accommodate 8ft. 0in. buses, and as there was no room for manoeuvres within the depot, trolleybuses had to reverse out into Bolton Road – an increasingly dangerous procedure. Next day the two routes welcomed modern amenities in the shape of A.E.C./E.E.C.s 654/664, Karriers 716/9, 'Llanelly' 784 and others: the 'utilities' were progressively withdrawn for rebodying, a further contract having been signed with East Lancs. for 29 bodies of the now-favoured forward-entrance layout.

First products of the new design were the 'Darlingtons' – the eight vehicles bought in 1957 and 'The Pup', formerly T403. Their transformation was complete and impressive: in place of their 33-seat

Top: Following experiments with Ohio Brass lightweight trolleys and trolley retrievers on ex-Darlington No. 788 (seen in 1959 at Bell Dean Road), British made retrievers were fitted to newly-rebodied Karriers, but repeated encounters with equally tall vehicles caused the project to be abandoned. This view also shows the well-balanced proportions of the new East Lancs forward-entrance bodywork. *Author*

Left: Comings and goings at Duckworth Lane on April 19th 1958 – ex-Notts. & Derby No. 588 (left) and No. 594 display their new East Lancs bodies. *Author*

Below: 'Silk purse from a sow's ear' – the author's opinion of the conversion of the wartime Karrier Ws into warm, comfortable vehicles with platform doors. Number 715 was photographed in Allerton Road on a rare visit. It had begun life with austere Park Royal utility body in 1945 but, transformed by East Lancs 12 years later, was to remain in service util 1970.

B.C.T./WYPTE/WYAS

single-deck 'utility' bodies they now bore 28ft.11in. x 8ft. 0in. forward-entrance bodies with air-operated jack-knife doors and 'Panelec' heating. Sunday morning strollers and passengers who beheld the debut of No. 793 on the Allerton service on December 7th, 1958, undoubtedly agreed that Mr. Humpidge had 'made a silk purse out of a sow's ear', as the large vehicle was fast and silent, and the doors were outstandingly efficient. Less impressed was the would-be passenger who attempted to jump on board a moving 'Darlington' only to find – by painful physical contact – that the entrance was no longer at the rear. But one could feel sympathy for the inebriated upper-deck passenger who enquired peevishly as to who had "removed the bl--dy staircase!"

The 'Darlingtons' were assigned to Duckworth Lane Depot, but were usually to be found on the Allerton and Thornton routes rather than the Duckworth Lane section with its tight turning-circle. Their greater body length stemmed from the fact that Karrier single-deck chassis had been designed with a longer wheelbase than those intended for double-deckers. Although they had a perfectly adequate turning lock – better than the B.U.T.s which even with full lock experienced difficulty in the terminal loop at the foot of Sunbridge Road and consequently were rarely seen on the route – drivers of the 'Darlingtons' were relieved that the tight turning-circle at Four Lane Ends had been replaced (June 8th 1958) by a larger circle embracing West Park Road, to which the inward-bound Allerton vehicles were now diverted.

Of the nine 'Darlingtons' 789-793 were equipped with 85 h.p. Metrovick motors; 785-8 with their 80 h.p. English Electric motors were somewhat underpowered and sluggish though able to tackle any gradient. Their arrival allowed the pre-war 'Notts. & Derbys', 580-6, to retire, having completed their role as 'floats' or spare vehicles during the rebodying programme; although dated, they had always provided extremely comfortable travel. For a while Duckworth Lane Depot housed a unique blend of ancient and modern – ex-Darlington 792 on one of its first ascents of Whetley Hill was closely pursued by 1934-vintage Brush-bodied 600, rebodied ' Notts. & Derby' 594 and 'Jo'burg' 700.

Although continuous attention to overhead line design had reduced trolley de-wirements to an extremely low level, the latter were still capable of causing damage and interruption to services. 'Darlington' 788 was therefore fitted with experimental Ohio Brass Co. lightweight trolley bases, booms, heads and spring-operated rope-hauled retrievers which pulled the booms down to roof level if they left the wire. Unsuccessful experiments with Hull-type retrievers had been tried with No. 773 in 1956.

Unobtrusively the two ex-Brighton B.U.T.s, numbered 802/3, entered service in April/May, 1959. Small but comfortable, with their 'Alhambrinal' patterned ceilings, concealed lighting and high seat-backs they were the most luxurious trolleybuses since 'Queenie'. They were followed by ex-St. Helens B.U.T.s Nos. 794-801, which had been so neglected in their native habitat that not only bushes and bearings

Ex-Darlington No. 787 with its long forward-entrance 71-seat body at the quiet terminus of the Greengates (via Idle) route.
Author

but the housings themselves had worn away. The chassis had therefore been thoroughly renovated at Thornbury (the angle of the drive being altered to eliminate the grating noise generated by B.U.T. worm wheels when they became well worn), whilst the bodies had been refurbished by C.H. Roe at a cost of £1058-10-0 each – an unusually high cost which, however, had to be increased by £148 per vehicle when the true extent of the body corrosion was realised. New seating was added to increase the capacity from 56 to 63; both batches joined the Thornbury depot fleet, and Nos. 797, 799 and 802, together with old 622, received a trial all-blue livery with one primrose band above the lower saloon windows, which proved too drab and was not repeated.

A significant link with the Wilkinson era ended with the retirement of Norman A. Scurrah, Rolling Stock Engineer, in December, 1958; his successor, K.E. Griffiths from Liverpool Corporation, was followed as Assistant Engineer by J.H. Maiden from the S.H.M.D. Joint Board.

The process of rebodying the remaining austerity Karrier Ws was now in hand at a cost of £94,243 for the 27 vehicles, i.e., the 1945/6 batches originally bearing Roe bodies (703-714 and 734-9) and the unrebodied survivors of the Park Royal series (721/5/6/8/9/30-33). Continuing the tradition that each consignment received from East Lancashire was better designed than its predecessor, the new deliveries were slightly shorter and more manoeuvrable than the 'Darlingtons', with 2ft. 4in. wide entrances (i.e. 4in. wider than on the 'Darlingtons'), a factor which speeded loading and unloading. Ministry regulations had been relaxed to permit them to have all-metal bodies with 'traction' (110v.) lighting, the lamps being enclosed in heatproof glass lampholders. Soon after arrival they displaced the ' Notts. & Derby' A.E.C./E.E.C.s (587-596) from Duckworth Lane Depot, converting the latter establishment into the first (and only) British all-forward-entrance trolleybus depot. The routes served from the depot were therefore monopolised by speedy, warm and comfortable vehicles quickly appreciated by the public. Following successful trials with the trolley retrievers on No. 788, British-made equipment attached to conventional trolley booms was fitted to the later deliveries, culminating in No. 705, the last of the contract, which returned from East Lancashire in July, 1960. Within the space of $4\frac{1}{2}$ years the percentage of 8ft. 0in. wide trolleybuses in the fleet had risen from 15% to 75%.

Land at City Road, Sunbridge Road and Jowett Street was acquired for a new, central trolleybus depot in February, 1959, (however, other sites were to be mooted before a contract for an ultra-modern Transport Interchange was signed in 1970). Each of the existing depots possessed different characteristics. Saltaire, the only depot outside the city boundary, took pride in its 'premier route' status and maintained its vehicles

Left: B.U.T. No. 801, the first of the ex-St. Helens vehicles to enter service collects Bingley passengers in Forster Square on March 14th 1959, when newly in service in Bradford. New in 1951, they were extensively reconditioned on arrival.
J. Copland

Below: Unlike many of the second-hand acquisitions the two Brighton vehicles needed little renovation before entering service. No. 803, in conventional Bradford livery, was seen at Thornbury on June 7th 1959. The B.U.T. chassis and Weymann bodywork were generally similar to the ex-Notts. & Derby vehicles, though older, dating from 1948, and having Brighton's more elaborate interior trim.
Author

accordingly. The staff of Duckworth Lane depot, despite cramped conditions, lack of modern facilities and inability to turn vehicles within the building, always turned out immaculate trolleybuses. Thornbury, a large but friendly establishment, played host to a wide variety of vehicles and not only tested vehicles newly out of the Works but also loaned trolleybuses to other depots when required.

The ever-resourceful Overhead Lines staff in their own depots at Aldermanbury (closed 1967) and Thornbury were something of a law unto themselves. Responsible for maintaining a round-the-clock vigil and for undertaking large-scale renewals after services had ceased and the power could be turned off, they were understandably wary of venturing out in bad weather. The foreman, suspicious that opportunities

Above: **When the Eccleshill route was extended down the Bank on August 9th 1959 the first trolleybus to reach the Faltis Square terminus was rebodied 1939 A.E.C. No. 675, carefully observed by an inspector and overhead lines staff.** *Author*

Below: **The 1959-60 rebodying programme included all the "native" Karrier Ws not previously dealt with. No. 730 on its maiden voyage, bearing trolleybus enthusiasts on their annual tour, paid its only visit to Harris Street on September 13th 1959, passing a 1937 Standard motor-car.** *Author*

for night work were being neglected even when the weather was fine, once ventured to remonstrate with the night shift on the grounds that the depot cat, newly returned from a nocturnal prowl, was perfectly dry. He invariably saw the animal in a damp bedraggled condition after that.

When the driver of a Thornton trolleybus collapsed at the wheel, Christopher Stalker (13) pluckily wriggled into the cab and halted the vehicle, for which he received a £25 reward. For a flying goose which unexpectedly swooped on a trolley-bus the only reward was a shattered windscreen and a broken neck.

Replacement of the remaining 7ft. 6in. wide pre-war A.E.C./E.E.C.s was now under consideration, as the few still retaining their English Electric bodies were restricted to weekday use. When the proposed acquisition of 27 new trolleybuses was again deferred by the Committee, Mr. Humpidge negotiated the purchase of 12 Hastings Tramways Sunbeam Ws for £250 each from the Maidstone and District company. Received without enthusiasm, as their 1946/7 Park Royal and Weymann bodies bore a regrettable resemblance to 'native' austerity bodies recently discarded, they were earmarked for modernisation and rebodying at a future date. The best of the 'Hastings', 814/5 (the latter in the predominantly blue experimental livery) were in service by August 1959 and proved to be sound vehicles with 95 h.p. motors. The slightly older 804-813 series with 85 h.p. motors needed considerable structural attention with the result that 805/8 did not appear before November, the remainder following spasmodically over an eighteen month period. Their reversed pedal positions (power on the right, brake on the left) did not endear them to drivers, and modifications were duly effected.

The remaining 1939 A.E.C./E.E.C.s still in original condition, Nos. 668/9, were allowed to retire on December 31st, 1959, although 668 lingered in the 'Tin Shed' until 1962 for possible preservation. An even older vehicle, No. 606, was withdrawn three months later, being the last austerity-bodied (Brush) vehicle in the fleet – assuming, of course, that one could count the 'Hastings' as genuine post-austerity products!

Meanwhile the remarkable extension of the Eccleshill route into the Thorpe Edge housing estate had opened on August 9th 1959. In narrow Stoney Lane bracket-arm suspension emphasised the old-world village atmosphere; at the 'Monkey Bridge' (formerly housing the village 'lockup') a blind corner on an unfavourable camber led to Victoria Road, from which the aptly-named Bank fell steeply away on a 1-in-8 gradient to the Faltis Square terminus. Very properly, the overhead line was planned and constructed with the utmost precision, as de-wirements would have left vehicles wholly dependent on their handbrakes. Strict speed limits were imposed; drivers were ordered to halt before descending the Bank, and the original terminus was retained for winter emergencies. It was therefore a tribute to the resilience of trolleybuses that the first passenger-carrying vehicle was 20-year old No. 675, (rebodied in 1956) whose 80 h.p. motor surmounted the fearsome gradient with quiet

Left: **Ex-Hastings Weymann-bodied Sunbeam W No. 814, a lively performer, is seen in Tyrrrel Street in 1962 with A.E.C. motor-bus No. 537 whose Northern Coachbuilders body matched those of many AEC/EEC 661T trolleybuses.**

Below: **The ever-changing face of Bradford: the demolition of Victorian warehouses in Leeds Road in 1961 opened up new vistas of Charles Street (centre), the Ritz Buildings (left) and the new C & A buildings (right). Ex-Hastings No. 815 wearing the experimental mostly-blue livery is in Leeds Road at its junction with Drake Street.**

Author (both)

determination. The extension cost £5,830, and the route name and number (Eccleshill, 33) remained unchanged.

Additional wiring and junctions were installed at Bolton Junction to permit Eccleshill (33), Saltaire (40) and Greengates (42) trolleybuses to enter service from Thornbury without having to traverse the City centre. The work incorporated two sets of interlaced points, a novel feature increasingly favoured by Bradford because it provided a smoother transition and could be set well back from major road junctions. A new substation was constructed at Bolton at a cost of £3,599.

Difficulties in recruiting and retaining platform staff, acute for a decade, worsened in March, 1960. Britain was on the verge of the period known retrospectively as 'The Affluent Age' in which 'unsocial' jobs found few takers. The maintenance of scheduled services became an acute problem aggravated by

rapidly-mounting traffic congestion, although most services were sufficiently frequent to absorb irregularities without hardship to passengers. Trolleybuses on the Eccleshill-St. Enoch's Road Top service, which had to cross the entire city centre, were noticeably less punctual than the peak-hour extras which ran to City only, whilst the short but intensive Duckworth Lane route was so disrupted that early in 1961 a short-working circle was inserted in Toller Lane (Whitby Road) in an effort to restore regularity. Increasingly concerned about the danger of turning Frizinghall (27) trolleybuses in the face of fast-moving traffic, the Department redesigned the Park Gates junction with access to and from the Saltaire direction and a new circle at the junction of Oak Lane and North Park Road; the Frizinghall vehicles were cut back to this point from November 14th to December 16th, 1960, displaying the destination 'Park Gates' but no route number. Difficulty in following the path of the circle in hours of darkness led to spectacular de-wirements, and the Frizinghall workings were resumed.

Overhead efficiency was nevertheless reaching new peaks of excellence in the pursuit of ever-greater efficiency. Miles of new running wire were strung up at Cottingley, Tong Street and Duckworth Lane, and new or sound second-hand poles replaced ex-tramway or small-diameter poles. Although the sinuous curves of Highfield Road and lower Bolton Road, with their steep cambers, never allowed maximum speeds, routes such as Manningham Lane, Wibsey and Bradford Moor boasted good, modern carriageways which encouraged drivers to push transmissions to the limit. Facing frogs were not designed to be negotiated at speeds up to 40 m.p.h., but they sometimes were, to the dismay of knowledgeable passengers, and on one occasion a city official paced a trolleybus descending upper Bolton Road at 50 m.p.h.!

Inevitably, in a period of high staff turnover, inexperience took its toll. Trolleybus 620, illicitly driven by its conductor, sped to disaster down the Avenue, Clayton; others ran off the road because the driver was adjusting the destination display while the vehicle was moving. Other incidents were not without humour. A newly-qualified driver was so shaken at having overshot the Crossflatts terminus that (when restored to his rightful wires) he returned to Bradford at a snail's pace, pausing at the Branch to see if his trolleys were still on

the wires - to the far from speechless fury of his overworked conductress who had to cope with the huge queues which had built up meanwhile. On another occasion, boarding a Thackley trolleybus whose staff were all too obviously searching skywards with the bamboo stick to retrieve errant trolley booms, a passenger naively enquired what they were doing. "We're not bl—dy having a cup of tea!" came the exasperated reply. No form of transport is perfect: all are constrained by practical limitations within which they perform to specification if properly handled.

In January 1959 it had been agreed that of the various authorised routes into the new Holme Wood estate the Knowles Lane approach was best suited to trolleybuses, and twelve months later a 'spur' from the Tong Cemetery route was ready for use at a cost of £12,630 for poles, brackets and overhead equipment. Modern town-planning having made no provision for proper turning facilities, a reversing triangle had to be provided at the terminus (reversing there in icy conditions a few years later Karrier 723 subsided gracefully into a suburban garden). Ex-St. Helens 794 was seen there on test on February 7th 1960, and on a bitterly-cold March 6th 'Llanelly' 781 inaugurated the new service (Holme Wood, 17), which replaced most Dudley Hill (19) workings, vehicles alternating with Tong Cemetery (18).

It was known that this extension would be one of the last (possibly the last of all) to be constructed, as all worthwhile routes were now covered, and the proposed

Bradford's farthest trolleybus outpost was at Crossflatts, only half a mile from the boundary of Keighley, which R.H. Wilkinson had hoped to reach by 'trackless' in the 1920s. Park-Royal bodied ex-Hastings No. 813 is seen enjoying a long 'layover' at Crossflatts terminus on May 21st 1960. It is not difficult to detect the derivation of this 1946 body design from the bodybuilders wartime utility products.
J. Copland

The network reached its peak on March 6th 1960 when 'Llanelly' No. 781 reached the new Holme Wood terminus, watched by a bevy of inspectors and attended by Karrier 'Eagle' tower-wagon parked in the reversing triangle. *Author*

Bierley route was not really suitable. Significantly, it was seen as the culmination of half a century of enlightened progress and not as a prelude to retrogression and contraction. The trolley- and motor-bus fleets were evenly matched: approximately 190 trolleybuses operated 47 1/2 miles of urban and suburban route whilst an equal number of motor-buses served $92\frac{1}{2}$ miles of road including services to neighbouring towns and cities. Both forms of tranport served the areas to which they were best suited, and each assisted the other when the need arose: in national emergencies the electric vehicles came to the fore, whilst the diesel buses helped to solve local crises such as blocked highways or power failures. An all-trolleybus Bradford would never have been feasible: an all-motor-bus Bradford was not desirable.

Changes in the political control of the City Council in May, 1960, for the first time since 1945, produced a new team of city fathers who reassuringly endorsed the accepted transport policies of their predecessors.

Meanwhile the decline of other undertakings continued to provide a harvest of bargains. Intent on standardising their fleet on Sunbeam/Karriers, Doncaster Corporation offered for sale six 1949-vintage 7ft. 6in. wide B.U.T.s which they had bought from Darlington in 1952 and whose East Lancashire bodies had become so decrepit that new bodies had been contemplated as early as 1955. Inspected by B.C.T. in January, 1960, they were bought for £120 each, ostensibly for spare parts (the motors alone were worth £400 apiece), though observers predicted that 'Humpy would never scrap a B.U.T.!' They were not kept waiting long: after a decent interval the chassis were pronounced 'too good to scrap' and were reserved for renovation and rebodying at a saving of £56,000 over new vehicles.

Similarly Grimsby-Cleethorpes B.U.T.s and Karrier Ws were inspected before withdrawal in June 1960; Walsall Corporation however bid higher for the B.U.T.s, leaving Bradford with the much less attractive Karriers. In a more promising vein the tidings that Glasgow's modern trolleybus system was to close by 1965 aroused in Bradford the anticipatory comment that "Humpy will have a beanfeast then!" More prosaically two Ashton-under-Lyne Sunbeam Ws, redundant since the demise of the Haughton Green service, were bought for £350 and stored at Thornbury where their peacock blue and yellow livery resembled the B.C.T. colours they were intended to assume.

This miscellaneous collection was assembled into a batch of a dozen for rebodying in 1961/2 and received fleet numbers matching their registration marks, i.e.,

Ex-Ashton Sunbeam Ws FTJ 400/1	820/1
Ex-Grimsby-Cleethorpes Karrier Ws AEE 22-5/7	822-5/7
Ex-Doncaster/Darlington B.U.T.s LHN 781-5	831-5

The numbers 816-9, 826 and 828-30 were not used, and the sixth B.U.T. (LHN 780) was dismantled to provide a spare EE 410 motor (there had never been a spare before, such was their reliability). Only six more chassis were required to replace the remaining 1934/5 A.E.C./E.E.C.s, after which nothing further would be needed until the 'Crossleys' were withdrawn in 1966.

City centre redevelopment in Forster Square was now approaching a climax: familiar, shabby buildings were vanishing daily with new vistas and visionary edifices arising in their place. No longer was it possible for spare trolleybuses to be parked in the Square for hours on end, as the whole area was being reshaped and realigned with a new link (Petergate) to Leeds Road. In view of the implications for the Bradford Moor-Crossflatts (24-7/30) and Eccleshill-St. Enoch's Road services (33/44) Mr. Humpidge prepared plans for a one-way trolleybus gyratory system via Petergate, Broadway and Forster Square, with Manningham Lane and Thornbury vehicles loading in Broadway, thus minimising possible conflict between multi-lane traffic flow and the special requirements of trolleybus operation.

Fleet modernisation was progressing equally rapidly - already the first chassis (833) of the contract for 12 bodies was ready for despatch to East Lancashire Coachworks, and more acquisitions were pending. In 1955 the Mexborough and Swinton Traction Company had offered to sell their fleet to Bradford for £500 per vehicle, but Mr. Humpidge had felt able to wait. Now his patience was rewarded, as twelve chassis were acquired for a mere £124 each including new spares.

Confusion reigned when Teesside received two chassis reputedly assigned to Bradford, but the final intake was FWX 911-7/9/20 and JWW 375-7 which it was conjectured would receive fleet numbers 836-847 or 841-7/9/50 and 855-7. With their longer wheelbase chassis they were suitable for 29ft. 0in. bodies and would allow the 'Notts. & Derby' B.U.T.s to be withdrawn for rebodying and the remaining 1934/5 vehicles to be scrapped.

As the remarkable decade drew to a close, preparations for the trolleybus Golden Jubilee, 1911-1961, began. This move gave much satisfaction, as it set the seal on all the long years of hard work, persuasion, ingenuity and innovation which had made Bradford a mecca for advocates of electric traction. The obvious success of the undertaking was reflected by its local popularity and national prestige, and when echoes of the old whisper, "Can it last?" were heard, the confident answer was, "Yes, it can – there's no reason why it shouldn't!" And there wasn't.

Top left: **A Bradford trolley-scape with Cawthras' modern factory and chimney in the background, Victorian shops and houses in local stone with stone-slabbed roofs, a 'slow-major road ahead' traffic sign adjacent to the section feeder for the trolleybus overhead wires, and rebodied 'Llanelly' Karrier W No. 783 about to cross the old Great Northern railway bridge in Knowles Lane on its way to Holme Wood.**

Top right: **as the last vehicle in the 1959-60 rebodying programme, No. 705 (a 1945 Karrier), was being prepared for service in Thornbury Works, it was joined by ex-Doncaster No. 378 (originally Darlington No. 68) which was the only ex-Doncaster B.U.T. to be dismantled for spare parts.**

Above: **Ex-Ashton Under Lyne No. 65, a Roe-bodied Sunbeam W, intended for rebodying as B.C.T. No. 821, outside the 1915 Railless shed at Thornbury on October 2nd 1960. As it turned out, neither of the two Ashton vehicles were used, though the motors were salvaged.**   *All author*

Chapter seven

Change and Decay

Twelve days after having announced the forth coming Jubilee Mr. Humpidge tendered his resignation, having accepted the managership of the large Sheffield Corporation and Joint Omnibus undertakings.

The shock was profound: the timing unfortunate. Although physical preparations for the new Forster Square were well advanced, construction of the redesigned overhead network could not begin until much later. And efficient though the trolleybus fleet was, it still contained too many 7ft. 6in. wide vehicles - the 29 Notts. & Derby, Brighton and Hastings vehicles due for rebodying about 1963, the 11 'Crossleys' and the few surviving 1934-9 A.E.C./E.E.C.s and Karrier/Weymanns. Despite all the achievements everything therefore depended on the choice of a new manager.

Before his departure on May 2nd 1961 Mr. Humpidge tied up all possible loose ends. A further contract worth £43,305 was placed with East Lancs. for the rebodying of the 12 Mexborough chassis: the lease of the Shipley 'tramways' was renewed; overhead equipment was bought for the future Forster Square layout; the chassis of 835 was despatched to the coachbuilders, and new late-night services were arranged for the 1961/2 winter season - 11.20 or 11.30p.m. and midnight departures to Allerton, Bradford Moor, Buttershaw, Clayton, Duckworth Lane, Greengates, Saltaire (via Manningham Lane), Holme Wood and Spring Head Road. Mr. Humpidge took with him the good wishes of all who appreciated the benefits he had conferred on the city through his clear foresight, patient planning and unfailing courtesy.

From a short-list which included the trolleybus-operating managers of Ashton and Grimsby-Cleethorpes an all-party sub-committee selected Mr. John C. Wake of St. Helens, having been impressed by his undertaking's financial prowess. Mr. L. L. Christie (Traffic Superintendent) was appointed to the position of Acting Manager until Mr. Wake took office on July 3rd.

By this time it was tacitly accepted that in the United Kingdom the cause of the trolleybus was hopeless. All undertakings except Bradford, Bournemouth, Doncaster, Huddersfield, Maidstone, Reading, Rotherham, Teesside and Walsall were contemplating abandonment, and production of new vehicles by B.U.T. and Sunbeam had almost ceased. Having digested the implications of the local developments, the author concluded (March 23rd 1961) that 1971 would see a very different Bradford.

Golden Jubilee, June 20th 1961: AEC/EEC No. 603 in 1911-style livery and Karrier E4 No. 687 restored to 1939 livery, with ex-Darlington No. 787 in the siding at Mulcott Road, Dudley Hill. On the overtaking wires AEC/EEC No. 626 prepares to pass on its way to Bankfoot .Number 603 was one of the oldest vehicles in the fleet, having entered service in November 1934 – it was to complete a million miles the following year – though its Northern Coachbuilders body dated from 1947. The Karrier E4 had its original English Electric body of 1939, albeit rebuilt by Samlesbury in 1951.

Author

The Golden Jubilee, its significance heightened by the growing uncertainty, was splendidly celebrated. Two trolleybuses - 1934 A.E.C./E.E.C. 603 in a 1911-style livery and 1938 Karrier E4 687 restored to the ultramarine and cream of its youth - conveyed the Transport Committee over the original route on the 50th anniversary of its opening (June 20th), when guests of honour were Mr. Wake, Mr. Humpidge and old employees Edgar Oughtibridge, George Naylor and Alderman John Shee. Four days later - the anniversary of the commencement of public service – Nos. 603, 687 and 787 bore enthusiasts on a city-wide tour, wafted on their jubilant way by public approval of a form of transport so closely identified with the city. Moreover, the undertaking had just been declared wholly debt-free: the years of prudent frugality had borne fruit at last.

As the golden day faded and the Jubilee dinner was digested, thoughts turned to the future. Was this indeed the Apotheosis of the Trolleybus? Opinions varied. Some believed existing policies would continue, others that all would be gone within five years; the author forecast that an abandonment plan based on 'economics' would be proposed within two years and completed in ten. L.L. Christie, with Scotch forthrightness, was more emphatic, "The writing is on the wall!" he said.

High summer was troubled by the first chill autumn breeze a mere fortnight later, when it became known that five of the newly-acquired Mexborough chassis were to be scrapped and their electrical equipment transferred to the lower-powered 'Darlingtons' (785-8). The seven Ashton and Grimsby vehicles had not been touched since their arrival, and it quickly transpired that the seven remaining 'Mexboroughs' were to replace them in the rebodying programme and that the latest contract for 12 bodies was being cancelled. Orders quietly circulated that the 'Doncaster' and 'Mexborough' chassis were to be completed as quickly as possible, the inference being that the sooner they re-entered service the sooner they could be written off: indeed, so great was the haste that the opportunity of lengthening the 'Mexborough' chassis to accommodate 71-seat bodies was lost.

On September 28th 1961 the Transport Committee's Deputy Chairman (Coun. H.A. Sissling) made public his belief that the trolleybus undertaking would be eliminated over a period of ten years, as there was 'no room' in Bradford for two types of transport. The public, not having shared the premonitions of 'those in the know', were frankly astounded, and the surprised comment of the Bradford press – 'Why, after investing a huge sum on trolleybus development, should there now be a change of policy?' – was echoed by a rapidly growing volume of protest. Although the Chairman (Ald. H. Clayton) cautiously defined his colleague's statement as a private opinion, the public rejected any form of reassurance, especially when the Chairman retired shortly afterwards and was succeeded by his deputy.

A brief summary of the arguments propounded by both sides may suffice:-

---

AGAINST TROLLEYBUSES

1) Trolleybuses are dearer to buy (£10,000) compared with motor buses (£7,500).
2) New trolleybuses are virtually unobtainable.
3) Trolleybuses are route-bound and extensions are costly.
4) Electricity charges are rising more rapidly than fuel oil costs.
5) Well maintained diesel buses emit no fumes.
6) The use of two forms of transport necessitates two sets of spare parts.

FOR TROLLEYBUSES

1) Trolleybuses last twice as long as motor-buses if rebodied after 15 years.
2) Sunbeam and B.U.T. are still willing to trade.
3) No extensions are planned or needed but routes can be altered if long-term need arises.
4) Electricity is not dependent on the goodwill of oil-producing nations.
5) Trolleybuses cannot emit fumes.
6) Trolleybuses, being mechanically simple, account for only a small percentage of spare parts.

At this juncture residents of Bradford Road, Clayton, petitioned for a direct service to City, having been denied motor-buses in 1951 and having seen trolleybus proposals thwarted a few years later by the inadequacy of the highway. This time the cost (unspecified) of providing overhead equipment was seen as an insuperable obstacle, and motor-buses to Thornaby Drive (replacing two Clayton trolleybuses) were decreed. The spectre dispelled ten years earlier had re-appeared.

Fortune, too, had ceased to smile. An unusual crop of trolley dewirements (one outside the manager's window) caused delays. In a normal year motor-bus failures exceeded trolleybus failures eleven months out of twelve, but in December, 1961, the trolleybus figures were less favourable than usual. Violent gales in February 1962, blew trees on to the overhead lines and disrupted power supplies in Shipley and Bingley. All these facts were carefully reported to the Committee.

Outwardly life continued normally. The annual ritual of pole-painting recommenced in the spring; overhead wires were re-aligned in Highfield Road, revised plans for the Forster Square network were aired; two Austin tower-wagons replaced elderly Bedfords; the proposed Thornton Road depot for 67 trolleybuses (and a few motor-buses) was solemnly re-affirmed, and when H.M. the Queen Mother attended festivities in honour of the Bradford-born composer Delius on March 29th, 1962, Thornbury trolleybuses terminated in West Street and Wibsey/Buttershaw vehicles in Victoria Square. Obscure short-workings continued, e.g. the 8.40 a.m. journey from Peel Park to Bradford Moor, the two morning journeys to Nab Wood (one from Saltaire Depot and the other from City) and a school journey from Thackley to Crossflatts

Descending Barkerend Road at speed on August 18th 1962, on the long run from Bradford Moor to Saltaire, ex-Darlington No. 787 passes between Hanson School and St. Clement's Church. *Author*

which dated from about 1956. On April 28th trolleybus 603 completed a million miles in service.

Signs and portents were not lacking, however. Minor damage to a 'frog' was followed by the removal of the outward-bound North Parade wiring, and in the name of 'depot output rationalisation' three evening peak trolleybus journeys were turned over to motor-buses with a theoretical annual reduction in capital expenditure of £3,000! In March the Huddersfield manager stated that the Bradford undertaking was to be abandoned, and rumour indicated the substitution of motor-buses for trolley-buses on the Eccleshill-St. Enoch's Road Top service because of 'difficulties'. Rumour was soon amply confirmed.

On June 4th 1962 'the General Manager reported in regard to the question of continuing to operate trolley vehicles across the city centre through Forster Square, the redevelopment of which would involve the realignment of overhead equipment at an estimated cost of between £15,000 and £20,000. It was resolved that the Eccleshill-St. Enoch's Road Top and Crossflatts-Bradford Moor services be converted to motor-buses'. Submitted to a critical Council on June 26th, the recommendation was promptly sent back for reconsideration.

Not surprisingly! The deceptively bland recommendation, airily dismissed as merely 'two services', represented a quarter of the entire network: without Forster Square it would be fatally dislocated and disadvantaged.

The ensuing storm of protest could be summarised as follows:-

i) the outlay of £15/20,000 was theoretical, as the material was already in stock, and the overhead lines staff had to be paid whether they were working in Forster Square or on routine maintenance,

ii) if the £15/20,000 were 'saved' by trolleybus abandonment, 30 replacement motor-buses costing £195,000 would be needed, and as their life was only half that of trolleybuses the minimum cost was £390,000 less the £20,000 = £370,000;

iii) many trolleybuses, miles of overhead equipment and nearly 1,000 poles would be scrapped years before they were life-expired;

iv) if the cross-city services were merely suspended during the alterations the dilemma would be avoided: the Eccleshill, St. Enoch's Road and Bradford Moor services could terminate in Bolton Road, Tyrrel Street and Hall Ings respectively, and a temporary terminus could be built at the foot of Cheapside for the Manningham Lane services.

In July, twelve months after taking up office, Mr. Wake was appointed manager at Nottingham with effect from December; his brief reign had been

Left: Standing at the Thornbury terminus resplendent with its new forward-entrance East Lancs body, B.U.T. No. 832 disguised its third-hand origins in the Darlington fleet very successfully, save for the registration number. Like all the ex-Doncaster trolleybuses it was thoroughly modernised.

Below: The new Forster Square is taking shape, but not entirely on the site of the old. The new glass-fronted buildings stand at the junction of Petergate and the extension of Cheapside, whereas the Bingley/Crossflatts loading-point at which B.U.T. No. 833 is waiting, was on the southern perimeter of te original Square - in exactly the same location as No. 746 (front cover). By the time that the carriageways had been realigned the trolleybuses had been banished.

Author (both)

controversial and frustrating, as his only major proposals - fares increases and trolleybus replacements had been referred back.

Nevertheless the process of policy-making ground on: excactly thirteen years after motor-buses began a temporary service to Bradford Moor in preparation for trolleybuses, the City Council voted 36-32 to reintroduce them. Motor-buses were also to operate the cross-city Eccleshill-St. Enoch's Road Top service (with peak-hour trolleybuses to and from City only), and the Crossflatts service was to be converted within a year. The debate was heated. In Committee the manager had commented that the annual trolleybus profits were challengeable, and repeated the statement in Council when invited to

do so. Jehovah-like, the City Treasurer rose to enquire, "Who is going to challenge them?" An awkward silence followed. As a token gesture it was conceded that the Bradford Moor wires (apart from Forster Square) would remain intact for a trial period.

Meanwhile at the height of the controversy the ex-Doncaster B.U.T.s (831-5) had returned from the East Lancashire Coach Builders. Their appearance in service on the doomed Bradford Moor route underlined the unwisdom of abandonment: as they soared up Church Bank like 'flying carpets' passengers were heard to marvel that anyone should wish to discard such a fine mode of travel. Extremely handsome and tastefully streamlined, they were the most advanced vehicles in the country with their fluorescent lighting, saloon heating, air-operated folding platform doors, automatic acceleration, easily-cleaned 'Darvic' ceilings and surfaces, and maximum-depth windscreens designed to give drivers a panoramic view, especially of the nearside. Their third-hand origins were impossible to detect.

The series of mishaps which had dogged the trolleybuses intermittently for over a year continued. A localised voltage drop on November 3rd trapped many trolleybuses in Forster Square, though the Eccleshill-St. Enoch's Road vehicles managed to struggle through. When full voltage returned after an hour the stranded vehicles quickly dispersed, leaving the Square empty of trolleybuses - a unique sight at a Saturday midday but a foretaste of the future - and trolleybuses were drafted in from Duckworth Lane and Bolton Road to provide shortworkings to Chelmsford Road and Park Gates as a means of restoring the schedules with minimum delay. On September 28th a collapse of scaffolding had closed Bridge Street: depot-bound vehicles were diverted via Well Street and Broadway, while the Thornbury service made use of West Street. But it was the last time that major diversions were possible: on November 3rd/4th the West Street loop was disconnected and the Well Street wires removed in preparation for the impending changes.

Two of the least-known services faded away on November 16th when 'Crossley' 691 performed the morning trip to Nab Wood and 'Hastings' 815 left Peel Park for Bradford Moor. The unfortunate Ashton and Grimsby vehicles had already departed to the scrapyard to create space in the 'Tin Shed' for trolleybuses about to become redundant.

In appropriately wintry weather the services through Forster Square operated for the last time on November 17th, 1962. After the busy throng of Karriers, Roe and Weymann B.U.T.s, 'Llanellies' and 'Doncasters' had melted away, the last departure, to Bradford Moor at 5 minutes past midnight (intentionally delayed by five minutes) was A.E.C./E.E.C 655 whose stablemates had inaugurated the Forster Square services in 1939. Now the glory had departed - a triumph of parsimony over progress.

Next morning the debut of the fierce, snarling A.E.C. Regent Vs at Bradford Moor was audible half a mile away, whilst in Cheapside (formerly Lower Kirkgate) the Manningham Lane trolleybuses were quietly sampling their neat new turning-circle only a stone's throw from the City terminus of the Bolton Road services but now permanently divorced from them. A posthumous attempt to be the last trolleybus in the Square was made on November 19th by Karrier 739 returning from Buttershaw to Thornbury: alas, the Broadway wires were dead (they were cut down a few days later), and the vehicle was ignominiously towed back to its authorised route by 0.32, one of the two new Austin tower-wagons. A week later Mr. Wake left Bradford, while in every available corner of Thornbury depot withdrawn trolleybuses slowly gathered dust - some of the shortlived 'Hastings', the last Northern Coachbuilders A.E.C./E.E.C.s and even 'Notts. &

Derby' B.U.T.s - the 7ft. 6in. wide fleet was almost extinct, opportunities for future rebodyings being lost.

The first day of December, 1962, saw the arrival of the first of the seven 'Mexboroughs' (841-7). Similar in appearance to the 'Doncasters' although slightly longer, they differed in having traction lighting (in heatproof units), no auto-acceleration and typical Sunbeam bouncy springing not apparent on modern road surfaces but discernible on routes such as Greengates. Number 842, the first to enter service, was also the first Sunbeam F4 in the fleet and the first to bear a West Riding registration mark (FWX 912), the 'native' trolleybuses having always borne Bradford County Borough marks. Entering service at monthly intervals, they took up residence at Thornbury. Few doubted that they would be the last additions to the fleet, although no formal decision to abondon the system had been taken: indeed, no such decision was made until it was a foregone conclusion.

Numbers 846 and 847, which took up duty on February 1st and March 1st, 1963, bore the name of the new manager, Mr. Edward Deakin, M.Inst.T., previously manager at Chesterfield, who had had long experience of all three types of transport at Huddersfield and Rotherham, having also served in the all-trolleybus Ipswich stronghold. A genial, courteous gentleman as well as a skilful negotiator whose decisions were the fruit of considerable study, he accepted the Council's unvoiced abandonment policy but saw no reason to expedite it, preferring to retain trolleybuses until the chassis or bodies (usually the latter) were worn out.

In the early months of 1963 – the longest and bitterest winter since 1947 – Crossflatts passengers deserted their unheated trolleybuses in favour of West Yorkshire Road Car's warmer buses, thus prompting the transfer to Saltaire Depot of forward-entrance trolleybuses with 'Panelec' heating. The 29 new arrivals comprised 13 rear-entrance 63-seaters (587-596 and 3 'native' A.E.C./E.E.C.s), 12 forward-entrance 66-seaters (the 'Doncasters' and 'Mexboroughs') and 4 forward-entrance 70-seaters (785-8) in place of B.U.T.s 740-751 and others.

City centre redevelopment was now moving elsewhere. Hall Ings, previously connecting Church Bank with Bridge Street and now diverted to Eastbrook Well, was being extended to Manchester Road, superseding Union Street. But whereas a year earlier trolleybus abandonments would have followed automatically, Mr. Deakin planned to use the new thoroughfare, and an era of pole-planting unfurled.

The municipal elections of May, 1963, restored to power the pre-1960 civic leaders, to whom a review of transport policies was suggested by the pro-trolleybus party. Suggestions included (i) restoration of the Bradford Moor service (using stored vehicles), (ii) retention of the Manningham Lane trolleybuses as far as Saltaire with an express motor-bus service to Bingley and Crossflatts to win back passengers lost to the West Yorkshire Road Car Co., (iii) a Saltaire-Clayton trolleybus link, (iv) a route through the Allerton housing estate, from Bell Dean Road to Allerton Road, using almost-new overhead equipment to be salvaged from Bingley, (v) an adjustment to the latest A.E.C. Ltd. contract for 100 motor-buses whereby the Corporation would take (say) 25 trolleybuses in place of diesel buses of an equivalent value. But although the Council leader (Ald. E. Newby) cautiously stated that each route would be judged on its merits, no move was made to reverse the policy, and consequently it was no surprise when the Transport Chairman (Coun. L. Dunne) announced on November 20th that in view of substantial increases in electricity charges the whole undertaking would probably have to be abandoned.

Earlier decisions, therefore, had to run their course. On October 31st 1963, trolleybuses ran for the last time on the 7-mile 'showpiece' Crossflatts route. In the evening new motor-buses flooded Saltaire Depot whilst departing trolleybuses reached Thornbury Depot via Thackley and Bolton. Regular travellers savoured to the last the swift ascent of Cheapside, the dignified glide along Manningham Lane, the fast run past the Park, the intricacies of the Saltaire circle, the long, sinuous journey past Nab Wood and Cottingley Bar, a glimpse of the River Aire, the wide ascent to Bingley with its Main Street and ancient church, and the final dash round the curves to distant Crossflatts. 'Mexborough' 842 made the final departure from the still-new city terminus; at Crossflatts an old man who had seen the first tram in 1914 now beheld the last

Right: Approaching Victoria Road, Saltaire, on May 11th 1963, are Roe bodied B.U.T. No. 751 bound for Crossflatts and 'Doncaster' B.U.T. No. 834 due to terminate in Saltaire.

Below: Latest in a long line, ex-Mexborough and Swinton Sunbeam No. 847 basks in the early spring sunshine at Bolton on March 2nd 1963, one day after entering service with the paintwork on its new East Lancs body gleaming. It was the 344th trolleybus to be placed in regular service in Bradford – and the last. *Author (both)*

Snow and bitterly cold weather early in 1963 affected passenger figures on the Crossflatts route beyond Saltaire. Climbing from Cottingley to Bingley on January 26th, AEC/EEC No. 651, rebodied by East Lancs in 1956 but unheated, is almost empty.

Author

trolleybus, 'Darlington' 786. The final vehicle to reverse at Bingley was 788, a conscious link with the last tram, which carried the number 88.

By thoughtful courtesy of Mr. Deakin the spectators at Saltaire were allowed to use the late-night staff vehicle, 'Doncaster' 831, which unexpectedly voyaged to Thornbury by way of Manningham Lane, North Parade, John Street, Sunbridge Road and Leeds Road.

Access to Saltaire Depot was retained for use by 'layovers' on the 'other' Saltaire (i.e., via Thackley) service. The removal of the miles of redundant wiring began: inside the City boundary the task was complete within five weeks (except the Park Gates wires which were salvaged in January, 1964, for further use); the Shipley wires remained until September 1964, and the Bingley wires a year longer because of disputes as to their value and ownership. Much of the almost-new wire was salvaged to replace the old round-section Allerton wire; the Bingley poles were carefully removed (some are now at Beamish museum) but the Shipley and most of the Bradford poles were cut up for scrap. The temporary reprieve of the disused Bradford Moor equipment also ended: the Church Bank, Harris Street and Barkerend Road installations were discarded in the 1963/4 winter, leaving the 'inward' Leeds Old Road wiring still used by vehicles entering service on the Tong Cemetery, Holme Wood and Bolton-Bankfoot routes.

But the Bolton-Bankfoot (34) service itself closed on February 19th, 1964, being wholly absorbed into the less punctual City Circle motor-bus service introduced a decade earlier. Every trolleybus since 240 had travelled over the route, and it was fitting that the last rites should be performed by one of the latest 'railless', No.

843. Most of the wiring, however, was still needed for depot journeys, and only the Dudley Hill-Bankfoot section could be dismantled.

Regular workings to Eccleshill (33) ceased on the same day, although unscheduled extras continued to operate at peak hours and Saturday afternoons until October 31st, when the service quietly ceased. The last trolleybus was probably 796, and the first public intimation came with the removal of the wires, the newest of which (from the 1959 extension) saw further service in Thornton Road. The remains of the West Street loop and also the Lidget Green circle, disused for nearly a year, were cut down in January, 1965, followed by the Bell Dean Road circle in May.

The fleet was shrinking too. 'Notts. & Derby' 760 was the only 7ft. 6in. vehicle to survive the Crossflatts closure, but it never ran again, and from April, 1964, only East Lancashire-bodied vehicles remained in use.

A long period of calm then ensued. Smartly repainted vehicles emerged from the Works at more frequent intervals: since October, 1960, trolleybuses had been repainted every 50,000 miles instead of the 100,000 miles interval favoured in the 1950s. Traction poles and spacer bars were also dealt with in regular rotation, whilst the stranded-steel spanwires were either greased or painted green, according to whichever tower-wagon team was on duty!

During the redevelopment of the area around the Town Hall (renamed City Hall in 1965) overhead wiring arrangements changed so frequently that one morning the driver of 'Darlington' 786 was seen to dismount from his cab to check whether his route had altered since the previous day. The extension of Hall Ings referred to above was completed in 1963, when the Wakefield Road trolleybuses (transferred there from

Union Street) were the first vehicles to use it on March 17th. On May 18th, 1964, trolleybuses returned to Town Hall Street for the first time since 1940 and simultaneously appeared for the first time in parts of Market Street and Bank Street, wiring having been erected to allow vehicles travelling to and from Thornbury Depot to avoid Bridge Street. On May 31st the Thornbury (89) trolleybuses were diverted from Bridge Street, where major excavations and road widening were taking place, to a temporary turning-circle at the junction of Bank Street and Broadway, but on November 1st a gyratory system around Britannia House was instituted, after which Thornbury vehicles travelled in a clockwise direction (instead of anti-clockwise as from 1952 to 1964), loading in Bank Street. The last major change in the area came on March 3rd, 1968, when the Town Hall Street section closed for the second time, being superseded next day by new wiring in front of City Hall (Bridge Street to Town Hall Square).

At the beginning of 1965 the licensed fleet comprised A.E.C./E.E.C.s 587-596, 634/8, 651/4/5/9, 664/6 and 674/5; 'Jo'burgs' 693-702, Karriers 703-739, 'Llanellies' 775-784, 'Darlingtons' 785-793, two 'St. Helens', 796/801, 'Doncasters' 831-5 and 'Mexboroughs' 841-7. Thus only 7 B.U.Ts (796, 801, 831-5) remained in service: the premature termination of the rebodying programme had relegated the remainder to the vehicle store or even the scrapyard. Meanwhile 27-year old 634 with its modern body laboured on.

The most extensive service alterations ever made by the Department occurred on March 14th, 1965; in the trolleybus sector the Thornton (7) and Thornbury (89) services were combined as a cross-city service (7) with peak-hour extras from Thornbury to Spring Head Road (6). In preparation for this the 'Mexboroughs' replaced the 'Darlingtons' at Duckworth Lane Depot, the entire service being worked from the latter establishment where spare capacity had been created by the replacement of some Allerton trolleybus journeys (16, previously 31) by a motor-bus service into the growing Allerton estate (15, previously 35).

In the same month a 24-hour timetable was introduced, and it is believed that Bradford were the first trolleybus operators to do so.

In May 1965, a right-hand curve from Bank Street into Hall Ings was re-erected for the **third** time (such was the pace of change) to allow 'school specials' to operate from St. Enoch's Road to Tong Cemetery, but a few weeks later the Tong Cemetery/Holme Wood services had to be motor-bus operated while the wreckage of a burnt-out mill was cleared out of Nelson Street. A similar blaze in Thornton Road diverted the Thornton service to Sunbridge Road for a few days.

The chronic high turnover of staff obliged the driving school to adapt three trolleybuses for dual-control, thus creating an opportunity for the return of Roe-bodied B.U.T.s 745 (replacing 597 as 0.60 on June 14th, 1964) and 743/6 as 0.62/63 on January 1st, 1966. As a precaution against a severe winter and resulting vehicle damage, Weymann-bodied B.U.T. 757 was prepared for service in November 1964, but as the winter was mild its return was delayed for a year, when it was joined by 753/8. With the exception of 800 all the

When city redevelopment swept away all the old property 'behind the Town Hall', Union Street was closed and the trolleybuses which had used it were transferred to a new extension of Hall Ings, where 'Llanelly' No. 775 and 'St. Helens' No. 796 are seen at the Holme Wood and Tong Cemetary loading points respectively.
Author

A vanished scene: Tong Cemetery-bound Karrier No. 708 (normally a Duckworth Lane vehicle) passing the Great Northern Hotel at the bottom of Wakefield Road on January 23rd 1965. A six-lane highway now covers the site. *Author*

St. Helens B.U.T.s reappeared after renovation in place of Karriers which were experiencing a spare parts shortage.

Remembrance Day 1965, saw what transpired to be the last enactment of an annual ritual. As the Cenotaph lay in Victoria Square through which the Wibsey and Buttershaw trolleybuses passed, two motor-buses provided a circuitous shuttle-service between Tyrrel Street and Park Avenue, connecting with trolleybuses which on their inward journey coasted out of Little Horton Lane into Park Avenue, used the overhead wires to reverse at the park gates and regained their normal wires by means of a skilful uphill fly-shunt. In following years motor-buses provided the entire service between 10.45 a.m. and 11.45, when trolleybuses took over again.

Spring fever in 1966 brought further livery experiments: three motor-buses received large areas of primrose paint whilst 'Doncaster' 835 emerged in a variant of 'Notts. & Derby' blue and broken white. The Department concluded that the standard livery was infinitely preferable.

Trolleybuses made a minor comeback in Forster Square on May 15th, 1966, when the Saltaire (40) and Greengates (42) services were transferred from Commercial Street to a new section of Canal Road.

In preparation for the impending reconstruction of Wakefield Road as a six-lane highway the Transport Committee had met Yorkshire Electricity Board representatives on January 11th, 1965, to discuss the provision of new underground feeder cables. However,

in view of the rising cost of trolleybus operation, the capital cost of the new cables and overhead equipment and the virtual impossibility of maintaining operation while reconstruction was in progress, a reluctant decision was made that the Tong Cemetery (18), Holme Wood (17) and Dudley Hill (19) services should be abandoned, though not until the last possible moment. Motor-buses were ordered to replace the trolleybuses in due season, but fate capriciously intervened on February 28th 1967, when the Dudley Hill sub-station broke down irretrievably. Sufficient motor-buses were mustered to provide a share of the journeys, as the power now supplied directly from Valley Road generating station was insufficient to support a full service except at weekends.

The Wakefield Road trolleybuses therefore ran for the last time on Saturday, April 1st, 1967, when A.E.C./E.E.C. 655 which had reputedly opened the Tong Cemetery route in 1938 was also permitted to close it. A 'Llanelly' (781) had inaugurated the Holme Wood route in 1960: another of the same breed (784) now performed the closing rites only seven years later. A sign of changing times was noted: immediately after the departure of 784 from Holme Wood terminus, the reversing-triangle with its valuable brass and copper fittings was dismantled to forestall enterprising residents who might have contemplated carrying out the work themselves.

Most of the overhead equipment (including the Laisterdyke-Dudley Hill wiring retained for depot journeys since 1964) was quickly removed: the almost new Holme Wood equipment saw further service, whilst the best of the Tong Street wiring enjoyed a new life in Listerhills Road. Unexpectedly the Bowling Yard driver-training facilities and the whole of the Wakefield Road installations from Hall Ings to Foundry Lane (except the frogs) were retained, enabling 0.60 to make its unobtrusive daily journey between Thornbury Depot and Bowling until December 5th, 1967, when advancing highway work necessitated the removal of the Wakefield Road wires. Undaunted, 0.60 took up residence in the Yard and continued its training duties with the aid of power fed from the nearest feeder until February 13th, 1968, when the adventure had to cease. Driver-training was then conducted exclusively on the Queen's Highway.

Vehicles compulsorily retired as a consequence of the closure were the 'Jo'burgs' (693-702) and the last of the 'native' A.E.C./E.E.C.s, (651/5). The 'Jo'burgs', which had survived their brothers in Nottingham and St. Helens by a decade, had been the first 8ft. 0in. wide vehicles in Bradford 25 years earlier; the A.E.C./E.E.C.s had been well-respected for almost three decades.

Manufacture of trolleybuses in the United Kingdom had long since dwindled to a trickle; no British orders had been placed since 1962 (Bournemouth). Consequently the supply of spare parts was slower than previously, and vehicles which developed faults were sometimes laid up for months: indeed, A.E.C./E.E.C. 638 had enjoyed a year-long holiday not long before final withdrawal. The equipment was ageing, and even the durable traction motors were feeling the strain. The few remaining E.E. 406 80 h.p. motors, long obsolete, tended to overheat because of the slenderness of their armatures, and the 1944-6 vintage Metrovick and B.T.H. 207 85 h.p. types were gradually 'cracking up'. The more modern 95 h.p. Metrovick 209 type continued to give good service in 'Darlingtons' 785-8 and 'Mexboroughs' 841-7, and identical units formerly used in Hull's 'Coronations' were being fitted to the 703-714 series and the remaining 'Darlingtons' (789-793). Unfortunately the MV 209 motors being discarded by Ashton and Manchester were incompatible, but contact was being made with Nottingham and Woverhampton, also with Huddersfield and Bournemouth for sundry items.

Salvation lay in the mighty EE 410 120 h.p. motors, robustly designed for all conditions and climates, of which dozens salvaged from scrapped B.U.T.s were still in stock. Moves were therefore made to fit them to vehicles likely to remain in use until the final closure. Unfortunately the 'Notts. & Derby' A.E.C./E.E.C.s, 587-596, resisted all attempts to equip them with EE 410 or even MV 207 units, with the result that the ten vehicles, last of a famous breed, were withdrawn one by one when their EE 406 motors failed. More success was achieved with the Karriers: in January, 1967, the resourceful fitters at Thornbury managed to equip forward-entrance 730 (and rear-entrance 716) with EE 410 units, a feat previously thought impossible. The improvement was noticeable, and Whetley Hill began to enjoy the surge of English Electric power (though not, unfortunately, married to the supreme comfort of a

Despite route closures driver-training continued as usual. Learner vehicle O.60 (alias Roe-bodied B.U.T. No. 745) begins another circuit of Bowling Yard on April 7th 1967 – a week after the Wakefield Road route had officially ceased. *Author*

B.U.T. chassis save for brief periods, e.g. July 1964 when 'Doncaster' 834 was loaned to Duckworth Lane Depot.)

Delays to scheduled services and a continual need for improvements to highways and junctions were forced on the city by the relentless pressure of ever-increasing traffic flows. At Thornbury a large new gyratory system superseded the roundabout provided for the Bradford Moor trolleybuses in 1949, and an anti-clockwise turning-circle via Leeds Old Road and Hawthorne Street came into use on November 5th, 1967, trolleybuses on the Thornbury-Thornton (6/7) service thenceforth used the old Bradford Moor loading point. From June 23rd, 1968, outward-bound Duckworth Lane (8) vehicles were routed via new wiring in Barry Street, Godwin Street having been converted into an inward-bound one-way thoroughfare. Pressure from the Highways Department to divert inward-bound Allerton trolleybuses via Barry Street and Godwin Street was firmly resisted, as the diversion would have entailed an impossibly long 'dead section' where the Allerton and Duckworth Lane wires would have crossed on the steep ascent of Barry Street.

With the advent of each spring an annual programme of pole repainting began. Techniques changed over the years. Until about 1954 the painting teams had relied on long ladders, one at each side of a pole, resting on the bracket arm or the pole itself. The longer bracket arms, the topmost portion of the extra-tall poles between Forster Square and Crossflatts, and the wooden or metal spacer bars on the overhead line were the prerogative of the tower-wagon staff. Subsequently, however, the entire pole-painting operation was undertaken by the latter, who, by skilful adjustment of the hydraulic valve were able to ensure that the rate of descent of the platform matched the speed of painting, an unusual but effective example of 'time and motion'. The 1968 programme (which turned out to be the last) covered the new poles at Thornbury, a few at Allerton omitted previously because of roadworks, the City-Greengates route and the City-Wibsey and Park Avenue sections. From Five Lane Ends to Greengates and along Park Avenue a new plastic-based lime green paint was used, but aesthetic tastes must have been offended, as when the St. Enoch's Road poles were treated similarly they were hastily overpainted in the customary emerald colour.

Old favourites continued to emerge from the shadows when the call of duty sounded. Another Roe/B.U.T., No. 749, returned to service in March, 1968, after four years storage; more amazingly, No. 745, ex-0.60 – the driver-training vehicle stationed in the open air at Bowling Yard a year earlier – reappeared partly repainted and fully re-seated. But in September the end of trolleybus operation was foreshadowed when the Transport Committee was authorised to proceed with the purchase of ninety motor-buses over a three-year period.

On Christmas Day 1968 the usual skeleton services were provided. All trolleybus journeys were worked from Thornbury Depot, thus creating the unusual spectacle of a rear-entrance Karrier, 727, and a 'Doncaster' B.U.T., 833, on the Duckworth Lane Route, normally the exclusive preserve of forward-entrance Karriers and Sunbeams.

The onward march of city re-development around City Hall involved the sweeping-away of old, shabby property (as well as a few good buildings) and the creation of a new highway pattern. Victoria Square and New Victoria Street ceased to exist as such, being superseded by a new dual-carriage thoroughfare – Princes Way – linking Thornton Road and a re-aligned Manchester Road. The lower portions of Little Horton Lane and Morley Street became one-way roads with a new connecting link called Glydegate. As each section was completed the Wibsey and Buttershaw routes were diverted, making use of ex-Bingley poles and a few old Morley Street poles which had slumbered since the end of the Queensbury trams in 1949.

Glydegate and Morley Street came into use on May 18th 1969, followed by Princes Way (inward on August 18th and outward on September 21st). New loading sidings were erected for the Clayton Service in the remains of Town Hall Square (renamed 'The Tyrls' in January, 1972) and the Thornton service (outside the Gaumont cinema, later renamed the Odeon) on February 9th and March 3rd, 1970, respectively. With the energising of a new automatic 'frog' at the Thornton Road/Princes Way junction on April 19th, 1970, the long process of development and improvement of trolleybus overhead equipment in Bradford came to an end after six decades of progressive change and innovation.

Ever since the introduction of public transport one of the well known features of late-night travel had been the convivial snatches of song and mild truculence inspired by alcoholic excesses. At the end of the 'affluent 'sixties' the familiar phenomenon took a regrettable turn for the worse when senseless attacks on transport staff made an unacceptable appearance. In self-defence the Transport Department equipped four trolleybuses with two-way radios for use on late-night services; Nos. 842, 846, 845 and lastly 841 were the recipients of the equipment (which was also used for the reporting of delays and overhead damage) between April and December 1970.

A late spate of damage and disaster demonstrated that human nature was still capable of thwarting all sensible attempts to promote road safety. Descending St. Enoch's Road at great speed on May 2nd, 1970, B.U.T. 745 broke not one but both trolley booms in a drastic dewirement; 'Doncaster' 833 negotiating the ill-cambered curves of lower Bolton Road with a similar lack of caution brought down the wires on May 19th; on November 14th Karrier 738 halted the Thornton-Thornbury service when it rammed a pole and overturned near Thornton terminus, and 'Doncaster' 832 ended its career embedded in a pole on the wrong side of Highfield Road on May 2nd, 1971. No defects capable of wreaking such havoc were found when the vehicles were examined afterwards, leaving the inescapable conclusion that trolleybuses, like all other vehicles, were perfectly safe and roadworthy when driven as they were intended to be driven.

Above: Roe-bodied B.U.T. No. 749, seen at Greengates (Albion Road) on March 30th 1968, had just re-entered service after several years in store.
Below: The last section of new trolleybus overhead equipment, in Princes Way (Thornton Road to Little Horton Lane) was inaugurated by Wibsey-bound Karrier W No. 722 on September 21st 1969. *Author (both)*

One final accident – a tragedy – befell Thornton-bound Karrier 725 on August 11th 1970 when its trolley booms were inadvertently switched on to the diverging Allerton wires at the Four Lane Ends junction. As the vehicle accelerated across the junction the booms were inevitably dragged from the wires with considerable force, rebounding against a pole with an impact which snapped them in two. The shattered ends fell on and killed two small boys sitting on a seat outside the 'Craven Heifer'. Fearing that faulty equipment might have been the cause of the fatality the Department immediately converted the remaining 'auto-frogs' (at

Four Lane Ends and Princes Way) to manual operation; although at the ensuing inquest a verdict of 'Accidental Death' was returned, the question of how three warning signals – two visual and one audible – had apparently gone unheeded was not resolved.

The Clayton (37) service was cut back to the original (1926-1956) terminus at Town End when a new motor-bus service (36) to The Avenue via Bradford Road (proposed for trolleybuses in 1955 but never implemented) began on May 31st 1970. On the previous evening 'Llanelly' 782 had performed the last service journey up The Avenue with 'Mexborough' 844 following as a late-night special. The first trolleybus to revert to Town End, Roe/B.U.T. 749, was unfortunately wrecked three days later by a West Yorkshire Road Car bus. Regular scheduled short-workings to Chapel Lane (16), Thackley (41) and Little Horton (47) ceased when new schedules took effect in May, 1970.

Decimalisation Day for Bradford City Transport came on February 21st, 1971, a week later the official currency changeover, when the long-accustomed fares expressed in shillings and pence (s. and d.) were simultaneously increased and transformed into new pence (p); e.g., the Allerton fare was converted from 1/- to 6p. But decimal fares on Allerton trolleybuses lasted only a week, as the service operated for the last time, in a swirling snowstorm, on February 27th, 1971, when the Transport Committee rode on the last scheduled vehicle, 842, which was followed at midnight by a late-night extra, 'Darlington' 791. This, the 'old man's route', so-called because its leisurely schedules suited elderly staff better than the hectic pace of the Duckworth Lane 'money spinner', had been the first tram-to-trolleybus conversion in 1929. As a courteous gesture the Department left the power on for a further day to enable enthusiasts to take 'Mexborough' 843 on a farewell tour to Allerton and Chapel Lane. The overhead wires from Squire Lane to the terminus, salvaged a few years previously from the Bingley route, were again removed for use elsewhere – possibly in Thornton Road (Listerhills Road-City Road) in May, 1971, when Thornton trolleybuses were temporarily diverted via Sunbridge Road which had not seen regular service since the Allerton closure. At Clayton the overhead curves at the park were renewed in mid-July.

To its secret embarrassment the Department had been obliged to renew the Bolton Road wiring (Cliffe Road-Bolton Junction) in September, 1970, at a time when there was no salvaged wire in stock. Concerned at the worn condition of the 1948-vintage wiring the Overhead Lines Superintendent had confronted the Department with three choices – (1) that the Saltaire (40) and Greengates (42) services should cease forthwith, (2) that a 20 m.p.h. speed limit should be imposed, (3) that new wiring should be erected. Option (1) was ruled out by a lack of motor-buses; option (2) would have aroused public criticism. Option (3) was therefore unavoidable, and for the last time the gleam of new cadmium-copper wire was seen as a specially-hired Huddersfield overhead line crew – redundant in their own town since 1968 – enthusiastically renewed the section at dead of night.

Ironically a spare parts shortage compelled the Department to supplement the Saltaire and Greengates services with motor-buses for a few months, but the closure of the Allerton route and the simultaneous cessation of the Springhead Road (6) journeys released sufficient vehicles to allow a full trolleybus service to be resumed. For a brief, unique period Duckworth Lane Depot vehicles were lent out for use on the Bolton Road routes, but from March 1st, 1971, the Wibsey (45) and Buttershaw (46) duties were transferred to Duckworth Lane Depot, to the dismay of the shedmen who found themselves confronted by 'the work of the seat carvers and felt pen artists of Buttershaw'. Thornbury Depot trolleybus workings were therefore confined to the Clayton and Pasture Lane (37/8) and Saltaire and Greengates (40/2) services.

The approach of winter for the Bradford trolleybus system – ex-Darlington Karrier No. 791 closed the public service to Allerton at 15 minutes past midnight on February 28th 1971. *Author*

Chapter eight
The Golden Evening

With the final closure of the Teesside trolleybus system on April 18th 1971 Bradford became the last trolleybus operator in the United Kingdom. Once British trolleybuses had numbered 2,500, but now only 56 survivors – sought after by transport connoisseurs – remained in public service.

But for Bradford too the tide was ebbing. Long gone were the days of good-quality second-hand acquisitions when other systems closed: the last occasion had been in October, 1970, when Bradford had acquired two Metrovick MV 207 motors from Teesside in exchange for Karrier/Sunbeam differential units; regrettably the latter undertaking's fine ex-Reading Sunbeams, like Walsall's ex-Cleethorpes B.U.T.s a year earlier, were not destined to wear a South Sea blue and primrose livery.

The Diamond Jubilee of trolleybus operation was celebrated in a defiant swansong on June 20th 1971 when B.U.T. 758, 'Mexboroughs' 844/847 and Karrier 717 were hired for a tour of the whole network except the Saltaire route beyond Thackley where the power fed from Shipley sub-station was judged to be insufficient for four fully-laden vehicles superimposed on the normal service. The occasion was felt to be in the nature of a farewell, as the remaining routes were due for closure in the forseeable future.

Thereafter events moved swiftly. Only ten days later the Saltaire and Greengates routes closed, bringing to an end trolleybus operation outside the city. On the final day B.C.T. staff loyally ensured that any vehicle which developed a defect was replaced by another trolleybus and not a motor-bus. The last layover in Saltaire Depot was performed by 'St. Helens' 799, though Karrier 717 was thoroughly washed there preparatory to carrying members of Shipley U.D.C. on

the last trolleybus journey in their area. The Transport Committee rode on the last vehicle to make the round trip from City to Saltaire and back (834); whilst the last journey on any part of the route (City- Bolton-Greengates-Killinghall Road-Laisterdyke- Thornbury Depot) was undertaken by 'Doncaster' 831.

Next day all the remaining rear-entrance trolleybuses were withdrawn, except, for sentimental reasons, B.U.T. 758. Only one route remained on the schedules board at Thornbury Depot – Clayton/Pasture Lane (37/38), served by a sad handful of the throngs which had once filled the shed – 758, 'Darlingtons' 785/8/9, 792/3, 'Doncasters' 831/3/4/5 and 'Mexborough' 846. Two other 'Mexboroughs' 844 and 847 joined their fellows at Duckworth Lane Depot to work the Thornton (7), Duckworth Lane (8), Wibsey (45) and Buttershaw (46) routes.

For one further month Thornbury's varied fleet sped quietly up and down Listerhills Road and wove its way around the twists, turns and inclines of Pasture Lane and Green End to 'Bull Hill', Clayton. Then following the delivery of the bulk of an order for 70 Daimler Fleetlines and Leyland Atlanteans, in one night of drastic change the Clayton, Pasture Lane, Wibsey and Buttershaw services closed simultaneously on July 31st, 1971. A minor lighting defect prevented 758, the last rear-entrance trolleybus, from working the final Clayton journey, its place being filled very adequately by fellow B.U.T., 'Doncaster' 834, while 'Darlington' 793 carried the last Pasture Lane passengers. Duckworth Lane-based Karrier 732 closed the Wibsey route, closely followed by 'Mexborough' 841 to Buttershaw. 'Darlington' 785, the erstwhile single-decker T403 of remarkable memory, was retained as an extra to Little Horton, but its services were not

Frequent curves and steep cambers were particular features of the Thackley and Idle areas. Ex-Mexborough and Swinton No. 844 pauses near Idle Church on a return journey from Saltaire with its route number (42) ready for its next journey from City to Greengates. The overhead feeder cable suspended between the trolley wires and the standard was unique in Bradford, where underground feeders were the rule.

Author

needed, as the Bradford holiday fortnight had dispersed the crowds which would normally have thronged these last journeys.

Not since the abandonment of the Forster Square services nine years earlier had a closure produced such a drastic outcome. Thornbury Depot, once host to 120 trolleybuses, finally closed its doors to them after six decades; Little Horton Lane reverted to the noisy diesel buses from which it had escaped 16 years previously, and not only the 'Darlingtons' but also the splendid B.U.T.s 758, 831/3/4/5 were taken out of service. The trolleybus driving school ceased simultaneously (the specially-adapted B.U.T.s 062/3 having succumbed previously) when Inspector Gobbi handed the last of the coveted 'pink slips' to Conductor G.S. Watson.

Public interest in the trolleybuses increased as their numbers waned, and the remaining vehicles found themselves celebrities. Some of the Karriers had already been dismantled, leaving only thirteen in addition to the seven 'Mexborough' Sunbeams as the sole occupants of Britain's last trolleybus depot. Cine cameras whirred in endless rotation; knots of spectators gathered outside the depot, and the staff good-humouredly coped with the constant queries.

But even this unsought fame was presently to be marred. In preparation for the relaying of a troublesome water main in Toller Lane, a handful of new motor-buses was transferred to Duckworth Lane Depot on November 8th, 1971, remaining there even after the work was finished in order to allow drivers to familiarise themselves with diesel vehicles. And all the while the unpalatable task of dismantling miles of overhead wire was being tackled unenthusiastically by the overhead line staff, on whom the success of modern trolleybus operation had depended so heavily and who now saw the era of their expertise drawing to a close.

On the first day of the last year of British trolleybuses the operational fleet comprised nine Karriers (703/6/11/12/13, 728, 731, 735/7) and seven Sunbeams (841-7), a total of sixteen, but No. 841 fell

prey to a defective worm-drive unit only a week later. Fast becoming collectors' items, withdrawn vehicles were passing into private hands, popular acquisitions being B.U.T. 746, 'Doncaster' 834 and 'St. Helens ' 799 (the last-mentioned emerged from the Works displaying 'Moss Bank, 4', a destination from its West Lancashire past which delighted its purchasers). A brief snowfall from January 30th to February 3rd was the last encountered by trolleybuses which, unlike the trams, had never felt at ease in wintry or foggy conditions.

Preparations for the ceremonial closure of the system, delegated to the Manager and Deputy Chairman, began on January 19th, 1972, the immediate problems being the cost of a commemorative brochure, the selection of a vehicle for the Corporation's Industrial Museum and the date and time of the closure itself. The first was resolved satisfactorily (it ran to two printings and made a good profit); the second was not agreed until after the closure, and the third was dependent on factors as diverse as Easter holidays, the termination of the Yorkshire Electricity Board contract, church services, Sunday tea, the availability of the Lord Mayor and departure times of the London trains! Agreement was quickly reached that a ceremonial trolleybus should embark on a final journey at 3 p.m. on Sunday March 26th, and that the vehicle should be either 737 (the best of the Karriers) or 835 (the best of the B.U.T.s, delicensed and in store), specially repainted in pre-1942 dark blue and cream.

Fate in the guise of the National Union of Mineworkers then intervened unexpectedly. Following the outbreak of a miners' strike and a consequential shortage of supplies, the Yorkshire Electricity Board began selective power cuts on February 11th. When a similar situation had arisen a year earlier, the Y.E.B. had averted excessive disruption to trolleybus services by the expedient of switching power from one sub-station to another, but the unions were no longer willing to countenance such an arrangement. Accordingly the remaining trolleybus services were

In the closing months of the Wibsey and Buttershaw routes the vehicles were supplied from Duckworth Lane Depot. Karrier W No.731 is nearing the top of St. Enoch's Road on its way to Buttershaw, May 1971.

Author

suspended at midnight on February 10th, the vehicles being ferried to storage in Thornbury Works when power supplies permitted. Significantly the last trolleybus to vacate Duckworth Lane Depot on the 18th was No. 737.

Would normal power supplies be restored in time for the planned closure date? Would trolleybuses ever run again in the streets of Bradford, and if not, what form should the closure ceremony take? Gloom descended, and pressure to surrender all the vehicle licences at the end of February had to be firmly resisted. The Y.E.B., however, guaranteed to supply power for the last day, emphasising that in any event the standing charge of £1,000 for staff and sub-stations for the month of March would still have to be paid. Alternative power sources such as batteries and motor-generators having been deemed inadequate, it was resolved that unless the standing charges were waived by February 28th trolleybuses would run again, no matter how briefly. However, the proposed repainting of a vehicle was cancelled, and 'Mexborough' 844 was selected as the last trolleybus on account of its smart condition, it having been the last trolleybus to receive a full repaint (April 4th 1971).

Principal guest at the Transport Department's 33rd annual dinner-dance was, appropriately, C.T. Humpidge, to whom the Deputy Chairman expressed regrets that they had never coincided as Manager and Chairman respectively, as they could have pursued some very progressive policies for Bradford's electric transport. With typical humour came the reply, "Yes, we could – but all the same, I gave them something to scrap!" - a late echo of the views expressed during the years of expansion: "The more routes there are, the longer it will take to scrap them!" On the next evening, February 25th, the power cut was briefer than previously; a day later the miners' strike ended. Hope returned.

On the morning of March 2nd Duckworth Lane Depot contained nothing but motor-buses – but the glow of red warning lamps indicated that the overhead wires were live again. In the afternoon trolleybuses 735,

842/4/5/6 came home in triumph, and 842 and 846 immediately resumed service on the Duckworth Lane route. Civilisation had returned.

Within a few days the depleted fleet was busily at work, although as the drivers were by this time fully conversant with both forms of transport, appearances did not conform to a pattern: on March 22nd all the fleet except 844 was in use, whereas next day 703 and 735 were inconspicuous among a swarm of motor-buses. Dual operation presented certain problems: the functions of trolley- and motor-bus pedals were not identical, and at 80 lb. per square inch the trolleybus air-brake pressure was lower than that of diesel buses twenty years younger. Some trolleybuses did not return from their sojourn at Thornbury Works: the licence of 737 had not been renewed when it expired on February 28th, and requests for the reinstatement of B.U.T. 835 were turned down on the grounds of a few trifling defects detected during a trip around the Bradford Moor test circuit on March 25th.

Interest mounted as the days dwindled. On March 19th No. 844 with newly touched-up paintwork was hired as a mobile studio wherein a television crew interviewed the Deputy Chairman and retired employees Edgar Oughtibridge (who had ridden on the first railless on a pre-opening run) and George McLaughlin (whose father had been at the controls on the opening day). Number 844 traversed the remaining routes (thrice around the Four Lane Ends circle!) including Leeds Old Road, and then entered Thornbury Works to don its flags and commemorative inscriptions and to be fitted with a new resistance. Back at Duckworth Lane No. 845 was treated to a one-coat lower deck repaint in case it had to deputise for 844.

Requests from transport enthusiasts for permission to run privately-owned preserved trolleybuses under Bradford wires were declined in case any of the vehicles possessed incompatible (e.g. regenerative) equipment, and remembering an incident of some years previously, the Department switched off the power each night to forestall illicit journeys in 'the small hours'.

Below: A happy return – No. 845 about to turn from Toller Lane into Little Lane on its way back to Duckworth Lane depot.
Both: J. Copland

Below: Karrier W No. 706 enters the tight turning-circle at Duckworth Lane Terminus on March 19th 1972. The Royal Infirmary, opened in 1936, is in the background.

Chapter nine
Auld Lang Syne

The morning of Friday, March 24th 1972 was like any other early spring morning in Bradford, with a host of laden trolleybuses hurrying their daily passengers towards the city centre, to office, shop and factory.

And yet there were already signs that it was, after all, to be a very different day. At 4 a.m., long before daybreak, enthusiasts were reported waiting outside Duckworth Lane Depot, and the 8 o'clock national radio news heralded the last day of public service trolleybus operation in Britain. All day the vehicles were well filled, and at teatime crowds gathered to watch fully-laden Karrier 712 leave Thornbury on the last cross-city journey to Thornton. At least 100 people waited for the last City to Thornton trolleybus at 10.57 p.m., but as no duplicate was provided, many were left behind when No. 843 departed with a maximum load of 76 passengers. Those who had caught the last City to Duckworth Lane trolleybus (706) five minutes earlier were therefore privileged to join the throng which saw 843 return to Duckworth Lane by way of Squire Lane and enter the depot for the last time.

Next morning trolleybus rides cost £1 each, for this was the start of the Last Trolleybus Weekend, and all public service journeys were thenceforth performed by motor-buses. From 9.30 a.m. until late afternoon special trolleybuses conveyed passengers on a circular tour from Thornton Road to Thornton, Squire Lane, Duckworth Lane, City, Thornbury and back to City. Progress was leisurely, with photographic halts on request and visits to a 'shop' in trolleybus 737 outside Thornbury Depot, where the Rolling Stock Engineer (Mr. B.B. Browne) and colleagues sold brochures and mementoes. The venture was most successful: shop sales realised £379 and the tours £880. Many well known names in the transport world were in Bradford that day, notably W.A. Camwell, the famous tramway photographer, and G.G. Hilditch, manager at nearby Halifax.

The tour vehicles did not return to Duckworth Lane, which had succumbed to its diesel destiny: they joined gleaming 844 and other vehicles not in use that day inside Thornbury Works, which thus became for the first and last time an operational depot.

Overnight showers gave way to bright sunshine in time for the two final tours, the last of which, requiring eight trolleybuses, set out at 11.30 a.m. on Sunday, March 26th, 1972 – the last of the last days. Then, their duty done forever, they quietly re-entered Thornbury Works.

One more journey remained: the most spectacular of all. From all corners of the kingdom visitors and enthusiasts had flooded in, some with their own preserved motor-buses, most with cameras and seemingly endless supplies of film. Press and television were conspicuously in evidence, and from Belfast the City Transport Manager, R.W. Adams, himself a trolleybus operator until 1968, found time amid the troubles of his city to send a kind message to his Bradford colleagues. By early afternoon most of the long route to be taken by the civic party was lined with spectators.

'Auld Lang Syne' and the three o'clock chimes pealed overhead as trolleybus 844, beflagged and bedecked, pulled away from the front entrance of City Hall bearing three of the senior members of the City Council. At the Thornton loading point the civic party and their guests were waiting – members and past members of the Transport Executive Group and Municipal Undertakings Committee, the General Manager, City Treasurer, senior Transport Department staff, eminent former colleagues such as N.A. Scurrah (retired Rolling Stock Superintendent, a survivor of the R.H. Wilkinson era) and R. Edgley Cox (assistant engineer until 1943 and subsequently manager at St. Helens and Walsall, who was greeted ecstatically by his old B.C.T. staff), and representatives of trolleybus enthusiast organisations. Last to arrive was the Lord Mayor (Ald. H. Moran, J.P.) whose car had been delayed by the dense throngs.

Cameras whirred and motor-cars dashed past frantically as 844 made its stately progress to Thornton, where two halts were made. The first was at the terminus for purposes of fresh air, photography, camaraderie and the rescue of a small boy who had fallen from a tree. The second was outside the home of 98 year old Walter Hodgson, freeman of the city, former alderman and Chairman of the Transport Committee (1930-4, 1935-1945) who as Lord Mayor had inaugurated the Thornton trolleybuses thirty-seven years previously; his civic successor presented a bouquet as the old gentleman waved farewell.

At Kipping Lane the trolleybus passed a horsedrawn cart – final echo of the distant days when 'railless' 240 posed alongside similar conveyances to demonstrate its flexibility – and surmounting the steep crest of Squire Lane passed slowly in front of Duckworth Lane Depot whose staff 'presented arms' with a large flag attached to a bamboo trolley stick, to the delight of the dignitaries. Back in the city 844 circumnavigated the tight Tyrrel Street turning-circle before treading the less familiar path of Bridge Street for access to Market Street and Leeds Road.

On the approaches to Thornbury parked vehicles jammed every side-street, and amidst a vast crowd outside the depot a solitary Leeds Corporation motor-bus lay becalmed, not, like its 1911 dual-gauge tramway predecessor, waiting to convey the civic party to a Leeds luncheon, even though its owners were hopefully experimenting with a battery-electric bus as a possible successor to diesel buses.

Number 844 came to rest inside the Works, the crowd following like a whirlwind and filling all the available space. There, for a last, nostalgic half-hour, they listened to speeches. The Chairman of the Municipal

Above: The last normal scheduled journey, March 24th 1972, – Sunbeam F4 No. 843, still carrying passengers, returns from Thornton and turns into Allerton Road for the final run to the depot.   *J. Copland*

Below: A tour on Saturday March 25th 1972 with Karrier W No. 712, filled with passengers at £1 a head, arrives at Thornton to find the lay-by occupied by replacing Leyland 'Atlantean' motor-bus No. 468.   *J. Copland*

Undertakings Committee (Ald. F. Hillam) congratulated the staff for six decades of dedication; the Chairman of the Transport Executive Group (Coun. J.W. Pell) reviewed the remarkable story of the trolleybuses; the Lord Mayor (himself a former trolleybus driver) declared the system officially closed; the Deputy Transport Chairman (Coun. J.S. King) thanked the enthusiasts for their support and recalled famous names such as Spencer, Wilkinson, Owen Silvers, Tom Bamford and Edgley Cox who, against all the odds, had pioneered and proved the worth of the 'trackless'. Reference was also made to the 1911 partnership with the neighbouring city, but unaccountably no one present could recall the name of the place! The General Manager (Mr. E. Deakin) presented 844's schedule board to its driver (Mr. Fred Kelly). At the long-forgotten ceremony at Laisterdyke the Lord Mayor had closed a switch to begin trolleybus operation in the city; now, as his successor opened a similar switch, the Bradford Corporation trolleybus undertaking died.

A civic reception at City Hall, not on the 1911 scale, concluded sixty-and-a-half years of what could reasonably be called the most civilised form of transport known to man.

Left: Almost time to go. The City Hall bells in the distance prepare to strike three o'clock on Sunday, March, 26th 1972 as the crowds watch the civic party boarding No. 844 in Thornton Road. *Telegraph & Argus*

Below: Appropriately emblazoned and beflagged, Bradford's and Britain's last trolleybus, No. 844 pauses at the top of Thornbury Works siding for inspection by Mr. R. Edgley Cox (wearing a trilby hat – contributor of the Foreward to this book). *K. Rankowski*

Chapter ten
Will ye no Come Back Again?

It is always easier to destroy than create. Whereas the planning and perfecting of trolleybus installations had involved decades of work, the disposal of their remains was quick and easy. The last length of wire, at the bottom of Carr Lane, Windhill, was ceremonially cut down on August 13th 1972.

Chief beneficiaries were scrap-merchants, who welcomed countless tons of steel, copper and aluminium into their yards. A few items escaped: Blackpool bought a quantity of wire; some poles went to Tyne and Wear Metro and numerous vehicles to museums. Karrier 737 was chosen for the new Bradford Industrial Museum on account of its all-Bradford ancestry while its rival, B.U.T. 835, discounted for its minor earth leak, defective steering box and non-Bradford (i.e. Darlington) registration mark, departed for an active life at the Sandtoft Transport Centre. However, many hundreds of former trolleybus poles survived as street lighting standards, a factor which was to become significant in a surprisingly short time.

Public reaction to the end of operation was mixed. Many rejoiced to see the end of overhead clutter, trolley dewirements and the cautious crawl at road junctions: the trolleybus, they averred, had no place in modern traffic conditions. Others mourned the passing of a quiet, quick, clean form of transport and maintained that operation should have continued.

In the light of all that has transpired since abandonment was first mooted in 1961, is it still possible in 1993 to believe that the trolleybuses could indeed have survived? Although hindsight is an unforgivable tool for historians, it is nevertheless likely that had proposals which were submitted informally to the City Council by the Author been accepted in 1962, the system would easily have 'bridged the gap' between the then current trends of thought and the post-1976 realisation that electric transport would have to return one day. See Appendix page 109.

The proposals related chiefly to the purchase and stockpiling of B.U.T. chassis from the Portsmouth and Manchester undertakings whose closure had been decided. Apart from the obvious cost savings when compared with new vehicles (electric or diesel), such acquisitions would have deferred until 1981 the need to buy new trolleybus chassis. Naturally the network itself would not have escaped unscathed: decreasing use of public transport would have necessitated frequency reductions and, in a few instances, route closures. But the post-1981 chassis purchases would have been of the front-entrance thyristor controlled conductorless type ideally suited for operation into the 21st century, giving Bradford a service second to none.

Nevertheless, when the year 1981 actually dawned the Bradford Telegraph & Argus were already observing in February that,

'It is hard to conceal a shudder at the amount of money which could have been saved if the Council had heeded the nostalgic views of the transport buffs.

Sentiment isn't all mistaken'. The conclusion was correct even if the recollection was faulty: the pro-trolleybus campaign had been based not on nostalgia but on a desire to maintain progressive policies. More importantly, however, the press comment related to the fact that a trolleybus revival was already under way.

Long-held doubts as to the stability and finite nature of the world's oil resources had been disturbingly reinforced by the 1976 Middle East oil crisis which had brought to an end the era of cheap fuel. In Saudi Arabia Sheikh Yamani had called for international research into alternative power sources as a means of averting global conflict when supplies began to dwindle and die.

British reaction was summarised in the document, 'Energy for Transport – Long Term Possibilities (H.M.S.O., April, 1978) which soberly predicted a 'post-oil period' as early as the 1990s and concluded that electric propulsion in the form of tramcars and trolleybuses was inevitable in the long run. Within two months the West Yorkshire Passenger Transport Authority – post-1974 successor to the Bradford, Calderdale, Huddersfield and Leeds municipal undertakings – had begun a study, and a year later the existence of ex-trolleybus standards in the streets of Bradford was being cited as a reason for reinstating the vehicles which had once used them.

A formal proposal for trolleybuses in Bradford was adopted on October 8th, 1980, by the West Yorkshire Metropolitan County Council Passenger Transport Sub-Committee (alias the P.T.A.) on the motion of its chairman, County Coun. W.A. Proom. Imprudently the Sub-Committee made no proposal to provide the necessary capital, and when the Government displayed an equal reluctance the matter dragged on interminably. Nevertheless technical studies revealed the plan to be soundly based, and an Act was obtained for trolleybus operation on the Eccleshill, Greengates, Wibsey and Buttershaw routes whose lengths were for the first time expressed in Continental kilometres instead of the customary miles, furlongs and chains.

Similar plans for Leeds had been evolved by the time that the short-lived County Council was abolished, its transport functions devolving on April 1st, 1986, on the West Yorkshire Passenger Transport Authority whose members were now councillors appointed by the five District Councils of West Yorkshire. Now envisaged as a new form of inter-city link from Buttershaw to Leeds via Bradford and Thornbury, 'electrobuses' (not a new name of course, see Chapter 1) were adopted by the P.T.A. with all-party support, thus enabling the 75th anniversary of trolleybuses in the two cities (June 1986) to be marked by a symbolic journey from Leeds to Thornbury by West Yorkshire P.T.E. motor-bus 5035 (in a version of the 1911 Leeds trolleybus livery) and thence to Bradford by trolleybus 844, powered by a trailer-mounted diesel generator and still displaying its 'Last Trolleybus' slogans. Ironically B.U.T. 835 had once again failed to achieve the limelight, as its

120 h.p. motor had overtaxed the capacity of the generator, unlike the 95 h.p. unit of 844.

Patience finally had its reward. On September 25th, 1987, the P.T.A. resolved to proceed with the City-Buttershaw (via Reevy Road and Beacon Road) section, and following intricate negotiations to settle financial and operational obstacles, the Secretary of State for Transport (Mr. Paul Channon, M.P.) announced his approval on October 11th, 1988.

Deregulation of public transport having occurred two years earlier, the P.T.A. agreed that they would provide and maintain the fixed structures for whose use they would charge a rental to the selected operator, who in turn would purchase and maintain the vehicles.

Detailed plans were drawn up by experienced consultants. Vehicles were to load in a pedestrianised Forster Square and move outwards via Market Street, returning via Market Street, Hall Ings and Petergate.

Professional opinion preferred dual-mode trolleybuses, i.e., vehicles equipped with an auxilliary diesel engine capable of propelling them up St. Enoch's Road at normal service speeds if the overhead power supply should fail. Obviously the extra, cost, weight and mechanical complexity would be considerable.

It is perhaps worthy of note that such sophisticated safeguards have not been thought necessary for the Manchester Metrolink, Sheffield Supertram and the Inter-City electric trains which are, of course, equally dependent on overhead power supplies.

In 1985 South Yorkshire P.T.A./P.T.E. followed West Yorkshire and obtained general powers through its own Act for trolleybus operation anywhere in the County (including Barnsley!) and specific powers for routes in Doncaster and Rotherham. The first British-built trolleybus for 30 years was shown on the Hestair Dennis stand at the 1984 Birmingham Motor Show. On August 8th 1985 it took to the specially built test track adjacent to Doncaster Racecourse. The vehicle, 2450, was an otherwise standard S.Y.P.T.E. bus of the period – Dennis Dominator chassis with a 78-seat Alexander 'R' type body. This co-operative project included Balfour Beatty, Insul-8, I.C.I. and British Telecom with G.E.C. supplying the 600v electrical equipment including the 177 h.p. motor. There was also a 3-cylinder Dorman Diesel engine giving the vehicle an off-line capacity. Unfortunately by the time all was ready, thoughts were occupied by the demise of the Metropolitan County Councils and deregulation of the buses. The unique Dennis trolleybus is still in Doncaster garage.

Extensive trolleybus systems are operating in Switzerland, Austria, China, Russia and other former Eastern Bloc countries as well as in several Italian cities and in the Athens/Piraeus area. Interest re-awakened in France (Nancy and Grenoble) to complement those cities that had retained them, for example Lyon. Utrecht remained unique in the Netherlands retaining its loyalty to the trolleybus and Ghent has introduced trolleybuses. After an on-off history, Toronto decided to retain its network and Vancouver still has one of the largest systems in the developed world. Trolleybus operation continued in a number of Brazilian cities with a new standard thyristor-controlled design being introduced

in the early 1980s. Sao Paulo has an extensive and expanding system.

Against this background it was disappointing that little interest was shown by British or European manufacturers when actual negotiations began, although there were some heartening exceptions. Most potential suppliers chose to believe that the project would never progress further than the trial route, and declined to construct a small number of specially designed or adapted chassis without a guarantee of further orders.

It should therefore be stressed that the P.T.E./P.T.A. have not spent twelve years in research and preparation without intending to carry the project to its logical conclusion. In Bradford the Greengates (via Idle), Eccleshill, Clayton, Allerton and Duckworth Lane routes would be prime candidates for electrification, and in Leeds and other cities the potential is just as great. All that is needed is the success of the trial route – a success which is easily attainable.

In the short term nothing can be done until the Bradford-Leeds railway electrification scheme has matured, probably in 1994, as the P.T.E./P.T.A. could not face two major projects simultaneously.

Nevertheless the Bradford Trolleybus Project remains firmly embodied in the P.T.E./P.T.A. Capital Programme and continues to enjoy the support of all who are concerned with the quality of urban life.

However, future happenings are a tale still to be told, and in looking forward to the second birth of the Bradford Trolleybus we can reflect, like the prophet of old, that,

'The thing that hath been, it is that which shall be; and that which is done is that which shall be done: and there is no new thing under the sun. Is there anything whereof it may be said, See, this is new? It hath been already of old time, which was before us.'
(Ecclesiastes Ch.1, vv.9-10)

Above: Overhead ingenuity – a neat three-way crossing at the junction of Manningham Lane and Oak Lane which number 844 has negotiated at speed.

Below: Although a stranger at Bolton Junction, Duckworth Lane-based Karrier W 721 picks its way confidently through the complex but well-used frogs and crossings. Were these a blot on the landscape? Not at all – sensible people do not gaze skywards at a busy road junction.

Author (both)

TROLLEY BUS FLEET

Fleet Number	Registration	Chassis Number	Entered Service	Withdrawn	Notes and Disposals (See Page 109 for notes)	

R.E.T. Cars: Alldays & Onions 13' 0" wheelbase chassis; Siemens 2 x 20 h.p. shunt field motors; Siemens hand control (9 fwd., 6 rev. notches) series/parallel. Traction lighting (as all vehicles until 597). Hurst Nelson B28R body, 20' 3" x 7' 0" x 10' 8". Spoked wheels, solid rubber tyres (as all vehicles until 1926). U.W. 5t 3cwt.

Fleet Number	Registration	Chassis Number	Entered Service	Withdrawn	Notes and Disposals	
240	-	-	20/6/11	5/16	1912 renumbered 502.	WV
241	-	-	7/11	9/18	1912 renumbered 501	WV

B.C.T. Cars: David Brown chassis; motors as 240/1; controllers as 240/1; BCT B29R bodies 23' 2" long. UW 3t 19cwt 2qr.

Fleet Number	Registration	Chassis Number	Entered Service	Withdrawn	Notes and Disposals	
503	AK 9629	-	4/13	9/24		BC
504	AK 9635	-	6/14	3/23		BC
505	AK 9636	-	7/14	3/29	GW 15/11/29-1/10/30	S
506	AK 9637	-	7/14	6/28		S
507	AK 9632	-	6/14	6/28		S
508	AK 9633	-	6/14	12/28	GW 22/1/29-21/10/30	S
509	AK 9631	-	6/14	6/28		S
510	AK 9628	-	7/14	10/29	GW 15/11/29-29/8/30	S
511	AK 9630	-	7/14	10/29	GW 15/11/29-17/6/30	S
512	AK 9634	-	6/14	3/29	GW 22/11/29	
513	AK 9625	-	8/14	10/28		S
514	AK 9626	-	9/14	9/28	DT 9/28-1/10/30	S
515	AK 9627	-	9/14	12/28	GW 22/1/29-8/30	BIM
516	AK 9622	-	10/14	4/23		BC
517	AK 9623	-	11/14	4/23		BC
518	AK 9624	-	12/16	1/26		BC
519	AK 9639	-	4/19	5/23		S
520	AK 9621	-	4/19	5/23		BC

B.C.T. 4-wheel double-decker: BCT/Kirkstall Forge chassis, wheelbase 13' 0"; DK31B 45 h.p. motor and controls; BCT H 51 (26/25) R; 23' 1" x 7' 0" x 15' 4", UW 7t 8cwt 3qr.

Fleet Number	Registration	Chassis Number	Entered Service	Withdrawn	Notes and Disposals	
521	AK 9638	-	3/11/20	10/28		S

B.C.T. 6-wheel double-decker: BCT/Kirkstall Forge twin-steering chassis, wheelbase 13' 0"; Metrovick 70 h.p. motor, foot controller; BCT H 59 (33/26) R; 23' 10" x 7' 5" x 14' 7"; UW 7t.

Fleet Number	Registration	Chassis Number	Entered Service	Withdrawn	Notes and Disposals	
522	AK 9963	-	1/22	1/27	Chassis S; body S 4/11/30	

B.C.T. "one-manners": AEC 603/Kirkstall Forge chassis; wheelbase 14' 0"; DK31B 45 h.p. motor and hand-controller; worm drive (as all subsequent vehicles); BCT B30FD (13 smoking, 17 non-smoking); 21' 2½" x 7' 6" x 11' 0" (to trolley base), UW 5t 5cwt 1qr.

Fleet Number	Registration	Chassis Number	Entered Service	Withdrawn	Notes and Disposals	
523	KU 1161	-	12/22	30/9/30	1/10/30	S
524	KU 1162	-	2/23	31/5/30	6/30	S
525	KU 1163	-	3/23	30/9/30	1/10/30	S
526	KU 1164	-	3/23	31/3/31	4/31	S
527	KU 1165	-	5/23	30/6/31	7/31	S
528	KU 1166	-	6/23	30/9/30	1/10/30	S

A.D.C. (Associated Daimler 607) – the first commercially-produced B.C.T. trolleybuses. Pneumatic tyres and electric windscreen wipers and Klaxon horn (as all subsequent vehicles) and foot-gong (as all previous vehicles). Wheelbase 14' 6"; Bull 55 h.p. motor (E. R. & F. Turner, Ipswich), EMB "T" foot controller, 5 series notches and 1 AEC weak-field notch; Westinghouse air brakes (the first); Strachan B37C, 25' 10" x 7' 6"; UW 5t 2cwt.

Fleet Number	Registration	Chassis Number	Entered Service	Withdrawn	Notes and Disposals	
529	KU 9104	607001?	1/8/26	31/12/37	GW O.43 to 16/12/44	
530	KU 9105	607003	9/26	30/6/38	7/11/38	R
531	KU 9106	607002?	9/26	5/4/38		BC

Fleet Number	Registration	Chassis Number	Entered Service	Withdrawn	Notes and Disposals	

Garrett type "O"; wheelbase 15' 6"? BTH 50 h.p. motor and equipment (series/weak-field); Roe B31C; 26'0" x 7' 6" x 6' 2" (body height only) UW 5t? (532-4). 535 identical but B35C. 537-9 B30F, Bull 50 h.p. motor

Fleet Number	Registration	Chassis Number	Entered Service	Withdrawn	Notes and Disposals	
532	KU 9101	263	8/26	6/12/35	28/1/36	MW
533	KU 9102	264	9/26	30/12/35	28/1/36	MW
534	KU 9103	265	9/26	1/8/34	10/12/34	F
535	RT 1345	262	11/26	12/35	Ex-demonstrator; 28/1/36	MW
537	KW 204	325	10/27	31/12/34	31/3/35	B
538	KW 205	326	10/27	31/12/34	31/3/35	B
539	KW 206	327	9/27	12/33	29/3/34	C

Garrett "S" type: the first Garrett trolleybus, exhibited Olympia 1925, demonstrator; basically as 532-5/7/8/9/ but Bull 50 h.p. motor and Garrett controller (series/weak-field)

Fleet Number	Registration	Chassis Number	Entered Service	Withdrawn	Notes and Disposals	
536	UM 1755	261	2/27	13/5/31	Bought 10/27; 17/3/33	H

A.D.C. type 603; wheelbase 14' 6" (540) 13' 6" (541-3); Bull 50 h.p. motor; series/weak-field; Strachan bodies B37C (540) and B30F (541-3). Also quoted as type 607 (540) and 605 (541-3)

Fleet Number	Registration	Chassis Number	Entered Service	Withdrawn	Notes and Disposals	
540	KW 200	?	12/26	30/6/38	(Ex-demonstrator) 7/11/38	R
541	KW 201	?	9/27	30/6/38	7/11/38	R
542	KW 202	?	10/27	30/6/38	7/11/38	R
543	KW 203	?	10/27	30/6/38	7/11/38	R

E. E. (English Electric) Leyland Lion PLSC1 modified chassis; DK 106 60 h.p. motor; DK WS2 Form A controller; 16' 3" trolley booms; 3-pedal (power, rheostatic and mechanical brakes); EE B36C body. Front profile "bulbous" (544-553), slightly V-shaped (554-559). Perimeter seats for 34 in 1939 (552-557)

Fleet Number	Registration	Chassis Number	Entered Service	Withdrawn	Notes and Disposals	
544	KW 2601	46287	2/28	29/8/38		Co
545	KW 2602	46286	2/28	30/6/38	5/39	Fi
546	KW 2603	46289	2/28	31/8/38	10/2/39	BC
547	KW 2604	46288	29/2/28	16/8/38	14/3/39	BC
548	KW 2605	46290	3/28	30/6/38	5/11/38	St
549	KW 2606	46292	25/3/28	31/10/38	GW.047 to 30/10/45	
550	KW 2607	46294	3/4/28	31/10/38	GW.048 to 21/11/44	
551	KW 2608	46293	4/4/28	31/8/38	17/4/39	BC
552	KW 2609	46295	14/5/28	30/8/40	26/11/40	L
553	KW 2610	46291	16/3/28	31/7/40	20/12/40	B
554	KW 4600	47696	8/2/29	31/7/40	20/12/40	B
555	KW 4601	47680	6/2/29	31/7/40	20/12/40	B
556	KW 4602	47681	12/2/29	30/8/40	20/12/40	Ho
557	KW 4603	47684	1/3/29	31/7/40	20/12/40	B
558	KW 4604	47683	28/3/29	31/12/38	1/4/39	Hd
559	KW 4605	47682	30/3/29	31/12/38	21/4/39	B

Leyland Lion PLSC1 modified (first trolleybus marketed by Leyland; only trolleybus classified as Leyland by B.C.T., E.E. Co. "demonstration bus FSE 164"; ran at Ashton (6 months) and Maidstone (from 25/7/28) EE DK 106 63 h.p. interpole motor, DK WS2 controller (notch regulator); double-reduction; B31 or 32C.

Fleet Number	Registration	Chassis Number	Entered Service	Withdrawn	Notes and Disposals	
560	CK 3898	6001	29/3/29	31/12/38		D

English Electric type A based on Leyland Lion PLSC1 chassis, EE DK 121 60 h.p. motor, DK WS2 controller; pedals as 544-559; EE B34F body.

Fleet Number	Registration	Chassis Number	Entered Service	Withdrawn	Notes and Disposals	
561	KW 6051	1001	1/12/29	12/6/44		N
562	KW 6052	1002	9/11/29	27/1/45		N
563	KW 6053	1003	6/11/29	17/2/45	15/3/45	Sr
564	KW 6054	1004	1/12/29	17/3/45		Bu
565	KW 6055	1006	1/12/29	31/5/45	4/2/46	A
566	KW 6056	1005	22/12/29	31/8/45	4/2/46	A
567	KW 6057	1008	3/12/29	17/3/45	27/1/46	N
568	KW 6058	1007	9/12/29	31/10/45	4/2/46	A
569	KW 6059	1009	18/12/29	31/10/45	29/1/46	Cr
570	KW 6060	1011	4/1/30	30/11/45	4/2/46	W
571	KW 6061	1012	4/1/30	30/11/45	4/2/46 scrapped 1961	W

English Electric type E11 3 axle (Rubery Owen frames) EE DK122 80 h.p. twin-type motors; DK WD1 series/parallel/weak-field control (notch regulator); 3 pedals; EE H56 (30/26)R body, 28' 0" x 7' 6" x 15' 8; UW 8t 7cwt

Fleet Number	Registration	Chassis Number	Entered Service	Withdrawn		Notes and Disposals
572	KW 6062	101	15/8/29	30/4/46	22/5/46	N
573	KW 6063	105	4/12/29	30/6/42	21/12/42	NCT 306
574	KW 6064	108	9/1/30	31/12/45	4/2/46	A
575	KW 6065	109	7/3/30	5/1/46	4/2/46	A
576	KW 6066	110	25/3/30	30/4/46	22/5/46	N
577	KW 6067	107	1/12/29	31/10/45	4/2/46	A
578	KW 6654	103	1/11/29	20/12/45	4/2/46	A
579	KW 6655	102	26/10/29	31/10/42	21/12/42	NCT 309
580	KW 6656	104	2/11/29	29/9/42	21/12/42	NCT 308
581	KW 6657	106	3/12/29	30/4/46	22/5/46	N
582	KW 6658	111	27/3/30	15/5/45	14/5/46	SSCT 237
583	KW 6659	112	7/3/30	21/3/46	22/5/46	N

English Electric type E11 3-axle (Rubery Owen Frames); EE DK 122D 100 h.p. twin-type motors; electro-mechanical series/parallel control; EE body as 572-583 but bow front and raked rear elevation; 28' 0" x 7' 6" x 15' 9½" (probably as 572-583). First electric bell-pushes.

Fleet Number	Registration	Chassis Number	Entered Service	Withdrawn		Notes and Disposals
584	KW 9453	142	5/2/31	31/7/42	21/12/42	NCT 303
585	KW 9454	143	13/2/31	31/7/42	21/12/42	NCT 304
586	KW 9455	144	6/3/31	29/9/42	21/12/42	NCT 305
587	KW 9456	145	7/3/31	31/5/45	4/2/46	A
588	KW 9457	146	24/3/31	25/5/34	4/1/35, equip to 582	S*
589	KW 9458	147	24/3/31	30/4/45	4/2/46	A
590	KW 9459	152	3/8/31	19/5/45	22/5/45	SSCT 238
591	KW 9460	151	7/7/31	31/7/42	21/12/42	NCT 307
592	KW 9461	153	9/6/31	31/7/42	21/12/42	NCT 301
593	KW 9462	148	13/5/31	30/4/45	4/2/46	A
594	KW 9463	150	1/5/31	19/6/42?	21/12/42	NCT 302
595	KW 9464	149	4/5/31	29/6/42	2/12/42	NCT 300

English Electric type E11 3-axle (as 572-595); electrical equipment as 584-595; body similar to 572-583; exhibited at Olympia 1929; demonstrator originally registered CK 4257

Fleet Number	Registration	Chassis Number	Entered Service	Withdrawn		Notes and Disposals
596	KY 1360	113	25/3/32	28/5/45	28/5/45	SSCT 239

A.E.C. type 661T "Regens": EE 405/10DC1 80 h.p. compound motor with regenerative ("regenostatic") and air braking; double reduction rear axle; 24 volt lighting via motor-generator; EE H60 (32/28) R body with all-metal construction and safety-glass (the first); trolley de-wirement indicator (as all subsequent vehicles); 26' 0" x 7' 6" x 15' 7"; UW 6t 12cwt 1qr. Modifications: c.1937 full-width cab (632 may have been built thus) reducing seating to 58; 1947-55 regeneration limited; 1944-9 Brush UH58R boidies; 1946-6 NCB Mk. 1 H56R bodies; 1947-9 21 NCB Mk.2 H56R bodies; 1955-8: most re-seated to 57/58. 1954-60 most re-motored to EE 406E, EE 406J or MV 207C1 with single reduction. No. 603 achieved 1 million miles 28/4/62.

Fleet Number	Registration	Chassis Number	Entered Service	Rebodied		Withdrawn		Notes and Disposals
597	KY 8200	661T 033	21/11/34	NCB2	1/7/48	31/7/62	14/10/65	To O.60
598	KY 8201	661T 044	21/11/34	NCB2	1/4/48	28/2/60	16/7/60	Ba
599	KY 8202	661T 046	21/11/34	Brush	15/7/44	8/9/53	5/12/53	S(*)
600	KY 8203	661T 038	21/11/34	Brush	28/6/44	31/12/59	8/4/60	T
601	KY 8204	661T 040	21/11/34	Brush	21/5/44	31/8/59	22/10/59	Ho
602	KY 8205	661T 039	21/11/34	NCB2	1/7/48	30/11/62	1/2/63	Au
603	KY 8206	661T 052	21/11/34	NCB2	18/10/47	30/6/62	12/11/62	Au
604	KY 8207	661T 035	21/11/34	NCB2	11/4/48	30/6/62	12/11/62	Au
605	KY 8208	661T 037	21/11/34	Brush	1/4/44	30/6/59	24/8/59	Ba
606	KY 8209	661T 047	21/11/34	Brush	8/4/44	31/5/60	16/7/60	Ba
607	KY 8210	661T 036	21/11/34	NCB1	4/9/46	26/9/57	26/9/57	S
608	KY8211	661T 050	21/11/34	Brush	4/6/44	17/7/59	24/8/59	Ba
609	KY 8212	661T 051	26/11/34	Brush	1/7/44	5/3/57	8/7/57	N
610	KY 8213	661T 043	3/12/34	NCB2	31/12/49	30/11/62	1/2/63	Au
611	KY 8214	661T 034	1/12/34	NCB2	1/10/47	31/12/60	15/2/61	Au

Fleet Number	Registration	Chassis Number	Entered Service	Rebodied		Withdrawn	Notes and Disposals	
612	KY 8215	661T 045	4/12/34	Brush	1/5/44	31/12/58	15/2/59	Tu
613	KY 8216	661T 048	15/12/34	Brush	16/4/44	15/6/56	8/2/57	N
614	KY 8217	661T 042	12/12/34	NCB1	1/7/47	31/12/60	15/2/61	Au
615	KY 8218	661T 041	19/12/34	NCB1	5/10/46	30/7/60	15/2/61	Au
616	KY 8219	661T 049	20/12/34	NCB1	1/7/46	31/12/60	29/4/61	Au
617	KY 8220	661T 053	21/2/35	NCB2	1/11/47	30/6/62	12/11/62	Au
618	AAK 420	661T 054	5/7/35	NCB2	5/10/47	23/12/55	Body to 639	
619	AAK 421	661T 058	2/10/35	NCB2	1/11/47	29/3/61	16/6/61	Au
620	AAK 422	661T 055	12/8/35	NCB2	3/12/49	1/5/58	19/7/58	Ca*
621	AAK 423	661T 057	2/10/35	NCB1	21/6/46	28/2/61	10/6/61	Au
622	AAK 424	661T 059	2/10/35	NCB1	8/6/46	30/11/62	1/2/63	Au
623	AAK 425	661T 056	2/10/35	NCB2	1/7/49	14/6/62	12/11/62	Au
624	AAK 426	661T 061	2/10/35	NCB2	5/10/47	31/7/62	29/8/62	Au
625	AAK 427	661T 062	2/10/35	NCB2	3/11/47	31/7/62	29/8/62	Au
626	AAK 428	661T 065	3/10/35	NCB2	14/5/49	30/11/62	1/2/63	Au
627	AAK 429	661T 060	2/10/35	NCB2	9/4/48	24/1/60	6/5/60	T
628	AAK 430	661T 064	3/10/35	NCB2	25/10/47	30/11/62	1/2/63	Au
629	AAK431	661T 066	2/10/35	NCB2	19/10/47	30/11/62	1/2/63	Au
630	AAK 432	661T 063	8/10/35	NCB2	1/10/47	16/5/60	16/7/60	Ba
631	AAK 433	661T 067	12/10/35	NCB2	5/12/49	6/1/56	16/2/56	N
632	AAK 434	661T 068	5/11/35	NCB2	11/4/48	6/1/56	16/2/56	N

A.E.C. type 761T "Q"; wheelbase 15' 10"; chassis downswept at front for low loading (step height 13"); turning-circle 60' 0". EE 405/3 80 h.p. motor on offside chassis frame; contactors on nearside frame; master controller under driver's seat (as 597-632 and all later vehicles). EE H63(33/30)F, no platform door; concealed lighting (motor generator); single rear wheels; 25' 8½" x 7' 6" x 15' 7". Exhibited at Olympia October 1933; purchased B.C.T. 24/9/1934

Fleet Number	Registration	Chassis Number	Entered Service	Rebodied		Withdrawn	Notes and Disposals	
633	KY 6210	761T 001	2/2/34	-		31/12/41?	19/1/42	SSCT 235

A.E.C. type 661T; motors EE 406/1B1, probably 1E1 later (634), EE 406/2E1 (others), 80 h.p. compound, series/dynamic and air braking; single-reduction rear-axles (as all later vehicles except 697, 706); 24-volt battery lighting; EE H58(32/26)R body (634) and H56(30/26)R (others). 26' 0" x 7' 6" x 15' 6". UW 7t 4cwt 2qr (634), 6t 17cwt 2qr (635), 6t 16cwt 2qr (others). 634 on trial from 22/1/37; Commercial Motor Show 10/37. 635 was prototype for others. Modifications: 1952: 5 Crossley H59(33/26)R bodies 26' 0" x 7' 6", UW 7t 17cwt 3qr, 1956 10 E. Lancs H63(35/28)R bodies 27' 0" x 8' 0"; UW 8t 4cwt 1qr.

Fleet Number	Registration	Chassis Number	Entered Service	Rebodied		Withdrawn	Notes and Disposals	
634	BAK 934	661T 187	25/11/37	EL	1/6/56	30/11/65	22/6/68	HJ
635	CAK 635	661T 208	7/1/38	C	2/3/52	31/10/63	31/1/64	Hy
636	CAK 636	661T 214	4/7/38	C	2/3/52	31/12/62	31/1/64	Hy
637	CAK 637	661T 215	1/7/38	C	2/3/52	31/10/63	31/1/64	Hy
638	CAK 638	661T 216	1/7/38	EL	1/6/56	30/4/67		
639	CAK 639	661T 217	1/7/38	Ex 618	4/2/56	30/12/61	7/3/62	Au
640	CAK 640	661T 218	1/7/38	C	2/3/52	31/10/63	31/1/64	Hy
641	CAK 641	661T 219	1/7/38			22/12/55	4/9/56	N
642	CAK 642	661T 220	1/7/38			30/6/59	24/8/59	Ba
643	CAK 643	661T 221	5/7/38			30/12/55	16/2/56	N
644	CAK 644	661T 222	1/7/38			31/5/56	1/2/57	Ho
645	CAK 645	661T 223	1/7/38			30/5/56	1/2/57	Ho
646	CAK 646	661T 224	1/7/38			26/1/56	4/9/56	N
647	CAK 647	661T 225	1/7/38			30/12/55	16/2/56	N
648	CAK 648	661T 226	1/7/38			28/2/58	20/8/58	Ca
649	CAK 649	661T 227	1/7/38			10/4/56	4/9/56	N
650	CAK 650	661T 228	1/7/38			29/5/56	1/2/57	Ho
651	CAK 651	661T 229	5/7/38	EL	1/6/56	30/6/67	22/6/68	HJ
652	CAK 652	661T 230	11/7/38	C	8/3/52	31/8/63	31/1/64	Hy
653	CAK 653	661T 231	8/7/38			21/1/58	25/6/68	Ca
654	CAK 654	661T 232	11/7/38	EL	1/6/56	28/1/66	19/4/68	Br
655	CAK 655	661T 233	7/7/38	EL	25/7/56	30/6/67	22/6/68	HJ
656	CAK 656	661T 234	1/10/38			30/11/58	15/2/59	T
657	CAK 657	661T 235	1/10/38			31/5/56	1/2/57	Ho
658	CAK 658	661T 236	1/10/38			30/4/57	8/7/57	N
659	CAK 659	661T 237	1/11/38	EL	1/6/56	28/2/66	22/2/68	HJ
660	CAK 660	661T 238	1/11/38			10/2/58	20/8/58	Ca

Fleet Number	Registration	Chassis Number	Entered Service	Rebodied		Withdrawn		Notes and Disposals
661	CAK 661	661T 239	3/5/39			26/6/56	1/2/57	Ho
662	CAK 662	661T 240	7/5/39			25/3/59	10/6/59	Ba
663	CAK 663	661T 241	2/5/39			19/9/57	20/8/58	Ca
664	CAK 664	661T 242	2/5/39	EL	7/6/56	28/2/66	22/2/68	HJ
665	CAK 665	661T 243	13/5/39			7/2/56	4/9/56	N
666	CAK 666	661T 244	2/5/39	EL	1/6/56	31/12/66	19/4/68	Br
667	CAK 667	661T 245	3/5/39			31/1/59	10/6/59	Ba
668	CAK 668	661T 246	4/5/39			31/12/59	7/3/62	Au
669	CAK 669	661T 247	1/5/39			31/12/59	8/4/60	T
670	CAK 670	661T 248	1/5/39			21/4/58	25/6/58	Ca
671	CAK 671	661T 249	3/5/39			31/8/59	22/10/59	Ho
672	CAK 672	661T 250	1/5/39			25/5/59	10/6/59	Ba
673	CAK 673	661T 251	2/5/39			30/6/59	24/8/59	Ba
674	CAK 674	661T 252	1/5/39	EL	1/6/56	31/5/65	19/4/68	Br
675	CAK 675	661T 253	2/5/39	EL	1/6/56	31/5/67	19/4/68	Br
676	CAK 676	661T 254	2/5/39			28/2/59	24/8/59	Ba

Karrier E4, wheelbase 16' 0", deep-section chassis frame giving minimum turning-circle; dimensions and electrical equipment as 635-676 except 10-notch control (635-676 only 8 notches), later multinotch; Weymann H56(30/26)R body, UW 6t 16cwt 8qr. Modifications: 1950: 4 bodies reconstructed by Samlesbury Engineering Co. with sliding windows and no rainscreens above windows. 1952: 7Crossley bodies (as 635-etc.) No. 692, the last double-deck E4 to be built, identical with 677-691 except front destination layout, headlamp position and outward-flared lower deck side and rear panels.

Fleet Number	Registration	Chassis Number	Entered Service	Rebodied		Withdrawn		Notes and Disposals
677	CAK 677	30033	6/9/38	C	2/3/52	31/10/63	31/1/64	Hy
678	CAK 678	30034	1/9/38	C	2/3/52	31/10/63	31/1/64	Hy
679	CAK 679	30035	2/9/38	(Sa	4/11/50)	31/12/60	14/2/61	Au
680	CAK 680	30036	1/1/39			28/4/54	16/2/56	N
681	CAK 681	30037	1/1/39	(Sa	4/11/50)	5/5/61	24/6/61	Ba
682	CAK 682	30038	5/5/39	C	2/3/52	30/11/62	31/1/64	Hy
683	CAK 683	30039	10/1/39			16/5/53	16/2/56	N
684	CAK 684	30040	6/5/39	C	2/3/52	31/8/63	31/1/64	Hy
685	CAK 685	30041	11/1/39	C	3/3/52	31/10/63	31/1/64	Hy
686	CAK 686	30042	10/1/39			31/12/55	16/2/56	N
687	CAK 687	30043	3/5/39	(Sa	1/1/51)	31/5/62	12/11/62	Au
688	CAK 688	30044	4/5/39	C	3/3/52	31/10/63	31/1/64	Hy
689	CAK 689	30045	4/5/39	(Sa	4/1/51)	7/5/61	24/6/61	Ba
690	CAK 690	30046	5/5/39			30/12/55	16/2/56	N
691	CAK 691	30047	5/5/39	C	2/3/52	30/11/62	31/1/64	Hy
692	DKU 692	30050	17/1/40	C	3/3/52	30/11/62	31/1/64	Hy

"Johannesburg" Sunbeam MF2: BTH 206E1 103 h.p. motor; regenerative braking on power-pedal; rheostatic and air on brake pedal; run-back brake; 24-volt battery lighting; Weymann "utility" (austerity specification) UH 56(30/26)R body composite; 26' 0" x 8' 0" x 15' 6" (the first 8' 0" wide bodies); UW 8 tons. Modifications: 1944 – series/dynamic and air braking; 1946/7 glazed upper deck rear windows; 1951 most vehicles improved destination layout; 1956 E. Lancs bodies (as 634 etc.), 701 sliding platform doors, 697 epicyclic gears (to 706, 1960). Chassis ordered 1939 by Johannesburg.

Fleet Number	Registration	Chassis Number	Entered Service	Rebodied		Withdrawn		Notes and Disposals
693	DKW 993	13087	10/7/42	EL	6/1/56	28/2/67	7/67	HJ
694	DKW 994	13088	3/7/42	EL	1/1/56	31/8/66	7/67	HJ
695	DKW 995	13089	10/7/42	EL	1/1/56	28/2/67	7/67	HJ
696	DKW 996	13090	25/6/42	EL	2/1/56	28/2/67	7/67	HJ
697	DKW 997	13091	11/8/42	EL	1/1/56	28/2/67	7/67	HJ
698	DKW 998	13092	24/6/42	EL	1/1/56	28/2/67	9/67	Au
699	DKW 999	13093	1/8/42	EL	1/1/56	28/2/67	9/67	Au
700	DKY 2	13094	28/10/42	EL	2/1/56	28/2/67	9/67	Au
701	DKY 3	13095	21/8/42	EL	4/1/56	30/3/67	9/67	Au
702	DKY 4	13096	1/9/42	EL	6/1/56	28/4/67	9/67	Au

Karrier W, wheelbase 16' 3"; motors MV 207 A3 85 h.p. (703-714, 720-739), EE 406E 80 h.p. (715-719), all 10 notches and series/dynamic braking; traction (110 volt) lighting 703-714, 720-739; 24 volt battery lighting (715-719); bodies Roe utility UH 56(30/26)R (703-14); Park Royal utility UH 56(30/26)R (715-733); Roe semi-utility UH 56(30/26)R (734-739); 26' 0" x 7' 6" x 15' 2" (15' 3" 734-739); UW 7t 3cwt 6qr (703-714) 7t 11cwt (715-719), 7t 10cwt (720-6), 7t 6cwt (727-739). Modifications – seating: upholstered 703-714 (1951), to 59,

Fleet Number	Registration	Chassis Number	Entered Service	Rebodied		Withdrawn	Notes and Disposals	

Roe bodies (1955/7); motors: EE 409 715-719 (1955/7), EE 406 716 (1962), EE 410 716 (1947-52), 715/6/9/725/8/9/730/1/2/3/5/7 (1965-9), MV 209 703-714, 729 (1965-9); East Lancs. rear-entrance bodies with platform doors B63(35/28)RD 715-720/2/3/4/7 1957; East Lancs forward-entrance bodies B65(37/28)FD or (37/29) 703-714, 721/5/6/. 728-739 27' 6" x 8' 0" (1959-60); trolley retrievers 703/5/7/11-13 (1960-3).

Fleet Number	Registration	Chassis Number	Entered Service	Rebodied		Withdrawn	Notes and Disposals	
703	DKY 703	50170	4/5/45	EL/FD	30/3/60	26/3/72	25/2/73	Sp
704	DKY 704	50171	27/5/45	EL/FD	16/10/59	30/11/71	24/2/73	NTA
705	DKY 705	50172	27/5/45	EL/FD	1/8/60	30/7/71	26/4/72	Ro
706	DKY 706	50173	27/5/45	EL/FD	1/2/60	26/3/72	12/8/72	BTA
707	DKY 707	50174	1/6/45	EL/FD	1/7/60	28/7/71	18/4/73	Ro
708	DKY 708	50175	3/7/45	EL/FD	1/3/60	13/11/70	5/71	Au
709	DKY 709	50176	14/5/45	EL/FD	1/2/60	19/6/71	20/8/71	Sy
710	DKY 710	50177	2/8/45	EL/FD	1/3/60	30/11/71	24/1/72	Ro
711	DKY 711	50178	12/6/45	EL/FD	1/6/60	26/3/72	23/2/73	NTA
712	DKY 712	50179	2/7/45	EL/FD	2/5/60	26/3/72	24/2/73	NTA
713	DKY 713	50180	1/8/45	EL/FD	18/5/60	26/3/72	31/3/73	Sp
714	DKY 714	50181	1/8/45	EL/FD	10/7/59	30/7/71	26/4/72	GS
715	DKY 715	50236	1/11/45	EL/RD	4/12/57	28/2/70	2/7/70	Au
716	DKY 716	50237	1/11/45	EL/RD	18/11/57	31/7/70	25/11/70	Au
717	DKY 717	50238	1/12/45	EL/RD	12/11/57	30/6/71	20/8/71	Au
718	DKY 718	50239	1/12/45	EL/RD	13/11/57	29/4/70	2/7/70	Ro
719	DKY 719	50240	1/12/45	EL/RD	1/12/57	30/6/71	20/8/71	Au
720	DKY 720	50241	1/1/46	EL/RD	18/1/58	31/5/69	2/7/70	Au
721	DKY 721	50242	1/1/46	EL/FD	4/9/59	31/7/71	28/2/73	Ro
722	DKY 722	50243	1/1/46	EL/RD	19/1/58	30/6/71	20/8/71	Au
723	DKY 723	50244	1/2/46	EL/RD	24/1/58	30/6/71	20/8/71	Au
724	DKY 724	50245	1/2/46	EL/RD	24/1/58	4/10/70	10/12/70	Au
725	DKY 725	50246	1/2/46	EL/FD	1/7/59	31/7/71	21/1/72	Ro
726	DKY 726	50247	1/2/46	EL/FD	1/9/59	31/7/71	19/11/71	Au
727	DKY 727	50248	13/4/46	EL/RD	20/1/58	31/5/71	6/8/71	Au
728	DKY 728	50249	4/5/46	EL/FD	8/7/59	31/12/71	3/4/73	Au
729	DKY 729	50250	4/5/46	EL/FD	1/8/59	31/7/71	26/4/72	Ro
730	DKY 730	50251	22/4/46	EL/FD	11/9/59	31/7/71	5/3/73	Au
731	DKY 731	50252	6/5/46	EL/FD	1/11/59	10/2/72	23/9/72	BTA
732	DKY 732	50253	13/5/46	EL/FD	3/10/59	30/11/71	24/1/72	Ro
733	DKY 733	50254	15/5/46	EL/FD	1/7/59	30/11/71	5/3/73	Au
734	DKY 734	50255	8/4/46	EL/FD	13/11/59	31/7/71	19/11/71	Au
735	DKY 735	50256	10/4/46	EL/FD	12/10/59	26/3/72	7/4/73	BTA
736	DKY 736	50257	13/4/46	EL/ED	1/2/59	31/7/71	19/11/71	Au
737	DKY 737	50258	16/4/46	EL/FD	1/1/60	10/2/72	11/3/75	BIM
738	DKY 738	50259	20/4/46	EL/FD	1/7/59	14/11/70	5/71	Au
739	DKY 739	50260	10/5/46	EL/FD	1/1/60	28/7/71	26/4/72	GS

B.U.T. (British United Traction) 9611T: wheelbase 16' 4"; motors EE 410 120 h.p.; 12 power-notches; series/dynamic braking (as all subsequent vehicles); resistances: BTH (740-751), Walsh (752-9) "Rheostatic" Satchwell (760-774). 24-volt lighting. Traction batteries under stairs, 1949-55 (760-774); bodies: Roe B56(31/25)R (740-751), Weymann B56(30/26)R (752-774; dimensions 26' 0" x 8' 0" x 15' 2$\frac{1}{2}$" (740-759), 26' 0" x 7' 6" x 15' 6" (760-774); UW 8t 9cwt 2qr (740-751), 8t 7cwt (752-9); 8t 7cwt 2qr (760-774). Nos. 760-774 new May/June, 1949 to **Notts and Derby Traction Co.** (Nos. 343-357). Modifications: May 1952 758 first British bus with flashing indicators. 1953-60 fitted with auto-acceleration. Reseated to 58 (740-751, 760-774) and 59 (752-9) 1955/6. 740-751 delivered 31/12/48-28/2/49.

Fleet Number	Registration	Chassis Number	Entered Service	Rebodied	Withdrawn	Notes and Disposals	
740	EKU 740	9611T 009	3/5/49	-	29/2/64	6/6/68	WD
741	EKU 741	9611T 010	1/12/49	-	29/2/64	4/6/70	WD
742	EKU 742	9611T 011	1/12/49	-	29/2/64	4/6/70	FF
743	EKU 743	9611T 012	1/12/49	-	31/12/70	23/2/73	(0.62)NTA
744	EKU 744	9611T 013	3/12/49	-	29/2/64	10/12/68	Au
745	EKU 745	9611T 014	3/12/49	-	31/5/71	24/1/72	(0.60)Ro
746	EKU 746	9611T 015	3/12/49	-	30/7/71	8/71	(0.63)M
747	EKU 747	9611T 016	1/12/49	-	2/8/63	10/6/68	GS
748	EKU 748	9611T 017	1/12/49	-	29/2/64	10/12/68	Au
749	EKU 749	9611T 018	1/12/49	-	3/6/70	25/11/70	FF*
750	EKU 750	9611T 019	3/12/49	-	4/10/63	4/10/63	GS
751	EKU 751	9611T 020	3/12/49	-	31/10/63	6/6/68	WD

Fleet Number	Registration	Chassis Number	Entered Service	Rebodied		Withdrawn	Notes and Disposals	
752	FKU 752	9611T 108	4/11/50	-		29/2/64	13/12/68	GS
753	FKU 753	9611T 109	4/11/50	-		18/9/70	10/12/70	GS
754	FKU 754	9611T 110	1/1/51	-		3/10/63	29/10/68	GS
755	FKU 755	9611T 111	4/11/50	-		31/3/64	29/10/68	GS
756	FKU 756	9611T 112	4/11/50	-		29/2/64	25/11/70	GS
757	FKU 757	9611T 113	1/1/51	-		30/4/71	6/8/71	Au
758	FKU 758	9611T 114	1/1/51	-		31/7/71	24/6/72	M
759	FKU 759	9611T 115	1/1/51	-		29/2/64	12/68	HJ
760	NNU 224	9611T 116	1/7/53	-		18/1/64	5/65	I
761	NNU 225	9611T 117	2/7/53	-		31/10/63	19/6/67	HJ
762	NNU 226	9611T 118	3/7/53	-		31/10/63	31/3/67	K
763	NNU 227	9611T 119	1/7/53	-		15/2/63	5/65	I
764	NNU 228	9611T 120	1/6/53	-		31/10/63	31/3/67	K
765	NNU 229	9611T 121	8/6/53	-		31/10/63	31/3/67	K
766	NNU 230	9611T 122	1/6/53	-		8/3/62	5/65	I
767	NNU 231	9611T 123	1/6/53	-		30/11/62	31/3/67	K
768	NNU 232	9611T 124	1/6/53	-		18/6/62	5/65	I
769	NNU 233	9611T 125	1/6/53	-		31/10/63	3/6/67	HJ
770	NNU 234	9611T 126	1/7/53	-		31/10/63	3/6/67	NTA
771	NNU 235	9611T 127	1/6/53	-		31/10/63	31/3/67	K
772	NNU 236	9611T 128	9/6/53	-		30/11/62	3/6/67	HJ
773	NNU 237	9611T 129	1/7/53	-		31/10/63	3/6/67	HJ
774	NNU 238	9611T 130	22/4/53	-		31/10/63	8/67	EM

"Notts & Derby" A.E.C. 661Ts: motors EE 406J (when new classified as 406 A1 (580/1) and 406A6 (582-6) 80 h.p.; "Rheostatic" Satchwell resistances; traction batteries under stairs (removed c.1955); 24-volt lighting; Weymann H56(30/26)R; 26' 0" x 7' 6" x 15' 5"; new to Notts & Derby 1937 (580-6) as 301-5, 332, and 1941/2 (587-96) as 333-342. Modification: EE 409 100 h.p. motor, ex Newcastle, 1955-7 (593). East Lancs H63(35/28)RD bodies 27' 0" x 8' 0" x 15' 6", UW 8t 3cwt 2qr and EE 406E motors ex BCT AEC/EEC, 1958.

Fleet Number	Registration	Chassis Number	Entered Service	Rebodied		Withdrawn	Notes and Disposals	
580	DRB 616	661T 198	13/10/54	-		24/4/58	25/6/58	Ca
581	DRB 617	661T 199	3/11/54	-		30/11/58	15/2/59	T
582	DRB 618	661T 209	1/12/54	-		2/7/58	20/8/58	Ca
583	DRB 619	661T 210	1/3/55	-		30/11/58	15/2/59	T
584	DRB 620	661T 211	29/3/55	-		31/5/58	20/8/58	Ca
585	DRB 621	661T 212	8/4/55	-		28/4/58	25/6/58	Ca
586	DRB 622	661T213	7/6/55	-		31/12/58	15/2/59	T
587	HNU 826	661T 377	24/8/53	EL	2/5/58	30/4/65	23/8/68	FF
588	HNU 827	661T 376	4/9/53	EL	4/4/58	31/7/68	24/10/68	Au
589	HNU 828	661T 379	1/3/54	EL	1/6/58	31/7/68	20/6/69	HJ
590	HNU 829	661T 378	1/5/54	EL	3/2/58	30/9/65	23/8/68	FF
591	HNU 830	661T 373	1/6/54	EL	12/1/58	31/12/64	23/8/68	FF
592	HNU 970	661T 380	9/8/54	EL	3/2/58	31/7/68	20/6/69	HJ
593	HNU 971	661T 374	13/8/54	EL	19/1/58	31/5/65	10/12/68	Au
594	HNU 972	661T 381	3/9/54	EL	11/12/58	30/11/66	10/12/68	Au
595	HNU 973	661T 375	10/9/54	EL	12/3/58	28/1/66	10/12/68	Au
596	HNU 974	661T 382	8/5/53	EL	12/3/58	30/4/65	23/8/68	FF

Fleet Number	Registration	Chassis Number	Entered Service	Withdrawn	Notes and Disposals	

"Llanelly" Karrier Ws: new 1945/6 to Llanelly & District Traction Co., Carmarthenshire (later SouthWales Transport) as 37/8, 41-8; chassis (as BCT 703-739) bought and rebuilt by BCT 1952. Motors: BTH 207 A3 85 h.p. (775-8), MV 207 A3 85 h.p. (779-784); MV 11-notch controllers: Satchwell and fin-type resistances; motor-generator lighting (basically as 597-632). New East Lancs. bodies (as 693-700/2) 27' 0" x 8' 0" x 15' 6" before entering service. UW 8t 4cwt 1qt. 1956/7 BTH pendulum-relay auto acceleration (775-8 only)

Fleet Number	Registration	Chassis Number	Entered Service	Withdrawn	Notes and Disposals	
775	CBX 530	50127	25/3/56	31/5/69	2/7/70	Ro
776	CBX 531	50128	14/2/56	30/6/71	20/8/71	Au
777	CBX 600	50125	25/3/56	30/6/71	20/8/71	Au
778	CBX 601	50126	25/3/56	2/11/70	10/12/70	Au
779	CBX 909	50287	11/2/56	31/12/66	4/6/70	FF
780	CBX 910	50288	11/2/56	31/10/68	4/6/70	Ro
781	CBX 911	50289	3/3/56	30/4/67	30/4/67	Ro

Fleet Number	Registration	Chassis Number	Entered Service	Withdrawn	Notes and Disposals	
782	CBX 912	50291	3/2/56	30/6/71	20/8/71	Au
783	CBX 913	50290	10/3/56	30/11/69	13/7/70	FF
784	CBX 914	50292	4/2/56	31/10/70	10/12/70	Au

Ex-Darlington Karrier Ws: W/base 17' 6"; EE 406/8M 80 h.p.; traction lighting; Brush UB30C, 7' 6".

Fleet Number	Registration	Chassis Number	Entered Service	Withdrawn	Notes and Disposals
T403	GHN 403	50002	18/1/57	31/1/58	To 785

W/base 17' 6"; EE 406/8M, 80 h.p. (785-8), MV 207 A3 85 h.p. (789-793); new 1944; traction lighting E. Lancs. composite H71(39/32)FD, 28' 11$\frac{1}{2}$" x 8' 0". UW 8t 5cwt.

Fleet Number	Registration	Chassis Number	Entered Service	Withdrawn	Notes and Disposals	
785	GHN 403	(as above)	1/2/59	31/7/71	19/11/71	Au
786	GHN 563	50077	1/2/59	31/7/70	10/12/70	Au
787	GHN 564	50078	1/12/58	15/4/71	6/8/71	Au
788	GHN 566	50080	1/2/59	30/7/71	19/11/71	Au
789	GHN 569	50101	1/1/59	30/7/71	19/11/71	Au
790	GHN 570	50102	1/1/59	28/2/71	5/71	Au
791	GHN 571	50103	1/1/59	31/3/71	5/71	Au
792	GHN 574	50106	1/12/58	31/7/71	8/1/72	WRTS
793	GHN 575	50107	4/12/58	31/7/71	28/2/73	Ro

Modifications: 788 OB lightweight booms and retrievers. All 70 seats 1960. 1962: 785-8 MV 209 AY3 95 h.p. ex Mexborough. 1965: 790-793 MV 209 AY3 95 h.p. ex Hull.

Ex-St. Helens B.U.T. 9611Ts: EE 410 120 h.p.; battery lighting; E. Lancs. all-metal H63(35/28)R, 26' 0" x 8' 0" x 15' 3" UW 8t 5cwt. St. Helens Nos. 182-9 (later 382-9) and licence Nos. 140-6 new 1/1/51. Refurbished prior to B.C.T. service by Roe (bodies) and B.C.T. (chassis and equipment); new seats, trolleys, indicators.

Fleet Number	Registration	Chassis Number	Entered Service	Withdrawn	Notes and Disposals	
794	BDJ 82	9611T 001	1/7/59	31/5/68	25/11/70	GS
795	BDJ 83	9611T 002	1/6/59	30/6/71	10/1/72	Au
796	BDJ 84	9611T 003	10/4/59	31/3/67	20/6/69	HJ
797	BDJ 85	9611T 004	2/5/59	30/11/65	20/6/69	HJ
798	BDJ 86	9611T 005	1/7/59	31/7/67	20/6/69	HJ
799	BDJ 87	9611T 006	2/5/59	30/6/71	8/10/71	SH
800	BDJ 88	9611T 007	1/7/59	31/3/67	25/11/70	Au
801	BDJ 89	9611T 008	25/3/59	12/12/70	5/71	Au

Modifications: 1959-60 Auto-acceleration

Ex-Brighton B.U.T. 9611Ts; new 5/48 (Nos. 49/50). EE 410 120 h.p. motor; 24-volt battery lighting; Weymann all-metal H59 (33/26)R bodies, 26' 0" x 7' 6" x 15' 6"; UW 8t 10cwt. Prior to B.C.T. service new trolleys and destinations, auto-acceleration and re-seated from 56.

Fleet Number	Registration	Chassis Number	Entered Service	Withdrawn	Notes and Disposals	
802	HUF 49	9611T 031	11/4/59	1/6/63	1/5/65	I*
803	HUF 50	9611T 032	1/5/59	30/11/62	1/5/65	I*

Ex-Hastings (Maidstone & District) Sunbeam Ws; BTH 207 A3 85 h.p. motors (804-813), BTH 209 95 h.p. motors (814/5); foot-pedals in reversed position (left brake, right power); traction lighting; Park Royal semi-utility H56(30/26)R bodies (804-813), Weymann composite H56R bodies (814/5); 26' 0" x 7' 6" x 15' 6", UW 7t 14cwt. New 1946 (804-813-HTC 29/30/21-8), 1947 (814/5, HTC 45/40). Pedal positions altered 1961.

Fleet Number	Registration	Chassis Number	Entered Service	Withdrawn	Notes and Disposals	
804	BDY 804	50285	1/6/60	31/8/63	14/4/64	Hy
805	BDY 805	50286	1/12/59	30/11/62	14/4/64	Hy
806	BDY 796	50277	12/7/60	30/11/62	14/4/64	Hy
807	BDY 797	50278	1/4/61	31/8/63	14/4/64	Hy
808	BDY 798	50279	6/11/59	31/8/63	14/4/64	Hy
809	BDY 799	50280	1/5/61	31/8/63	14/4/64	Hy
810	BDY 800	50281	2/6/61	31/10/63	14/4/64	Hy
811	BDY 801	50282	8/2/61	31/10/63	14/4/64	Hy
812	BDY 802	50283	1/1/61	30/11/62	14/4/64	Hy
813	BDY 803	50284	13/5/60	30/11/62	14/4/64	Hy
814	BDY 820	50446	3/10/59	31/10/63	14/4/64	Hy
815	BDY 815	50441	15/8/59	30/11/62	14/4/64	Hy

Fleet Number	Registration	Chassis Number	Entered Service	Withdrawn	Notes and Disposals	

Ex-Ashton-under-Lyne and Grimsby (Grimsby-Cleethorpes Transport) Sunbeam Ws (820/1 and Karrier Ws (822-5/7), MV 207 A3 85 h.p. motors; traction lighting; Roe semi-utility H56 (30/26) bodies (820/1), Roe H56 (30/26) bodies (822-5/7), new Feb/March 1946 (820/1), Feb/March 1947 (822-5/7); bought by B.C.T. July 1960 (822-5/7) and Sept. 1960 (820/1) for rebodying with East Lancs. 27' 6" x 8' 0" H66FD bodies. Not used; motors salvaged for re-use.

Fleet Number	Registration	Chassis Number	Entered Service	Withdrawn	Notes and Disposals	
[820]	FTJ 400	50325	-	-	12/11/62	Au
[821]	FTJ 401	50324	-	-	12/11/62	Au
[822]	AEE 22	50336	-	-	12/11/62	Au
[823]	AEE 23	50337	-	-	12/11/62	Au
[824]	AEE 24	50338	-	-	12/11/62	Au
[825]	AEE 25	50339	-	-	12/11/62	Au
[827]	AEE 27	50341	-	-	12/11/62	Au

Ex-Doncaster (ex-Darlington) B.U.T. 9611Ts; wheelbase 16' 4"; EE 410 120 h.p. motors. New April/May 1949 to Darlington (69-73) with East Lancs. composite H56R 7' 6" body; sold 1952 to Doncaster (379-383); bought by Bradford 1959, bodies scrapped and chassis rebuilt to take East Lancs. H66(37/29)FD bodies, auto-acceleration and fluorescent lighting (24 volts). Trolley retrievers planned but not fitted. 27' 6" x 8' 0" x 15' 6"; UW 7t 19cwt 3qr.

Fleet Number	Registration	Chassis Number	Entered Service	Withdrawn	Notes and Disposals	
831	LHN 781	9611T 022	1/8/62	30/7/71	5/3/73	Au
832	LHN 782	9611T 023	1/7/62	2/5/71	6/8/71*	Au
833	LHN 783	9611T 024	1/8/62	31/7/71	28/2/73	Ro
834	LHN 784	9611T 025	2/7/62	31/7/71	11/10/71	BTA
835	LHN 785	9611T 026	1/8/62	31/7/71	2/9/72	BTA

Ex-Mexborough and Swinton Traction Co. Sunbeam F4s, wheelbase 17' 7"; BTH 209 AY3 95 h.p. motors; traction lighting. New Aug/Sept 1948 (M&S 27-30) and Aug 1950 (M&S 37-9) with Brush centre-entrance single-deck bodies (No. 29 last M&S trolleybus 26/3/61) Chassis bought 1961 by B.C.T. for rebuilding and fitting with East Lancs. H70FD 28' 11" x 8' 0" x 15' 6" bodies, but chassis not lengthened – bodies therefore 28' 6, 66 seats. No auto-acceleration. Trolley retrievers planned but not fitted. UW 7t 19cwt 3qr. Two-way radios fitted 1970 to 841/2/5/6. No. 844 last trolleybus 26/3/72; travelled from Thornbury to Interchange 24/6/86 towing diesel-electric generator.

Fleet Number	Registration	Chassis Number	Entered Service	Withdrawn	Notes and Disposals	
841	FWX 911	50564	1/1/63	31/12/71	3/4/73	Au
842	FWX 912	50565	3/12/62	26/3/72	7/4/73	Bw
843	FWX 913	50566	4/1/63	26/3/72	31/3/73	BTA
844	FWX 914	50567	1/1/63	26/3/72	31/3/73	BTA
845	JWW375	50729	3/12/62	26/3/72	19/8/72	BTA
846	JWW 376	50730	1/2/63	26/3/72	31/3/73	BTA
847	JWW 377	50731	1/3/63	10/2/72	12/8/72	BTA

Note: minor variations occur between the sources of information. For withdrawal dates some quote the date last used but others the licence expiry date, e.g. numerous vehicles were not used after 17/11/62 (Bradford Moor closure) but the licences were not surrendered until 30/11/62. Some disposal dates relate to the date when the sale was agreed; others when the vehicle was removed. The withdrawal date of 594 (KW 9463) refers to the date on which its sale to South Shields was agreed (19/6/42), whereas the author travelled on it from Bankfoot to Bolton twice in 10/42.

Hired Vehicles: Southend-on-Sea Corporation Transport Nos. 124-127 (BHJ 194-7), AEC 661T chassis (337-340); EE 406/4G1 80 h.p. motors; EE 9-notch control; traction lighting; Strachan H56 (30/26)R 7' 6" bodies. New 1939; on hire 9/40 to 2/42; withdrawn by S.C.T. 10/54. Entered service in Bradford 4/9/40 (124), 9/9/40 (125/6), 14/9/40 (127).

Vehicles/Chassis Bought and Dismantled for Spares:
November 1954 – Darlington 11, Karrier E4S 30052/EE 406/8M, 80 h.p. (GHN 322)
November 1954 – Darlington 17/19/15/23/1/47/8 (GHN 401/2/4/5/6/7/8), Karrier W 50006/1/3/4/5/7/8, EE 406/8M, 80 h.p. and 16 (GHN 572), Karrier W 50104, MV 207 A3, 85 h.p.
October 1956 – Darlington 2/3/6/13/18/22 (GHN 561/2/5/8/573/4), Karrier W 50075/6/9/82/105/108, MV 207 A3, 85 h.p.
March 1960 – Doncaster (ex Darlington 378) 68 (LHN 780), BUT 9611T 021, EE 410 120 h.p.
April 1961 – Mexborough 31-3/5/6 (FWX 915-7/9/920, Sunbeam F4 50568-70/2/3), MV 209 AY3 95 h.p.

Overhead Repair Vehicles (Motor Tower Waggons)

Fleet Number	Registration	Chassis Number	Entered Service	Withdrawn	Notes and Disposals
0.9	AK 3974	Tilling TS3	28/1/21	24/3/48	Ex Parcels Dept.
0.10	AK 8116	AEC YC	28/1/21	20/4/39	
0.11	AK 5591	AEC YC	28/1/21	/44	
-	AK 5590	AEC YC	6/19	19/10/34	S
0.12	KW 4548	Leyland GH2	15/10/28	/48	(Leyland Badger)
0.30	YG 2105	Ford AA	22/3/35	4/39	To Stores van; to NFS 1940
0.44	KW 6360	Leyland TA3	4/39	/49	Ex Parcels Dept. 0.5
0.35	AKW 906	Karrier CK2	25/4/36	/53	To Stores Van 0.19
0.36	AKW 907	Karrier CK2	6/5/36	/54	
0.86	EKY 593	Karrier CK3	1/8/47	31/12/62	
0.87	EKY 594	Karrier CK3	22/9/47	1/3/69	Sandtoft
0.89	FKW 972	Karrier CK3	16/3/49	29/8/64	Sandtoft
0.90	FKW 973	Karrier CK3	11/3/49	6/9/58	
0.37	KUG 577	Bedford OLBG	4/2/54	/72	(Ex Leeds); B.I.M.
0.32	XKW 833	Austin FGK60	1/11/62		To West Yorks PTE 1/4/74
0.33	XKW 832	Austin FGK60	22/9/62		To West Yorks PTE 1/4/74

Re-numberings: in 1953 0.35/36/86-90 became 0.31-6
in 1963 0.32 became 0.33; in 1971 0.37 became 0.34;
in 3/72 0.32-4 became 0.29/30/28.

Maximum Fleet Strength (1955): 203 in stock; 188 operational

Bradford Corporation Electricity Department – Estimated trolleybus power consumption at Friday tea-times in August, 1944 based on number of vehicles in service per route:- Allerton 8, Eccleshill/Greengates/Thackley boundary 18, Bolton to Bankfoot 12, Clayton 14, Duckworth Lane 9, Frizinghall (boundary) 15, Thornton 14, Tong Cemetery 11 – total 101 x 7,200 amps @ 500 volts = 3,600 Kw.

Notes – Explanation of Abbreviations – Vehicle Disposals

A	–	Autowrecks	I	–	Irving, Huddersfield
Au	–	Autospares, Bingley	K	–	Knutton
BC	–	other Corporation departments	L	–	Lambert, Bradford
BIM	–	now at Bradford Industrial Museum	M	–	David Mitchell
B	–	Bentley	MW	–	Motor Wreckers
Ba	–	Blamires	N	–	North, Leeds
Br	–	Barraclough	NCT	–	Newcastle Transport
Bu	–	Burrows	NTA	–	National Trolleybus Association
Bw	–	Tom Bowden	R	–	Robinson, Huddersfield
BTA	–	Bradford Trolleybus Association	Ro	–	Rollinson
C	–	C. Champness	S	–	Scrapped by B.C.T.
Ca	–	Cambridge	SSCT	–	South Shields Transport
Co	–	Cole	SH	–	St. Helens Trolleybus Association
Cr	–	F. Croft, Bradford	Sr	–	Stratham
DT	–	to Driver-Training	St	–	Stephenson, Bradford
D	–	Dalby, Bradford	Sp	–	Steamport
EM	–	East Midlands Transport Museum	Sy	–	P. Sykes
F	–	Foulds, Bingley	T	–	W. Taylor
FF	–	Fisher and Ford	Ta	–	A. L. Taylor
Fi	–	Firth, Bradford	W	–	Dismantlers Autos
GW	–	to Grit- Waggon	WD	–	Wombwell Diesels (!)
GS	–	Goodwin and Smith	WRTS	–	W. Riding Trolleybus Society
H	–	Hepworth	WV	–	Converted to Trolley-Battery
Hd	–	Hodges			Lorries – 502 (AK4516)
HJ	–	Hardwick and Jones			scrapped 7/25; 501
Ho	–	Hornby			(AK 8090) sold to E.E. 17/11/30
Hy	–	C. Hoyle	(*)	–	Withdrawn following collision

Rebodying

From 1944, many of Bradford's trolleybuses were rebodied, beginning with some of the 1934 batch of AEC 661T, all of which were so treated by 1949, and continuing with subsequent batches, though only dealing with some vehicles where the original bodywork proved more durable, as applied to the 1938-39 English Electric bodies, some of which achieved 20 years service. None of the Roe or Weymann bodies purchased new from 1949 onwards was replaced. From 1956, a policy of fitting new bodywork to chassis acquired from other undertakings before placing them in service was adopted, though some also entered service unrebodied. A total of 147 vehicles was rebodied for the Bradford trolleybus undertaking – latterly most of the surviving fleet having been so treated.

Year	Bodybuilder	Body type	Fitted to chassistype	Fleet numbers involved	Quantity	Dates withdrawn
1944	Brush (utility)	H32/26R	AEC 661T	599, 600/1/5/6/8/9/12/13	9	1953-56
1946	Northern Coachbuilders	H30/26R	AEC 661T	607/14/15/16. 621/2	6	1957-62
1947-49	Northern Coachbuilders	H30/26R	AEC 661T	Remainder of 597-617 and 618-632	21	1955-62
1952	Crossley	H33/26R	AEC 661T	635/6/7/40/52	5	1962-63
1952	Crossley	H33/26R	Karrier E4	677/8/82/4/5/8/91, 692	8	1962-63
1956	East Lancs	H35/28R	AEC 661T	634, 638/51/4/5/9/64/6/74/5	10	1965-67
1956	East Lancs	H35/28R	Karrier W	775-784 (before entering service)	10	1966-71
1956	East Lancs	H35/28R	Sunbeam MF2	693-702	10	1966-67
1957-58	East Lancs	H35/28R	Karrier W	715-719, 720/2/3/4/7	10	1969-71
1958	East Lancs	H35/28R	AEC 661T	587-596 (ex Notts & Derby)	10	1964-68
1958-59	East Lancs	H39/32F	Karrier W	785-793 (before entering service)	9	1970-71
1959-60	East Lancs	H37/29 F (except 714/31/2/8 H37/28F)	Karrier W	703-714, 721/5/6/8-33, 734-739	27	1970-72
1962	East Lancs	H37/29F	But 9611T	831-835 (before entering service)	5	1971
1962-63	East Lancs	H37/29F	Sunbeam F4	841-847 (before entering service)	7	1971-72

In the quaintly-named Prune Park Lane, Allerton, ex-Mexborough & Swinton number 842, now rebodied, passed under a negative overhead feeder. A positive feeder and section-breaker can be seen further downhill. *Author*

NOTES TO THE FLEET LIST

The earlier vehicles tended to be ordered from one supplier, which sub-contracted others, or designed by Bradford City Tramways, again with some work sub-contracted, before the later pattern of separate chassis, body and electrical equipment orders emerged, Even then the English Electric Co., with its traction department located in the city, sometimes acted as main contractor, until the late 'thirties.

The first pair of vehicles of 1911, originally numbered 240 and 241, was purchased from the Railless Electric Traction Co., (RET), which obtained the chassis from Alldays and Onions, makers of cars and commercial vehicles, based in Birmingham, and the bodies from Hurst, Nelson Ltd., better known as tramcar bodybuilders. There were two Siemens 20 h.p. motors, each driving one rear wheel by a combination of worm and chain drive, the latter enclosed in an oil bath. A Siemens hand controller was used.

In 1912/3, the two RET vehicles were renumbered 501 and 502. The next batch, 503-520, were designed by Bradford City Tramways, the bodies being built in its workshops though the chassis were supplied by David Brown Ltd. of Huddersfield. The motors, drive and hand controller were as 240/1. These were quite small vehicles, 23ft. 2in. long, with an unladen weight of just under 4 tons. Maximum speed was 23 m.p.h., though the Board of Trade limit for trolleybuses was 12 m.p.h. until 1926.

Number 521 of 1920 was almost exactly the same length, at 23ft. 1in., but was a double-decker, some 15ft. 4in. high to the roof (nearly a foot more than a modern highbridge double-decker). It must be remembered that the covered-top double-deck motor bus, as a production vehicle, was still in the future, and hence it was the open-balcony tramcar that was the obvious reference source for its design.

However, recognition of the practicalities was evident in the inward taper (or tumble-home) of the upper deck, doubtless with the need to avoid risk of collision with the poles supporting the overhead wires, and also to improve stability, Even so, a maximum speed of 18 m.p.h. on the level doubtless seemed more than enough for such a vehicle on cobbled streets. This time the chassis as well as the 51-seat body was built in the B.C.T. workshops, though Kirkstall Forge supplied components, probably including items such as the axles in which that concern was to become a specialist supplier. Chain-drive was used, with a Dick, Kerr motor and hand controller.

The next vehicle, No. 522 of January 1922, carried the concept further and indeed was a true pioneer venture, being one of the first six-wheelers with twin steering axles of any kind and quite possible the first passenger-carrying example in the world – so far as is known, only one other trolleybus of this layout was produced, built by Leyland for London Transport in 1939. In other respects, it followed the pattern of No. 521, being B.C.T. designed and a double-decker with obvious tramcar influence in its appearance. Its length has been quoted as 23ft. 10in., only 9in. longer than the four-wheeler, but photographs convey an appreciable increase in length, with six-bay body instead of four-bay, and even if the bays were slightly shorter, it seems possible that the figure might have referred to the body structure excluding the rear platform.

As with No. 521, there was chain drive and a 'solid' rear axle, but this time the controller for the more powerful Metrovick 70 h.p. motor was foot-operated, though it may have been essentially the same as the previous hand-operated type. The vehicle weighed seven tons unladen, distributed equally between the rear axle and the front four wheels. Seating capacity was 59.

Succeeding batches of vehicles through most of the 'twenties were single-deckers with chassis generally derived from motor-bus equivalents, though the Garrett concern was primarily a steam wagon maker having no direct counterpart to its O-type trolleybus, with its low-built and up-to-date design. In 1929, however, the English Electric E11 six-wheel double-deckers took advantage of the availability by that date of suitable proprietary axles from Kirkstall, by then beginning to grow in importance in this field. Electrical control systems steadily improved, with more notches and the introduction of the weak field principle to give higher speed from the ADC vehicles 529-531 of 1926 and rheostatic braking on the English Electric single-deckers based on Leyland Lion chassis of 1928-9.

The A.E.C./English Electric 661T, beginning with the 597-617 batch of 1934-5 introduced a type of vehicle, the 'modern' two-axle double-decker with both electrical and air-pressure braking, that was to constitute virtually the whole of Bradford's subsequent fleet. On this and the following 618-632 batch, there was regenerative braking, powerful but rather fierce, producing audible protest from the double-reduction rear axle. The Q-type demonstrator, with its entrance at the extreme front, and side-mounted motor, was purchased but did not create a precedent in design terms. Instead, progress was more subtle, with the more controllable series-dynamic braking, permitting a return to the worm-drive axle, the latter itself subject to some development by A.E.C. to enable it to cope with the strong torque of trolleybus motors.

Power on the A.E.C. 661T vehicles remained at 80 h.p. until the war, when the diverted Sunbeam chassis intended for Johannesburg introduced 103 h.p. motors to suit their operating conditions and the extra weight of 8ft.-wide bodywork. The utilities reverted to 80 or 85 h.p., but the B.U.T. 9611T, as well as having much in common with the A.E.C. Regent III motor bus in chassis design, introduced 120 h.p. motors. In making comparisons with motor bus power ratings, it must be remembered that a trolleybus motor had quite different characteristics and a typical 80 h.p. double-deck trolleybus could offer much more brisk acceleration from a standing start and hill-climbing capability than a bus with, say, a Gardner 5LW engine of 85 b.h.p., partly because of its immense torque capability from rest and the absence of any pause for gear changes.

The pre-war maximum dimensions for two-axle double-deckers of 26ft. by 7ft. 6in. remained in force until 1946, when 8ft.-wide vehicles could be used on approved routes (the 'Johannesburg' Sunbeams had been operated by special dispensation). The B.U.T. trolleybuses bought new took advantage of this, but the ex-Notts. & Derby B.U.T. vehicles were 7ft. 6in. The ex-Llanelly Karrier W buses rebodied in 1956 were built to the 27ft. by 8ft. dimensions by then permissible, but that year the length limit went up to 30ft. The ex-Darlington vehicles, originally single-deck and 27ft. 6in. long with 17ft. 6in. wheelbase, were rebodied in 1948/9 to 28ft. 11½in. length, the maximum possible without exceeding the overhang limit. The 1962 rebodying of the ex-St. Helens B.U.T. chassis was to 27ft. 6in. length, these having been double-deckers with 16ft. 4in. wheelbase, but the final rebodied vehicles, on 17ft. 7in.-wheelbase ex Mexborough single-deck chassis, were 28ft. 6in.

THE ROUTES

Names in capital letters were displayed on destination indicator blinds. Route lengths in brackets are included in the total mileage.

Route	Opened	Closed	Route Length	First Known Bus	Last Known Bus
			mls. yds		
LAISTERDYKE to DUDLEY HILL	June 20, 1911 (a)	Feb 29, 1964 (b)	1 552	240	843 (b)
extended to BANKFOOT	July 17, 1914	Feb 29, 1964	1 1232		843
extended to BOLTON	Oct 13, 1914	Feb 29, 1964 (c)	1 1355		843 (c)
BIERLEY CHURCH turning circle	c.1930	Feb 29, 1964 (d)			
Greenhill Lane reversing triangle	March 1935	Feb 29, 1964			
Birch Lane turning circle	Jan 9, 1941				
and sidings	Feb 1948	Feb 29, 1964			
			4 1389		
ODSAL to OAKENSHAW	June 25, 1914	July 31, 1940	1 1211	505?	
extended to CITY	Oct 27, 1927	July 31, 1940	2 165		
			3 1376		
BOLTON WOODS and FRIZINGHALL	March 11, 1915	April 30, 1932	2 799		
Inward route via Gaisby Lane	March 11, 1915	Y/e 31.3.1919	433		
			2 1232		
CLAYTON (Town End)	Sept 4, 1926	July 31, 1971	(3 644)	529	834
extended to The Avenue	July 15, 1956	May 30, 1970	3 1529	605	844
Shortworking to PASTURE LANE	Feb 25, 1951 (e)	July 31, 1971	(2 352)		793
Shortworking to LIDGET GREEN	Dec 12, 1934 (e)	Nov 2, 1963 (f)	(1 944)		846
ALLERTON	Dec 1, 1929	Feb 27, 1971 (g)	3 1550		843
Shortworking to CHAPEL LANE	Dec 1, 1929	Feb 27, 1971 (g)	(2 1428)		843
Inward journey via West Park Rd.	June 8, 1958	Feb 27, 1971 (h)			
SALTAIRE (via Thackley)	March 30, 1930	June 30, 1971	6 789	576	717
Shortworking to THACKLEY	March 30, 1930	June 30, 1971	(3 1005)		0.63 (i)
GREENGATES (VIA IDLE)	March 22, 1931	June 30, 1971	3 1203		831
Shortworking to FIVE LANE ENDS	1931?	June 30, 1971	(2 559)		834
ECCLESHILL (Stony Lane)	May 30, 1934	Oct 31, 1964	(2 445)		796?
Shortworking to PEEL PARK	June 1, 1935	March 1967	(1 340)		
Extended to Faltis Square	Aug 9, 1959	Oct 31, 1964	2 1219	592	796?
Cross-city service to ST. ENOCH'S ROAD (TOP)	Nov 3, 1957	Nov 17, 1962		654	739
THORNTON	Nov 21, 1934 (j)	March 26, 1972 (k)	4 1709	604	844
Shortworking to FOUR LANE ENDS	Nov 21, 1934	March 26, 1972	(1 1239)		731/737
Shortworking to BELL DEAN ROAD	Nov 21, 1934	July 25, 1964 (k)	(2 1149)		
Shortworking to SPRING HEAD ROAD	Sept 6, 1940	March 26, 1972 (k)	(3 990)		703
Cross city service to THORNBURY	March 14, 1965	March 26, 1972		734	844
DUCKWORTH LANE (Depot)	*Oct 2, 1935	March 26, 1972 (k)	(1 1515)	602?	844
Extension to Royal Informary	April 20, 1936	March 26, 1972 (k)	{ 2 35		
			{ 2 104 (l)		844
Shortworking to Whitby Road	Dec, 1960	Sept 26, 1971	(1 1073)		735
Outward journey via Barry Street	June 23, 1968	March 24, 1972	(0 71)		706
TONG CEMETERY	July 6, 1938	April 1, 1967	3 5	655?	655
Shortworking to DUDLEY HILL	July 6, 1938	April 1, 1967	(1 1181)		
Spur to HOLME WOOD	March 6, 1970	April 1, 1967		794	784
Service from CITY to BIERLEY CHURCH	Dec 31, 1956	May 31, 1963		703	
CROSSFLATTS	May 7, 1939	Oct 31, 1963	6 1694	650	786
Shortworking to BINGLEY	May 7, 1939	Oct 31, 1963	(6 328)		788
Shortworking to NAB WOOD	May, 1939	Oct 31, 1963 (m)			691
Shortworking to SALTAIRE	May 7, 1939	Oct 31, 1963	(3 928)		842/831
Shortworking to FRIZINGHALL	Feb 23, 1944	Oct 31, 1963	(2 390)		589
Shortworking to PARK GATES	Nov 14, 1960 (n)	Dec 16, 1960 (n)			
Cross-city service to BRADFORD MOOR	Jan 1, 1950	Nov 17, 1962		696	751
BRADFORD MOOR	Dec 4, 1949	Nov 17, 1962	1 1504	729	655

*Trial run September 24th

THE ROUTES

Route	Opened	Closed	Route Length	First Known Bus	Last Known Bus
			mls. yds.		
Shortworking to CHELMSFORD ROAD	Dec 5, 1949	Nov 17, 1962	(1 298)		
Cross-city service to CROSSFLATTS etc	Jan 1, 1950	Nov 17, 1962		746	741
THORNBURY	March 2, 1952 (o)	March 26, 1972 (o)	2 169	640 (o)	844
Cross-city service to THORNTON etc	March 14, 1965	March 26, 1972 (o)		734	844
WIBSEY	April 24, 1955	July 31, 1971	2 920	754	732
Spur to BUTTERSHAW	April 8, 1956	July 31, 1971	1 281	701	841
Shortworking to ST. ENOCH'S ROAD (TOP)	April 24, 1955		(2 1761		
Shortworking to LITTLE HORTON	Nov 8, 1954	July 31, 1971	754	785	
Spur to Park Avenue SPORTS GROUND	May 6, 1957	July 2, 1969	580		
ST. ENOCH'S RD to ECCLESHILL, cross city	Nov 3, 1957	Nov 17, 1962	654	831	
Inward journey via Glydegate	May 18, 1969	July 31, 1971		841	
Inward journey via Princes Way	Aug 18, 1969	July 31, 1971		841	
Outward journey via Princes Way	Sept 21, 1969	July 31, 1971	722	785	
MISCELLANEOUS:					
Queen's Road (no service)	Jan, 1914	1926	503?		
Town Hall Street-southbound (p)	Oct 24, 1927	Aug 1, 1940			
Town Hall Street-northbound (p)	May 18, 1964	March 2, 1968			
New Victoria Street (q)	Sept 4, 1926	1953			
Well Street	1930	Nov 3, 1962			
Squire Lane	May 19 or Aug 9, 1947	March 26, 1972			844
Hall Ings (Bridge St-Leeds Rd)	Nov 7, 1946				
Broadway	June 20, 1954	Nov 17, 1962		588	831
Victoria Square	June 20 1954	(s)		588	
Canal Rd (Balme St-Forster Sq)	July 27, 1949				
Bowling Yard (no service)	May, 1956	Feb 13, 1968		749	0.60
West Street circle	April 15, 1957	Nov 2, 1962			628
Hall Ings (Norfolk Gardens)	March 17, 1963	March 2, 1968			
Bank Street	May 18, 1964	March 26, 1972			844
Canal Rd (replacing Commercial St.)	May 15, 1966	June 30, 1971			789
Hawthorne St., Thornbury	Nov 5, 1967	March 26, 1972 (t)		758	845
Market St. (towards Town Hall Sq.)	March 3, 1968	March 26, 1972			844
MAXIMUM ROUTE MILEAGE (1962)			**47.41**		

Notes:

(a) public service June 24

(b) depot use until April 1, 1967

(c) depot use until June 30, 1971 (Barrack Tavern-Bolton and March 25, 1972 (Barrack Tavern-Laisterdyke)

(d) little used after 1963

(e) original circle Nov 1937, regular service

(f) turning circle available until January 1965

(g) used by private tour February 28th

(h) available for depot journeys until March 24th, 1972

(i) 0.63 probably last vehicle to use the circle, June 29th, 1971

(j) formal opening November 20th, 1934

(k) regular service ceased March 24th, 1972 (Thornton and Duckworth Lane) and February, 1971 (Spring Head Road) but all wiring remained usuable until March 26th, 1972; Bell Dean Road circle used for driver training until May, 1965; Whitby Road circle occasionally used up to 1972; trial run to Duckworth Lane September 24th, 1935.

(l) extra mileage following diversion via Barry Street

(m) little used after November, 1962

(n) wiring used for sports specials 1939-1963

(o) first trolleybus over any part of the route was 240 in June, 1911; regular service ceased March 24th, 1972

(p) southbound for Oakenshaw; northbound for Thornton etc

(q) New Victoria Street later absorbed into Princes Way

(r) passengers allowed on depot journeys from April 14th, 1952 to March 24th, 1972

(s) Victoria Square absorbed into Princes Way (q.v.)

(t) last vehicle around test circuit (Leeds Road, Leeds Old Road, Killinghall Road and return to depot) 835, March 25th, 1972; last vehicle to reverse at Thornbury terminus 846, March 26th, 1972

TERMINOLOGY

The following terms relate to trolleybus technology as understood in Bradford, though often also applicable elsewhere.

Anchor
: backstay – the termination of a live wire by means of a clamp and span wire.
: ear – an outrigger securing the end of a length of line wire.

Auto-acceleration
: device to limit the rate of acceleration to a maximum acceptable to passengers, vehicle transmissions and power supplies.

Benjamin
: a street lighting unit used in the city centre 1938-1953.

Boom:
: see Trolley

Bracket Arm
: Consisted of 2" diameter steel tube clamped to traction standard. Span wires were attached to 'short brackets'; 'bracket arm suspension' involved tubes up to 16 feet long to which the trolley wires were attached by means of bowstring brackets as a substitute for span wires. Pre-1958 street lighting units were usually suspended from bracket arms.

Bridle
: a single 'saddle' (q.v.).

Bulldog
: a splicing ear to join lengths of line wire.

Bullring
: steel ring to which two or more span wires were fastened.

Butterfly
: street lighting unit used in certain thoroughfares 1927-1958.

Canopy switch
: circuit breaker in the driver's cab; 'tripping' or 'blowing' the switch denoted actions which caused the breaker to blow out and need resetting.

Catenary
(Nottingham-type)
: wire strung from top of pole to centre of span wire in order to lift it and retain the trolley wires in a level position.

Churchwarden
: key for tightening bolts in bulldogs.

Clamp
: iron casting clamped around pole, into which bracket arms were screwed.

Controller
: mechanism (mechanical or electro-magnetic) to control the flow of power to traction motors, thereby providing acceleration or breaking.

Corporation
: officially 'the Lord Mayor, Aldermen and Citizens of the City' : in practice the City Council.

Dead Section
: length of insulation inserted between wires of opposite polarity or between sections of line wire to isolate them from each other – a 'section breaker'.

Derrigo
: a post-1950 clip-on hanger.

Diamond
: centre of an overhead crossing unit.

Dropper (vertical dropper catenary)
: span wire strung between the top of two poles and lifting the lower span by means of a centrally-placed vertical 'dropper' wire.

Duck
: trolley head (q.v.)

Ear
: clip by which trolley wire is suspended from hangers.
: Clinch ear – fitted around the wire, usually on round-section wiring. Mechanical ear : two separate halves bolted together and clasping the wire by its groove to provide an uninterrupted path for the trolley head.

Feeder
: insulated cable feeding power into the overhead line from an underground conduit via a roadside section box.

Finial
: cap surmounting traction pole to exclude moisture; cast-iron from 1911, copper sheet from 1934 and aluminium from 1953; 'ball-and-spike' from 1911; 'Wilkinson' from 1922; 'Dearne District' 1934; plain caps thereafter.

Fly-shunt
: coasting without power, with trolleys removed from wires.

Frog
: overhead junction; 'facing' – diverging turnout; 'wayward' or 'trailing' – converging frog; 'pull-frog' – hand-operated facing frog: 'auto-frog' – remotely-operated facing frog; 'interlaced frog' – a facing frog positioned well in advance of a junction but retaining the diamond at the normal point of divergence; 'frog springer' – a device to spring derrigoes etc into place.

Globe strainer
: spherical composition insulator originally providing insulation for 'strain' or span wires.

Hanger
: insulated fitting attached to span wire or bowstring brackets until 1939 gunmetal but often aluminium or iron thereafter. Straight-line hangers : 'unequal arm' or R.E.T. (made by B.C.T. or Clay and Atkinson) 1911-1931; 'tramway type' by Brecknell, Willis 1934-1948; other types (OB, BICC etc) clipped on span wire.

	: Curved line hangers, 1911-1948 : 'single pull-offs' (one lug) or 'double pull-offs' (two lugs).
	: Twin hangers : designed to keep the twin wires horizontal and thus the ears vertical – Ohio Brass (OB), Wiseman BICC.
Insulators	: ('pots'), on span wire or bracket arms : porcelain or composition fittings insulating live wires from span wires, bracket arms or from each other.
Jumper	: length of insulated cable linking two otherwise separate sections of line wire, temporarily or otherwise.
Man on t'wall	: tool to pull line wire out to end of bracket arm when erecting wires on a curve.
Peg the light	: actuate auto-frogs.
Pole	: see Traction Pole.
Protective Fare	: surcharge to discourage short-distance passengers from using infrequent longer-distance services (eg Oakenshaw) when a more frequent alternative is available.
Railless (railless tramcar)	: term used for trolleybuses in early days.
Resistance	: device regulating volume of current fed to traction motor(s) by the action of the controller.
Saddle	: method of retaining line wires in a predetermined curve by the use of span wires attached to the pole and to each other to ensure that the spans were at 90 degrees to the line.
	: Bridle – a single saddle, on the outside of the curve.
	: Double saddle – on both sides of the curve.
Separation	: distance between the positive (inner) and negative (outer) line wire.
Series-parallel	: method of control on a two-motor vehicle.
Skate	: overhead – fitting on the positive line wire which, when contacted by a trolley head drawing current, actuated an automatic frog.
	: rail – cast-iron shoe or a wheel travelling in the groove of a tram rail to complete the electrical circuit in place of the negative trolley.
Skid	: sliding current collector; soft iron (1920s), carbon-insert (1942-1972) or ice-cutter (slotted steel block which removed ice from the line wire).
Space bar	: overhead fitting connecting two hangers; galvanised steel, larch, or steel-insert hickory.
Span (strain) wire	: galvanised stranded steel wire used for supporting the line wire and overhead fittings.
Strap	: plain – wrought-iron fitting clamped around a pole, to which a span wire was attached; substitute for or additional to a short bracket arm.
	: multiple – as above, but capable of accommodating up to a dozen span-wires.
Tower waggon	: vehicle with extendable tower for overhead repairs and maintenance; motor vehicles used throughout, but a few horse-drawn waggons available until about 1947.
Trackless (tram)	: name in vogue in the 1920s, superseding 'railless' and not replaced until about 1935 by 'trolleybus' in local popular usage.
Traction pole or standard	: tubular steel pole usually 31' long, of which 6' were embedded in the ground; graded according to top outside diameter, i.e., A (light) $5\frac{1}{2}$", B (medium) $6\frac{1}{2}$", C (heavy) $7\frac{1}{2}$", D (extra-heavy) $8\frac{1}{2}$", with 'long' (extra-tall) versions of B to D.
Trolley	: informal name for trolleybus
Trolley (boom)	: high-tensile steel tube (tapered until 1945 but two-part tubular gradually superseding) mounted on trolley base and pressing trolley head against underside of overhead wire.
Trolley Base	: roof-mounted sprung swivel base supporting trolley booms.
Trolleybus (trolley bus, trolleybus)	: omnibus propelled by electricity derived from an external source.
Trolley Gantry	: framework mounted on body pillars and supporting the trolley bases – a sound-insulating measure.
Trolley Head	: gunmetal swivel fitting attached to end of trolley boom, within which the trolley wheel rotated or the trolley skid slid.
Trolley Hook	: roof-mounted hooks used for anchoring trolley booms when lowered from wires.
Trolley Plank	: planks on roof for use by fitters.
Trolley Wheel	: grooved brass wheel running under the line wire.
Trolley Wire (line wire, running wire)	: hard-drawn copper, usually round-section, superseded by cadminum-copper grooved wire, electrically charged.

WHAT COULD HAVE BEEN....

Summary of informal proposals made by the Author to the City Council, November 1962, for the retention of trolleybuses.

1. REPLACEMENT DATES FOR EXISTING FLEET (excluding pre-war vehicles due to be replaced by "Mexbros" not yet in service)

	Chassis New	Rebodied	Due for Replacement	Total
Crossley-bodied AECs and Karrier E4s	1938/9	1952`	1963-6	13
East Lancs bodied AECs	1938/9	1956	1971	10
East Lancs bodied "Jo'burgs"	1942	1956	1971	10
East Lancs bodied AECs "Llanellys"	1945/6	1956	1971	10
East Lancs bodied AECs "Notts & Derbys"	1941	1958	1973	10
East Lancs bodied AECs (BCT) Karriers	1945/6	1957/8	1975/6	10
East Lancs bodied AECs "Darlingtons"	1943/4	1958/9	1973/4	9
East Lancs bodied Front-entrance	1945/6	1959/60	1975	27
Ex Hastings Sunbeam Ws	1946/7	(1965)	1977	12
Ex-Brighton B.U.T.s	1948	(1965)	1978	2
Ex-Notts & Derby B.U.T.s	1949	(1964)	1979	15
Bradford B.U.T.s	1949/51	(1965/6)	1979/80	20
Ex-St. Helens B.U.T.s	1950/1	1958/9*	1980	8
Ex Doncaster B.U.T.s	1949	1962	1980	5
Ex-Mexborough Sunbeam F4s	1948/50	1963	1981	7

* refurbished, not rebodied   168

2. OPTIONAL ESTIMATED CAPITAL EXPENDITURE ON ROLLING STOCK 1963-1984

(based on new motor-buses at £6,000, new trolleybuses at £7,500 and new bodies at £3,500, availability in 1963 of 13 Portsmouth B.U.T.s at £500 each for service in 1966 with new bodies and replacement in 1982, and availability in 1966 of 30 Manchester B.U.T.s at £1,000 each for service in 1972 with new bodies and replacement in 1986).

OPTION A : retain existing fleet proportions and buy new vehicles as replacements

	T/B	£1,477,000
	M/B	2,100,000
		£3,577,000

OPTION B : retain existing fleet proportions and buy new motor-buses, second-hand trolleybuses in 1963/6 and new ones thereafter

	T/B	£1,299,500
	M/B	2,100,000
		£3,399,000

OPTION C : convert Forster Square trolleybus routes to motor-bus but retain other routes

	T/B	£1,015,000
	M/B	2,571,720
		£3,586,720

OPTION D : Replace all trolleybuses by 1970   M/B   £4,111,720

MANAGEMENT

GENERAL MANAGERS

Christopher John Spencer, M.I.E.E., M.Inst.T., born Halifax December, 1875; apprenticed to the Blackpool electric tramways; General Manager of Bradford City Tramways 1898-1918; Manager of the Metropolitan Electric Tramways, South Metropolitan Electric Tramways and London United Tramways 1918-1933; manager of London Passenger Transport Board northern and western tramways 1933; manager of the North Metropolitan Electric Power Supply Co. 1933-1940. Died 1950.

Richard Henry Wilkinson, M.Inst.T., A.M.I.E.E., born Liverpool 1874, apprenticed to mechanical engineering with a Liverpool-based steamship company; obtained Board of Trade certificate in marine engineering 1898; assistant to Liverpool tramways manager 1898-1900; Oldham Tramways Superintendent 1900-2 and Manager 1902-4; Huddersfield Tramways Manager 1904-1918; Bradford Tramways General Manager 1918-1930; died December 13th, 1943.

Charles Richard Tattam, M.Inst.T., born Maidstone 1885; engineering apprentice 1902-1905; deputy works superintendent of Mainstone Corporation Electricity Department 1905-7; general assistant to Maidstone Tramways Manager 1907-10; Power Station Superintendent, Chichester, 1910-2; General Manager, Llanelly Tramways, 1912-4, H.H. Forces 1914-9; Mansfield District Tramways Manager 1919; Operations Manager for Balfour, Beatty, 1920-1931; General Manager of Bradford City Tramways (Bradford Corporation Passenger Transport from July, 1935) 1931-1951. Died May 25th, 1966.

Chaceley Thornton Humpidge, B.Sc.(Eng)., M.Inst.T., born Birmingham 1905; Birmingham City Tramways engineering assistant 1928-35; Liverpool Corporation Rolling Stock Engineer 1935-7; Portsmouth Corporation Transport Chief Assistant Engineer 1937-9; Nottingham City Transport Chief Engineer 1939-42; Rochdale Corporation Transport General Manager and Engineer 1942-51; General Manager of Bradford Corporation Passenger Transport (Bradford City Transport from February, 1952) 1951-1961; General Manager of Sheffield Transport and Secretary of Sheffield Join Omnibus Committee 1961; Church of England curate until his death in July, 1972 'The Apostle of the Trolleybus'.

John Cecil Wake, M.I.R.T., MInst.T., M.I.C.S., born Middlesbrough 1909: Middlesbrough Corporation Transport (latterly Assistant General Manager) 1925-50; Burton-on-Trent Corporation Transport Manager 1950-2; St. Helens Corporation Transport |Manager 1952-61; General Manager of Bradford City Transport July 3rd, 1961 to November 30th, 1962; subsequently Nottingham City Transport General Manager, now retired.

Edward Deakin, M.Inst.T., latterly F.C.I.T.) born Sheffield 1910; employed by Wilson Hough of Holmfirth (later as secretary and traffic manager) 1925-34; Huddersfield Corporation assistant traffic manager 1934-40; Ipswich Corporation traffic manager 1940-4; Rotherham Corporation traffic manager 1944-8; Chesterfield Corporation Deputy General Manager 1948-9 and General Manager 19490-62; General Manager of Bradford City Transport January 1st, 1963, to March 31st, 1974. Died February 16th, 1979.

ENGINEERS

C. J. Spencer and R. H. Wilkinson were Managers and Engineers. John William Dawson was engineering foreman at Thornbury from 1906, subsequently assistant electrical engineer and finally Works Superintendent until retirement in 1927. His successor, C. E. Barton, previously chief draughtsman, was appointed Rolling Stock Superintendent at Salford in 1929. N. A. Scurrah (q.v.) succeeded Mr. Barton, and on Mr. Wilkinson's retirement a Rolling Stock Superintendent and Engineer was appointed for the first time.

Henry James Troughton, A.M.I.C.E, employed by Westinghouse 1903 later with London County Council, Metropolitan Electric and London United tramways; director-general of Athens electric transport 1926-30; Bradford Rolling Stock Engineer 1931-7; General Manager at South Shields 1937-1948.

Norman A. Scurrah, technical assistant at Thornbury Works 1915-1929; Works Superintendent 1929-31; Car Works Superintendent 1931-7; Rolling Stock Engineer 1937-58 (retired).

Kenneth E. Griffiths M.C.I.T., M.I.R.T.E., (previously Assistant Engineer for Liverpool Corporation) Rolling Stock Engineer 1958-1963; subsequently General Manager at Ashton and Rotherham, latterly with South Yorkshire Passenger Transport Executive. Died suddenly 1987 "99% pro-trolleybus" (his words).

Alan Gurley, B.Sc.A.M.I.Mech.E., Rolling Stock Engineer 1963-5; subsequently Chief Engineer, Yorkshire Traction Co.; Chief Engineer, Hants & Dorset Motor Services Ltd.; Development Engineer, National Bus Company; Director Technical & Operations, Bus and Coach Council.

Bernard B. Browne, C. Eng., M.I.Mech. E., M.I.R.T.E.; Yorkshire Woollen District 1952-6; Technical Assistant to Bolton Corporation 1956-9; Technical Assistant to Liverpool Corporation 1959-62; Wallasey Corporation Rolling gStock Engineer 1962-5; Bradford Rolling Stock Engineer August, 1965 – March 31st, 1974; West Yorkshire Passenger Transport Executive Development Engineer 1974-82; Blackpool Transport chief Engineer from 1982.

TRAFFIC SUPERINTENDENTS

T. Stirk, successively conductor (1898), inspector, Assistant Traffic Superintendent and (1925) Traffic Superintendent; retired 1932.

Frank Evans, 1932-5, previously assistant to Mr. Stirk.

Eric Booth baxter, Assistant Traffic Superintendent at Blackpool 1924 and later at South Shields; Traffic Superintendent at Bournemouth; Bradford Traffic Superintendent 1935-8; General Manager at Stockport from 1938.

Leonard Lyle Christie, previously with Midland Red; Bradford Traffic Superintendent 1938-1962.

David R. Smith, M.Inst.T., Traffic Superintendent at Leicester 1959-62; Bradford Traffic Superintendent 1962-6; Deputy General Manager at Leicester from 1966 and later General Manager at Cardiff.

John H. Hill, M.C.I.T., previously with Wigan Corporation; Bradford Traffic Superintendent June 1st, 1966-March 31st, 1974; subsequently with West Yorkshire Passenger Transport Executive.

The Bradford Trolleybus System : 1911 to 1972

"Portamus" – "Always at your Service"

(Minor alterations and short-lived arrangements not shown)
```
••••    Proposed or authorised extensions
— —     Municipal Boundaries
✳ A-U   Electricity Sub-stations
Route numbers  24  Original
               26  Subsequent
```

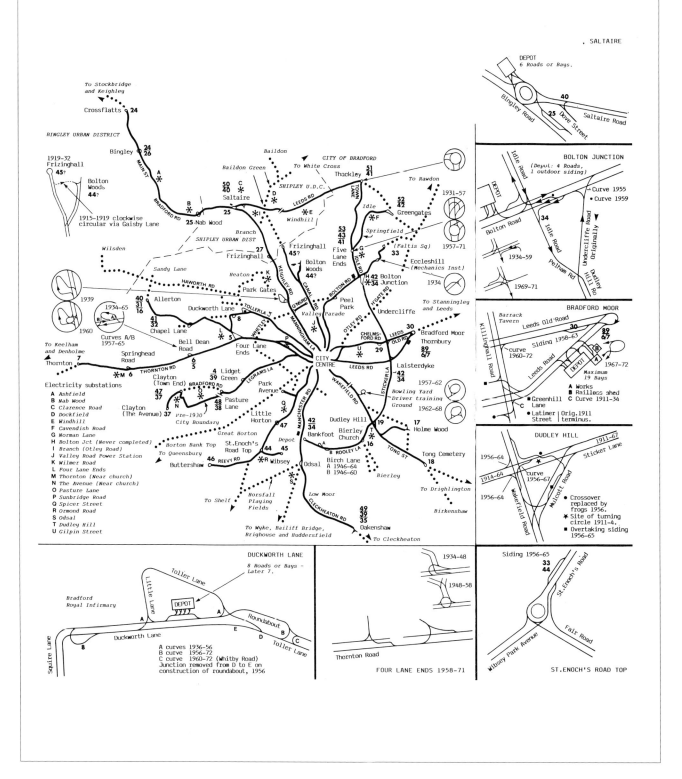

Electricity substations
A Ashfield
B Nab Wood
C Clarence Road
D Dockfield
E Windhill
F Cavendish Road
G Norman Lane
H Bolton Jct (Never completed)
I Branch (Otley Road)
J Valley Road Power Station
K Wilmer Road
L Four Lane Ends
M Thornton (Near church)
N The Avenue (Near church)
O Pasture Lane
P Sunbridge Road
Q Spicer Street
R Ormond Road
S Odsal
T Dudley Hill
U Gilpin Street

. SALTAIRE

DEPOT
6 Roads or Bays.

BOLTON JUNCTION
(Depot: 4 Roads,
1 outdoor siding)

BRADFORD MOOR

A Works
B Railless shed
C Curve 1911-34
■ Greenhill Lane Maximum 19 Bays
• Latimer | Orig.1911
Street | terminus.

DUDLEY HILL

• Crossover replaced by frogs 1956.
✳ Site of turning circle 1911-4.
■ Overtaking siding 1956-65

DUCKWORTH LANE

8 Roads or Bays –
Later 7.

Bradford Royal Infirmary

DEPOT

A curves 1936-56
B curve 1956-72
C curve 1960-72 (Whitby Road)
Junction removed from D to E on construction of roundabout, 1956

FOUR LANE ENDS 1958-71

ST.ENOCH'S ROAD TOP

118

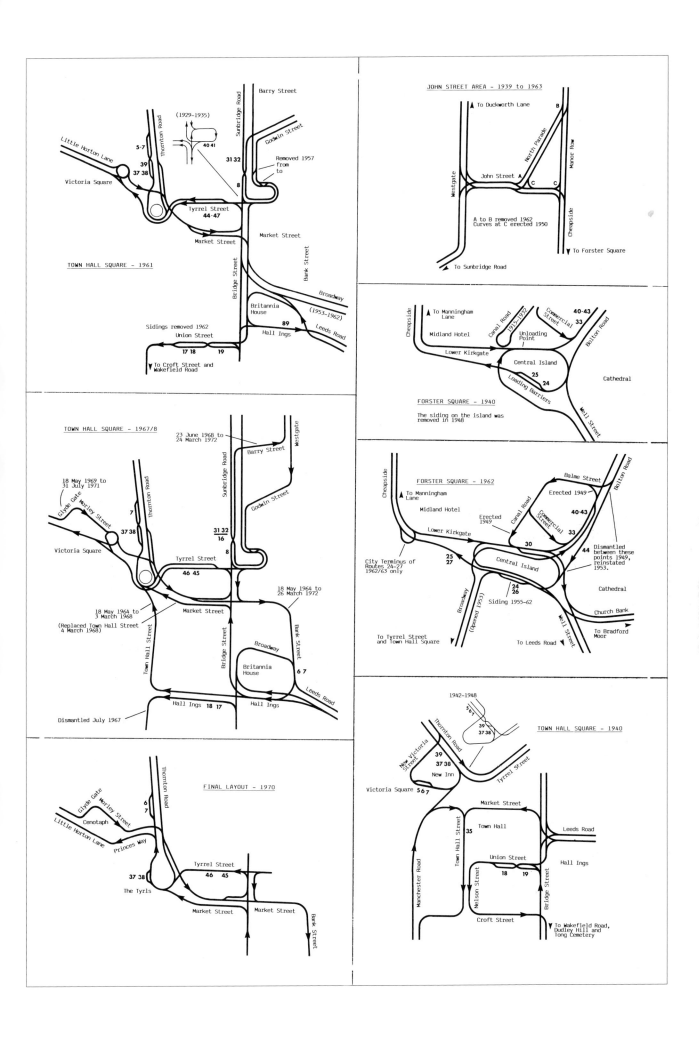

119

CHAIRMEN, CONVENERS & DEPUTIES

TRAMWAYS COMMITTEE

	Chairman	Deputy Chairman
1910-14	Coun. Enoch Priestley	Coun. Sydney C. T. Neumann
1914-16	Coun. Enoch Priestley	Coun. John Lund
1916-17	Coun. Enoch Priestley	Coun. Isaac F. Akeroyd
1917-21	Ald. Enoch Priestley, J.P.	Coun. Thomas Taylor
1923-26	Ald. Enoch Priestley, J.P.	Coun. Francis V. Gill
1926-30	Coun. Irvine Smith	Coun. Walter Hodgson
1930-34	Coun. Walter Hodgson	Coun. George R. Carter
1934-35	Coun. George R. Carter*	Coun. Edwin T. Bolland*

PASSENGER TRANSPORT COMMITTEE

	Chairman	Deputy Chairman
1935-36	Ald. Walter Hodgson	Ald. George R. Carter
1936-37	Ald. Walter Hodgson	Coun. Edwin T. Bolland**
1937-45	Ald. Walter Hodgson	Coun. George R. Carter
1945-49	Coun. Benjamin W. Berry	Coun. William C. Lacey
1949-50	Coun. Benjamin W. Berry	Coun. William C. Lacey
1949-50	Coun. Benjamin W. Berry	Coun. Arthur S. Downey
1950-52	Coun. Arthur S. Downey	Coun. Frank Huntley
1952-55	Coun. Arthur S. Downey	Coun. Frank Huntley
1952-55	Coun. Arthur S. Downey	Coun. Tom Wood
1955-57	Coun. Tom Wood	Coun. Arthur Stott
1957-60	Coun. Tom Wood	Coun. William C. Lacey
1960-62	Ald. Herbert Clayton	Coun. Henry A. Sissling
1962-63	Coun. Henry A.Sissling	Coun. Thomas E. Hall
1963-67	Coun. Lawrence Dunne	Coun. James Mallinson
1967-68	Coun. Henry A.Sissling	Coun. Brian Boldy

TRANSPORT EXECUTIVE GROUP

	Convener	Deputy Convener
1968-70	Coun. Herbert Lee, O.B.E.	Coun. Joseph W. Pell
1970-71	Coun. Joseph W. Pell.	Coun. Jack Mears
1971-72	Coun. Joseph W. Pell	Coun. J. Stanley King

*Temporary appointments during Coun. Hodgson's term as Lord Mayor
**   Temporary appointments during Ald. Carter's term as Lord Mayor.

MILEAGE BETWEEN OVERHAULS OF THE 'SALTAIRE' B.U.T. TROLLEYBUSES 740-759, RECORDED OCTOBER, 1961

740	–	97,000 miles	750	–	130,000 miles
741	–	130,000	751	–	128,000
742	–	132,000	752	–	131,000
743	–	121,000	753	–	128,000
744	–	114,000	754	–	134,000
745	–	121,000	755	–	120,000
746	–	131,000	756	–	104,000
747	–	124,000	757	–	122,000
748	–	125,000	758	–	117,000
749	–	119,000	759	–	130,000

Average for class: – 122,900 miles
Comparisons: – 'Darlington' Karrier Ws 120,000 miles.
      Motor-buses 50-60,000 miles or up to 65,000 if pushed hard!